Practice What You Preach

Virtues, Ethics,
and Power
in the Lives of
Pastoral Ministers
and Their Congregations

Practice What You Preach

*Virtues, Ethics,
and Power
in the Lives of
Pastoral Ministers
and Their Congregations*

**Edited by James F. Keenan, S.J.
and Joseph Kotva, Jr.**

SHEED & WARD

Franklin, Wisconsin

1999

Sheed & Ward
7373 South Lovers Lane Road
Franklin, Wisconsin 53132
1-800-266-5564

Printed in the United States of America

Cover and interior design: GrafixStudio, Inc.

Library of Congress Cataloging-in-Publication Data

Practice what you preach : virtues, ethics, and power in the lives of pastoral
    ministers and their congregations / edited by James F. Keenan and
    Joseph J. Kotva.
        p. cm.
    Includes bibliographical references.
    ISBN 1-58051-064-7 (pbk. alk. paper)
      1. Clergy—Professional ethics. 2. Christian ethics—Catholic
    authors. I. Keenan, James F. II. Kotva, Joseph J.
    BV4011.5 p73 1999
    241' .641—dc21   99-16894
                                              CIP

1 2 3 4 5 / 02 01 00 99

Contents

PART ONE:
PASTORAL MINISTERS AND POWER

SECTION ONE:
The Way Churches Train Their Pastors

A. Admissions and Candidacy Development

B. Ordination, Marriage, and Pastoral Assignments

SECTION TWO:
The Way Pastors Live

A. The Pastor and Personal Relationships

B. Context Affecting Self-Understanding

PART TWO:
CONGREGATIONS AND POWER

SECTION ONE:
The Way Communities Worship

A. Truth in Prayer and Preaching

B. Inclusive Language and Communion

SECTION TWO:
The Way Communities Behave

A. Empowering Leaders

B. Arbitrating Conflict

C. The Measure of Justice

To

Richard McCormick, S.J.

and

in memory of

John Howard Yoder

Acknowledgments

In many ways, theologians who ask whether church leaders and members treat one another ethically often feel like people asking a terribly rude question. The conviction that the question is right remains, however, in the hearts and minds of many ethicists who, like our contributors, try to set standards for the way the churches should behave. In the United States, two Christian ethicists really illustrated the courage and intelligence necessary to ask the question in the first place. To them, we dedicate this work.

We want to thank some people for their help and support. To our contributors who trusted us with their cases and analyses, we thank them for participating in this project. Our own institutions (Weston Jesuit School of Theology and First Mennonite Church, Allentown) provided us with the time and support to continue this project. Three people were especially helpful in making this project appear in print: Angela Senander of Boston College helped set up the project, Barbara Vorel of John Carroll's Religious Studies Department patiently downloaded many essays, and Laura Richter of Weston Jesuit took care of nearly everything else with great care and timing. John Carroll University provided Jim with the Walter and Mary Tuohy Chair where he finished the project. Finally, we are grateful to Sheed & Ward editor Jeremy Langford for taking this project.

Introduction

Why a Course on Virtue Ethics in Church Ministry?

When we began recruiting ethicists from around the country to reflect on the practices of their churches we discovered curious phenomena. First, most responded immediately by saying, "I have just the case!" These enthusiastic contributors also had an incredible diversity of cases in mind. Carlos Piar referred to Spanish-speaking immigrants excluded from ordination, while Vigen Guroian mentioned the lack of civility that occurred over a major doctrinal dispute within the Armenian Church. Samuel Roberts discussed how African American pastors are affected by a culture of deference; William Everett suggested a case regarding law and covenantal governance. Margaret Farley brought up intercommunion and Gilbert Meilaender talked about the appointment of married clergy. The diversified list goes on, but our first encounters with most was that they were happy to have a forum to address a question from their own experience with their church!

However, despite the enthusiasm of the contributors, most churches show little interest in ethics. For instance, in most of this book's cases, the ethicists became familiar with the case as observers. Our contributors were seldom called upon as persons with relevant expertise and skills; that the church person was an ethicist apparently made little difference in leaderships' own estimation. Indeed, within the churches ethicists are only occasionally constructively engaged, such as when church leaders wish to speak either to their congregations about their members' personal and social ethical obligations or to society at large about a type of conduct they find unacceptable. But ethicists are not involved in the nitty-gritty assessments of how leadership relates with its community members and how the actual congregation is itself behaving. The competency of the Christian ethicist rarely factors in when church leaders begin facing new issues affecting how they proceed in leadership.

Breaking Open the Field of Ministerial Ethics

This book wants to be among those attempts at remedying the churches' lack of interest in its ethical life. Still, this book is not meant to cover every issue in ministerial ethics. Rather, it seeks to break open a variety of cases that concern the way pastors lead and congregations live. It attempts to offer a first word, not a last word. It tries to make the case that when forming policy decisions about how their churches are proceeding, church ministers need to get into the habit of asking themselves, "but is it ethical?"

Moreover, the cases in this book demonstrate that bringing disciplined ethical reflection into the conversation about how the churches ought to proceed is a crucial and necessary move. As we will see, such reflection is just now beginning to have a significant role in the practice of ordinary church life. Three examples demonstrate this claim. The first is the tragic, highly harmful, and damaging experience of pederasty and the frequent subsequent cover-ups. The absence of self-critical moral reflection is seen not simply in the pederasty itself. Rather, it also appears in the inability of church leaders to know how to proceed in light of possibly suspicious and at times clearly evident sexual abuse. Individual pastors, superiors, bishops, and elders did not know how to proceed. Why not? A variety of reasons can be given: Incredulous (and unrealistic) understanding about the sinfulness of clergy; insufficient regard for the claims of individual members of the laity; the crisis management style of leaders who simply shuffle "troublesome" people elsewhere; inadequate guidance in sexual development of clergy and so on. Whatever the reasons, church leaders did not employ or seek out the resources of the ethical traditions that we teach our children to follow. Fortunately, we are beginning to see today a variety of dioceses and regions publishing their newly articulated policies regarding sexual harassment, which they developed with the help of local Christian ethicists.

Another case concerns the salaries of those in pastoral ministry. A good friend and wonderful colleague, M. Cathleen Kaveny, lectures and writes on a variety of ethical issues. Besides being a trained Christian ethicist, Kaveny is also a lawyer. When she turns to legal ethics, she does not look at some of those critical dilemma-oriented cases that concern made-for-TV instances of confidential privileges. Kaveny likes talking about the much less exotic topic of billable hours. She argues that the real ethical issues for lawyers are not those rare conflicts that make for good television drama; rather, lawyers' consciences are often challenged by their firm's policies on billing clients. This ordinary issue is critical and affects in a variety of ways questions about the purpose of law, the character of the lawyer, and the access of clients to equal justice. It is the meat-and-potato topic for lawyers' consciences.

Though the financial issues for those in church ministry are hardly the same as those for lawyers (would that they were!), money significantly impacts those in church ministry. Church ministers have been notoriously underpaid in a variety of contexts. Anne E. Patrick, for instance, provides two very disturbing cases of the treatment of Roman Catholic women religious in their apostolic work. Her cases are hardly unique.

It would be interesting to consider the genesis of the presupposition that employees ought to forego equitable pay for the sake of the church's work. Certainly, Catholic religious orders whose members had a vow of poverty elected to assume a variety of duties for missions that meant low remuneration. But what one elects for oneself and what one assumes for an employee are two very different things. This insight is all the more striking when applied to past history. Religious orders of women who controlled their own apostolate managed to maintain sufficient long-term financial security while still observing the vows of poverty and electing their own simple salaries. This was not the case for many who were employees of church leaders who presumed that for the sake of the mission their employees could work at below standard wages and without long-term benefits. This presumption was only recently challenged by employees who invoked papal social teachings that had been taught beyond church walls for more than one hundred and twenty years. The ethical standards that the churches preached preceded the practices they engaged.

Of course, inadequate pay is not an injustice found solely in Catholic quarters. Karen Lebacqz and Shirley Macemon narrate a simple, but all too familiar case that one finds in too many parishes: The recommendation by an employer that church employees ought to be patient with their meager pay for the sake of the mission. Employers in this case, like so many others, pair their call for patience with an equally artificial nod to piety, but as Lebacqz and Macemon make clear, unless patience is invoked for the sake of justice, it becomes an instrument for the continuation of injustice.

Finally, the discussions of the role of women in church leadership illustrate how new ethical discourse in church ministry is. For decades, the so-called secular world has been engaging in lively reflection and making significant choices about the equality of men and women in financial, social, medical, artistic, and legal forms of life. The quality of those discussions and selections may not be satisfactorily enlightening for many but they are remarkably luminous when compared to the work of the churches. Many may ask, "How could a believing community that saw women in positions of leadership early in its founding be so far behind the discussions about women today?" More pertinent for our book, however, is the fact that in many ecclesiastical traditions the question is rarely even raised. Rather than engaging an ethical question about whether our own identity as community is inhibited or not when we exclude certain members from leadership, many of the churches invoke past practices as normative policies simply on the grounds of their past consistency. But we can ask, "Is this an ethical way of reasoning?"

These three topics demonstrate that disciplined ethical reflection is just recently being recognized as an important resource for the making of church policy regarding its own way of proceeding. Those topics break open church life to show us that we can look anew at the way we Christians proceed and that ethics is a potentially healing guide. One would expect, moreover, that a Christian interest in mission would necessitate such reflection: Meaningful witness to the "world" requires authentic moral deliberation and practice "at home."

The essays in this volume try to do just that: Bring disciplined ethical reflection home to the church. The cases break open a variety of concerns that Christians have with the way we proceed: Who do we exclude from candidacy or ordination; how do we determine ministerial assignments; how do church leaders understand themselves particularly when context is so important? If worship is how we allow ourselves to be formed by God, how true is our prayer and how true to the Word is our preaching; how do we welcome others by our language and our communion?

Because church ministry is not a solitary profession, the following essays raise other types of questions as well. As a people called into communion, we see that we are shaped by our leaders and our leaders are shaped by our community. We need then cases that reflect on how pastors and communities are mutually constituted. We also must look at how community leaders are charged with certain deliberative tasks and how important it is for those leaders to examine not just the matters upon which they deliberate, but about who they are as they deliberate. Finally, we examine a variety of ways in which pastoral leadership must be asked whether its way of living out the response to the call of the gospel actually conforms to justice.

This shift to examining the ethical character and conduct of the agent is extraordinarily important because until recently ethics was basically focused on the moral decisions leaders made. The so-called turn to the subject in theology and philosophy has become equally important in ethics. Now ethics suggests that, generally speaking, before judging and acting, decision makers must first critically reflect on their own abilities both to understand themselves and to judge fairly and truthfully.

These cases then evidence the tremendous gap in the relationship between self-critical moral reflection and the churches. For while those in ministry instruct their members and the world on what is morally right, they do not critically ask whether their way of proceeding conforms to the very standards of ethics that they promote.

Bridging the Gap by Developing Character

This work is not a blanket indictment of the church's failure to assess critically its own ways of proceeding. Rather, the writers of these essays reveal a gap between what we teach and what we practice in order to bridge that gap.

The bridging of the gap is carefully done. We the editors are very concerned that church ministers and communities invoke their own resources to respond to the evident gap. We are concerned that in the absence of ethical guidelines, ministers and their communities might invoke the particular norms that are offered in a variety of professions and thus overlook the resources of their own tradition.

For that reason, we asked each contributor to appeal to the ethics of character and virtue. We know that today more and more people find in biblical passages and in the sermons on those passages an extraordinary resource regarding the building up of character. Whether instructing the young or old, families or individuals, pastors' and preachers' appeal to character and virtue is very effective because it emerges naturally from the gospel narratives, the prophets' injunctions, wisdom's anthropology, and the epistles' exhortation. We the editors have made the case elsewhere that virtue ethics is a suitable way of expressing and embodying the task that the Scriptures lay before us to "Come follow Christ." The call to become disciples involves a call to critically understand oneself before God and community and to see where each of us can become more true, more faithful, more responsible to the grace and call that we have been given.

Thus, we bridge the gap between our failure to examine ethically our own ministerial way of proceeding and our effective teaching and preaching of justice and the other virtues by extending the strengths of the latter into the realm of the former. These ethical guidelines then do not derive from outside our communities of faith. Rather, they have long been a part of our own way of understanding ourselves and of teaching one another how to proceed on the way of the Lord. Now by extension we want to see them applied to the way we govern ourselves.

Using These Cases

We hope that readers find great variety in our cases. They differ in several ways. First, they differ by their concern for the types of activity under consideration. For the most part, these essays are about the way we proceed with one another. Inasmuch as the evangelical instinct is extroverted, Christians often wear blinders about how they really treat one another. In this book's deliberate and focused turn to the subject, we try to provide to the reader, as the table of contents shows, a diversity of concerns about how church members proceed together. Second, though there are questions of women, of Hispanics, of African Americans, and of homosexuals in leadership, they are never treated as "them." The questions are more about how we treat one another. They are always about "us" and the way we are incorporated into the body of Christ.

Third, the essays differ on the level of governance. In one of the book's last sections on "arbitrating conflicts," each case is on a different level of governance. Pinches's case is a local congregation;

Everett's, a denomination's regional governance; and, Guroian's is the highest level of governance in a denomination.

Fourth, though many of the cases focus on pastors and their local congregations, not every case of pastoral ministry is restricted to that setting. For Copeland and Farley the context is a university campus, for Keenan and Patrick the setting concerns religious orders, and for Kay the place is prison. This variety of contexts stretches our imaginations to see that church life is not solely limited to parish life. In fact, so much pastoral ministry occurs in varying contexts and so many Christian communities arise in divergent locations, that we do ourselves a disservice if we limit our cases to the parish. We are called to witness to the gospel wherever we are gathered in Christ's name.

The reader will find other ways that the cases differ. But hopefully each essay and each case will be considered a beginning point, a point of departure to consider the subject matter with which each author is concerned. In that way, the reader might think of analogous cases or contexts to see how similar subject matter might play out. Or, the reader might want to change the circumstances of the original case to see if a change in circumstance leads to a moral difference. In any event, the cases are meant to break open a discussion about a field too long ignored.

Invoking the Virtues

The field of virtue ethics is hardly a monolith. Rather, it is comprised of those ethicists who are concerned about the priority of an ethics of *being* over an ethics of *doing* or an ethics of *character* over an ethics of *action*. Some of these ethicists take rather traditional reads on how Christians ought to conduct themselves; others see new horizons constantly being opened up. In either case, both are interested in character. Similarly, some are convinced of virtues that are more Aristotelian, others more Thomistic, yet others more Calvinistic. Each, however, is concerned with some type of character.

The reader therefore will read some cases with three sets of questions in mind. First, do you agree with the way the author describes a particular virtue? Is it adequately described? Is it too rigid, too loose? Second, are these the virtues you would have invoked to address the case? Are there other virtues that you would add? Third, do you rank the virtues in the same order or do you give greater priority to one over another?

The cases and virtues are meant then to generate discussions among those who understand that the call to follow Christ is a complex one that requires attention to self-understanding, reflection, judgment, and decisions. This book is designed not only to initiate those discussions but also to offer initial guidelines, particularly about the ways we Christians can become more alert to our way of proceeding.

James F. Keenan, S.J.
Joseph Kotva, Jr.

PART ONE

PASTORAL MINISTERS AND POWER

SECTION ONE

The Way Churches Train Their Pastors

Introduction

Good virtue ethics starts at the beginning of a person's formation of character. For that reason, this collection begins with church ministry cases that examine the admissions, candidacy, and appointments processes. Rather than simply outlining the personal traits that someone becoming a pastoral leader ought to have, these four essays look at the way that church institutions prepare themselves for this work.

Good virtue ethics always happens in a context, and in the life of ministry that context is a community of believers who help one another hear and respond to the call of Jesus Christ. Often, in calling forth from the community persons who are willing to develop the skills to become a pastoral minister, a variety of institutional committees are established to screen, evaluate, guide, and assign these persons. Just as often, these committees make a variety of policies and set several standards.

Virtue ethics looks to those committee decisions not only for the impact they have on the aspirant, but more importantly for how those decisions embody the long-term goals of the church that the committee represents. In interviewing candidates, these committees are meeting their potential future; the policies and standards that they set are then indicators of the direction that they wish to go in their journey in faith. Thus, inasmuch as virtue ethics calls agents to reflect on the significance of their actions for their own development, they do the same when examining the decisions of a collective.

These candidates are not themselves disembodied. Rather, as we see in the cases to follow, they pursue their vocations through these committees. In many ways, the candidates bring newness. Incorporating that newness into an institution that has just entered its third millennium requires a significant amount of prudence and hope.

In Richard Bondi's essay we get a glimpse of some of the contemporary concerns facing those committees charged with determining the admission of new candidates. In the case of an educated, professionally trained woman applying for a church appointment, we find in her all-male judges the embodiment of how evolutionary psychology plays an enormous role in the decision making of community leaders. Bondi highlights that the human is remarkably conditioned and provides a guideline of virtues for the woman to be a persistent agent of change in the face of long-held, unexamined, and fairly well-determined tribal presuppositions. Her experience is like all those in ministry who, through their stages of development, encounter church leaders who fundamentally resist newness. If she is to advance in service then she will have to be more curious and less judgmental about the inherent humanity of those whom she meets, whether they are in the pews, in positions of authority, or in the mirror.

James Keenan looks at a similar question from an almost opposite perspective. By focusing on the testing of candidates for HIV, he helps us to see the ramifications of committee decisions that articulate the bottom line for a qualified candidate. But like other virtue ethicists, Keenan also asks how this policy affects both the committee and the religious order. Selection process policies not only narrow the field of candidates, but they also narrow the projected identity of a community. More specifically, as more admission committees begin looking at projected health issues among their candidates, Keenan reminds us that those policies must reflect the charisms of the community that is interviewing its potential future.

Carlos Piar raises yet another question about the determinations that ordination committees make. Faced with a Hispanic congregational pastor whose economic opportunities have limited him to a middle school education, a committee must decide whether to ordain this otherwise experienced and able pastor. Like the other writers, Piar tries to offer a bridge between committee and candidate that helps the former to maintain its standards while at the same time promoting those virtues that are necessary for becoming a community of faithful and just disciples of Jesus Christ.

Finally, Gilbert Meilaender takes us away from committees to another relationship that candidates often have, that is, to their spouses. What is the virtuous ordering of relationality when a pastor is being offered a parish and the spouse has an opportunity for employment elsewhere? Which comes first, marriage or ministerial availability? Meilaender recognizes that too often pastors and their spouses find themselves caught between a specific call that matches the pastor's talent and community's need and a spouse's understandable resistance to the assignment. In the absence of both a discerning ethos and a set of theological guidelines, Meilaender leads the reader to consider that the two are not opposing vocations but rather constitutive of the pastor and spouse's one vocation of ministerial service.

A. Admissions and Candidacy Development

Chapter One

Christ and Darwin Go to Church
Ministerial Selection and the Candidacy Process

by Richard Bondi

An intelligent and hard-working woman (let's call her Ruth[1]) from a small southern town had grown up nurtured in the faith by her local congregation–let's call it First Church of Branchwater Creek. Ruth went to college, became a pediatric nurse, married a medical school student named Frank, and supported him through his internship. Soon after opening his own practice, Frank had a series of affairs and Ruth found out. They tried counseling, but Frank didn't try very hard. After the divorce Ruth returned home, worked in a local clinic, and experienced a lot of healing from the supportive members of First Church. She came to feel a call to ministry, a chance to give back what had been given to her, and so in her mid-thirties went to seminary. She enjoyed herself, did well, and soon after graduation found herself a candidate for a church appointment in the Big Denomination[2] to which her home church belonged.

Ruth tells her story from here.[3] "I approached the candidacy process with some trepidation. I'd never had any trouble getting a job as a nurse, but getting selected as a minister felt different. In seminary I'd tried to get a student appointment and been told point blank by an official involved in the process 'not to expect anything because women are the last to be picked.' Our male counterparts were getting valuable experience in their student pastorates while many women never got the chance. There were a lot of reasons, I suppose—a desire to give jobs to men who were 'heads of families,' resistance at the local church level, slowly changing prejudices among church leaders. But whatever the reasons, the consequence was we were less prepared when seminary was over and appointment time came around. I worried that the gap in 'practical experience' would work against me. I also worried that my home church and my seminary were widely perceived as 'more liberal than the rest of the church,' and I'd heard this had hurt the chances of other candidates in the past, regardless of gender.

"But I wasn't prepared for the gut reaction I had when I went before the group of people who would make the decision on my suitability for selection to the ministry. I entered the room and faced a panel of seven judges, all males.[4] *Now for the average male candidate this is daunting enough, but for a woman seeking to break through the gender line it is quite threatening on a more basic, primal level. The candidate comes into a room full of Alpha males.*[5] *The fear has nothing to do with reason, and everything to do with survival.*

"The interview began politely enough, with some of the men trying to put me at ease with questions about my call, the support from my home church, and my good grades in seminary. Then things shifted. One man asked why I had returned to school and given up a secure profession. Another questioned why I had left my home state (in a different region of Big Denomination) to attend seminary, and was trying to get a job in this region, adding that 'You know we've got to take care of our own.' Finally the leader of the panel, crossing his hands and looking very serious, talked about my divorce, ending with 'You don't think you're trying to be a pastor so you can lord it over the men in the church, do you? Maybe this is just a phase you'll get over.'

"Stunned, I looked around at these men of God. I couldn't see their faces, for each one was examining his shoes with great intensity. Sadly, I noticed some of their shoes were in need of repair. These men were dependent on the panel leader for their next appointment. In this region of the Big Denomination, where

there was over a $100,000.00 difference between the lowest and highest paid appointments[6], they were as trapped as I was. I don't remember much of the rest of the interview.

"Later I received a letter thanking me for my time, but telling me the panel had decided I would not make a 'good fit' with any of the currently open appointments. They suggested I look for something on my own and try again next year or, in what they said was my 'best interest,' go back to my home state and try there. They were sure the Lord would lead me to the best place for me to be."

Because of her good record in seminary and her nursing background, Ruth found a job as an associate minister (paying about one-third the amount made by the senior pastor in her church) with special responsibility for visitation. She felt lucky to find this position, as it turned out, for only one new appointment, male or female, was made that year from among the candidates in her region of Big Denomination. It seems there hadn't been as many retirements as had been expected, so fewer positions opened up. Two people who requested transfer from another region (and who had happened to have gone to the same seminary that most of the region's leaders had attended) were found to be "good fits" for certain appointments. Ruth spends her time visiting the sick, assisting the pastor, and pondering her future in the church.

What can we learn from Ruth's story? First of all, notice that I have cast her story really more in the form of a narrative than of a case study. It will become clear that within that narrative I have emphasized elements of an *ethics of character and virtue* on the one hand and of *evolutionary psychology* on the other hand. Taken together, these two perspectives can give us insight into Ruth's story and, at the same time, suggest ways of reflection that might provide fresh opportunities for church leadership today.

The discipline of ethics is often presented as if its major aim was to come up with a model of moral decision making. Whether applied to individuals or groups, this model would yield answers to questions like "What ought Ruth to do?" or "What is the right selection policy for Big Denomination to adopt?" As important as these questions are, there have always been people who thought that other questions were at least as important and perhaps existentially prior, such as "What kind of a person should I be?" or "What would it be like to live in a good society?" Instead of trying to come up with a model of moral decision making, these other folk have spent their energy trying to come up with practices of moral reflection. Instead of formulating moral principles, they've developed moral psychologies; instead of focusing on what's right for everyone, they've explored what's good for particular historical communities.[7]

Those developing an ethics of character and virtue, in other words, tend to be more interested in long-term dispositions than in isolated acts; in vision and interpretation rather than judgment; in the direction of our desires rather than in an isolated act of choice. An interest in character then is an interest in the self in relation to the world, and in the virtues necessary to live well and truly in that world.

In order to provide a descriptive account of the self in relation to the world over time, an ethics of character must depend on an adequate moral psychology. Elsewhere I have sketched the outline of a moral psychology based on our capacity for rational, intentional action; the necessary qualification of that capacity by our emotions and feelings; our subjection to the accidents of history (the genetic and cultural particularities of living in a specific time and place); and the unifying sense of purpose and calling we might call metaphorically our "heart."[8] Now I'd like to expand my account of the self in relation to the world with insights from the emerging discipline of evolutionary psychology.

Evolutionary psychology is ultimately indebted to Charles Darwin[9] and to the host of researchers and thinkers who have in his wake followed the notion that our creaturely nature and its evolution determines or influences our individual and social behavior.[10] Much ink continues to be spilt over whether "determines" or "influences" is the proper verb (and if so to what degree) and over the distinctions to be made between micro- and macro-behavior. Certainly it can be said that evolutionary psychology does not claim to provide exhaustive explanations of individual human behavior. It does claim to point the way to an understanding of human behavior in general and, in regard to specific traits, to make statements applicable to humanity at large.[11]

Of the many core ideas discussed in evolutionary psychology, the ones most relevant to expanding the depth and scope of an ethics of character and virtue are the following: Human beings today are creatures subject to the constraints of evolution from an earlier, ancestral situation. That means contemporary humans, both on the level of individual mind-body development[12] and on the level of social interaction,[13] act out of mind-body, personality, and social traits originally developed to aid in survival under conditions that may be very different from those we face today. We face Information Age quandaries with Stone Age capacities and impulses—overlain, to be sure, by thousands of years of cultural development, but present nonetheless.

Some of the most crucial of these underlying capacities and impulses include the cumulative working out of a natural selection for fitness and adaptability in the service of survival;[14] the importance of family and kin closeness in determining the actions (especially risky ones) that we will undertake for others; the use of covert and overt violence in defense of—not just survival of—a desired state of affairs for an individual or group; the differentiation of society by gender and the disproportionate value attached to male and female genders; and the way status hierarchies use shame, blame, and obedience to distribute desirable social resources in a way that perpetuates the hierarchy. Finally, lest we in despair or error assign only selfish traits to our creaturely nature, evolutionary psychology holds forth the possibility that the evolved virtues of empathy, friendship, altruism, and compassion may broaden the narrow scope of familial and status hierarchy allegiance, and in fact suggests that that's what ethics and religion should be about.[15]

Taken together, the combined picture looks something like this: We are the way we are due to a complex interaction of formative influences on our individual and communal character. Our basic temperament and personality,[16] the impact of our families of origin,[17] the role played by our wider cultures,[18] our participation in the status hierarchies within the enduring institutions of culture (family, government, the economy, the military, religion, education,[19] and, one might argue, sports and entertainment): All of these are underlain by the evolutionary traits enumerated above, and overlain by the systems of meaning and belief with their attendant narratives and virtues that have arisen over the course of human civilization. And all of this occurs within the problems and possibilities of a specific historical time and place. In order to undertake truly informed personal and social reflection on character and the good life, we need to include these factors in our awareness as much as possible.

So let's take a look at how themes from an ethics of character and virtue, when combined with observations from evolutionary psychology, might elucidate Ruth's story, and give some clues to their usefulness in reconsidering ethics and church leadership. Ruth's story was told in seven paragraphs, and I'll retell each in turn.

(1) We know little about Ruth's family of origin, temperaments, and personality, though we can infer she has fairly good self-esteem and a lot of persistence. We do know she grew up connected to a Christian faith community and experienced first hand its convictions about compassion and care even to one who, through divorce, might be seen to violate its official or unofficial norms. She had an early adulthood typical of many women who end up assisting men towards higher economic and social status and then are excluded from that status themselves. The beginning of her story also gives us a glimpse of her heart. She has been inspired to service in the church, and she begins this process with a sense of trust in the institution that lies behind the local church she knows so well.

(2) During seminary Ruth begins to be more aware of a gap between her desires as a candidate for ministry and the expectations (the standards for selection and survival as a minister) of the institution. She also experiences a gap between the seminary she chose to leave her home state to attend, and the organizational reality of Big Denomination in the region where she is trying to get an appointment. Apparently her seminary, even though based in the region where she wants to work, is considered too liberal by some influential members of the local denominational leadership. Ironically, had she stayed "at home" and gone to the more conservative seminary in that region, she might have been more acceptable to the panel she will now face. She also begins to experience gender differentiation, though is inclined to make allowances for much of it. Her heart remains set on full-time ministry.

(3) Ruth's fear actually is rational, though it feels (and also is) quite primal. How can this be? The visual picture of a wall of dominant males instantly engages her fight-or-flight neurotransmitters, and this (through mediation of the prefrontal cortex)[20] also engages her capacity for intentional action, leading her to interpret the situation as a threat to her survival as a candidate. Reason and emotion go hand-in-hand.

(4) The panel begins by asking about Ruth's vocation and training, but quickly moves to question her status rank, her character, and the "real" intentions in her heart. The ancestral impulse towards preferential treatment of those with closely related genes reappears in the preferential treatment of those who went to the same seminary or come from "our home state," and Ruth fits in neither category. Not being "our own" from the perspective of the panel, she will find it harder to enter the regional status hierarchy. Finally, the superior position of Alpha males, under question in the culture at large and possibly in this church body, is reasserted obliquely yet without doubt in the question posed to Ruth by the leader of the panel.

(5) Ruth, in reacting both intellectually and viscerally, sees more clearly than before the gap between her sense of calling and the concerns of the institution into which she is trying to be

admitted to fulfill that vocation. Her observation of the sorry state of some of the men's shoes reflects their impotence in the face of disapproval by the panel leader. A drive for higher status in the tribal grouping gave our successful ancestors greater access to food, shelter, and sexual activity. Today that drive may give some of us selective access to institutional authority, higher salaries, better living and working conditions, and better nutrition, as long as our relative status rank is accepted and the system supported.[21]

(6) The panel, representing the institutional church, fails to select Ruth as a candidate. In a word resonant with Darwinian overtones, she does not "fit." The letter contains suggestions that might be compassionate, pragmatic, dismissive, or a combination of all three, and ends by entrusting her future to the Lord. We don't know if this is genuine or a way to pass the buck.

(7) Continuing to show the virtues of perseverance and fortitude, Ruth does locate at least a temporary position, for which her background in nursing makes her a good fit. Although relieved to find a place to minister, she is disturbed to find how difficult it was for any of her peers to achieve higher rank. The smaller than usual number of retirements may have meant that some were holding on to their rank in hopes of increasing their pension or retirement funds—not an irrational move in a capitalist society. That some positions that did open up were filled by people transferring in from another region seemed to indicate that "family and kin" were determined more by joint social background and theological alliance than by geographical region. Such people entering the region would, of course, serve to strengthen the position of those making the selections of future candidates, and might even serve on such panels themselves. We say farewell to Ruth as she continues to follow her heart in the practice of ministry, but ponders how to do it in the hierarchy in which she finds herself at least a questionable fit for higher status.

Ruth's story and my interpretation of it may seem to have been stacked in favor of the pure-of-heart candidate versus the self-interested defenders of the status quo, but it reflects reality in more church situations than most of us would care to admit. One doesn't even have to attribute ill will or bad character to the panel members in the story. They have their own shoes to mend, and Ruth, after all, wants their approval and a higher place at the table.

The truth is that when Christ and Darwin go to church they always sit together. They're in the pew, in the choir, in the pulpit, and in the governing bodies of the congregation and the larger church. The wise church leader (and member) must attend to them both, and first and foremost to the way they intertwine in her or his own character. In outlining some features of an ethics of character and virtue informed by evolutionary psychology, my intent is not to discourage candidates or offend leaders. It is to stimulate more curiosity and less judgment. We need to know much more about the formation of our own character and the character of our lives together. Just imagine getting curious in each leadership situation about whether we are acting in tribal self-interest or fanning with Christ the equally ancestral flames of altruism and compassion. Getting to know better the Darwin in us all, I firmly believe, will empower us to ask critical questions that will open the way for Christ to flourish ever more fully in our hearts. And that is a consummation devoutly to be wished.

1. Ruth is, of course, a composite figure, though each aspect of her story is based on true events. I am grateful to the women and men (who must go unnamed) who have shared their stories and their concerns with me in the course of developing this essay.

2. The Big Denomination could be any Christian church with status hierarchies, which is to say all Christian churches to some degree.

3. What follows is a fictionalized blend of actual communications from several individuals. Some phrases have been preserved intact; so has the anonymity of my correspondents.

4. Such a "panel" and its "leaders" are a disguised but representative version of groups of church leaders who decide on candidate selection across a wide setting of Christian churches.

5. This phrase, used by one of my correspondents, refers to the dominant males (there can also be Alpha females) of a given pack, tribe, or troop. For examples of this see "Rank and Order," in Frans de Waal, *Good Natured: The Origins of Right and Wrong in Humans and Other Animals* (Cambridge: Harvard University Press, 1996), 89–132.

6. I am not providing an exact reference for this, partly to protect my correspondents but also in order to emphasize that this rough estimate would hold in any number of denominations; the spread would be smaller in some parts of the United States and larger in others. The gap in high/low clergy salaries is a result of the way clergy compensation mimics (though it may not keep pace with) status rank compensation in the secular world.

7. The past twenty-five years or so have been marked by a revival of interest in an ethics of character and virtue, stimulated in part by the work of Stanley Hauerwas, whose book *Vision and Virtue* (Notre Dame: Fides Press, 1973) became the first of many pieces by Hauerwas and others aimed at renovating an ethics of character in a contemporary American context.

8. See Richard Bondi, "The Elements of Character," in *Journal of Religious Ethics* 12:2 (1984): 201–18, and *Leading God's People* (Nashville: Abingdon Press, 1989).

9. Principally found in *On the Origin of the Species* (Cambridge: Harvard University Press, 1859/1964); *The Descent of Man, and Selection in Relation to Sex* (Princeton: Princeton University Press, 1971/1981); and *The Expression of the Emotions in Man and Animals* (Chicago: University of Chicago Press, 1872/1965).

10. The development of evolutionary psychology and its implications for ethical reflection are traced by de Waal, *Good Natured;* Robert Wright, *The Moral Animal* (New York: Pantheon Books, 1994); William Wright, *Born That Way: Genes, Behavior, Personality* (New York: Alfred A. Knopf, 1998); and Stephen Pinker, *How the Mind Works* (New York: W. W. Norton, 1997). Specifically Christian responses to this body of material, though not to each of these authors, can be found in Philip Hefner, *The Human Factor: Evolution, Culture, and Religion* (Minneapolis: Fortress Press, 1995) and Stephen Pope, "Descriptive and Normative Uses of Evolutionary Theory," in *Christian Ethics,* eds. Lisa Cahill and James Childress (Cleveland: Pilgrim Press, 1996), 166–82.

11. Perhaps the most visible contrast is between deeply skeptical (one might say cynical) perspectives such as that advocated by Richard Dawkins, *The Selfish Gene* (Oxford: Oxford University Press, 1976), who gives a picture of human nature as rather nasty, cold, brutish, short, and selfish, and on the other hand the more hopeful and generous depiction of de Waal, *Good Natured*, who finds evolutionary roots of positive virtues such as empathy, altruism, friendship, and compassion.

12. For a view of mind-body relations that supports the connection between reason and the emotions noted above, see Antonio Damasio, *Descartes' Error: Emotion, Reason, and the Human Brain* (New York: Putnam, 1994). See also W. Wright, *Born That Way* and Pinker, *How the Mind Works*.

13. See R. Wright, *The Moral Animal*, 155–310, and de Waal, *Good Natured*, 163–208.

14. Note I did not use the commonplace Darwinisms "survival of the fittest" or "nature red in tooth and claw." These cruder notions of natural selection have been largely superceded by less negative and more comprehensive views that include the selection of traits like altruism and compassion as well as aggression and selfishness. On this development see R. Wright, *The Moral Animal*, 313–78 and, especially well put, de Waal, *Good Natured*, 6–39.

15. For a summary of these points, see R. Wright, *The Moral Animal*, 316–82, and de Waal, *Good Natured*, 209–18.

16. See Jerome Kagan, *Galen's Prophecy: Temperament in Human Nature* (New York: Basic Books, 1994).

17. See the many references on this topic, a mainstay of contemporary family systems theory, in Edwin Friedman, *Generation to Generation* (New York: Guilford, 1986).

18. See Rafael Art. Javier and William G. Herron, eds., *Personality Development and Psychotherapy in Our Diverse Society: A Sourcebook* (Northvale, NJ: Jason Aaronson, 1998).

19. On this see the two volumes by Robert Bellah, et. al., *Habits of the Heart* (Berkeley: University of California Press, 1996) and *The Good Society* (New York: Vintage, 1992).

20. On this see Damasio, *Descartes' Error*.

21. As recent national events seem embarrassingly to prove, higher status probably also still grants access to greater sexual activity. Sadly, the church is not exempt from this phenomenon; see for example Marie Fortune, *Is Nothing Sacred?* (San Francisco: HarperCollins, 1992).

Chapter Two
Testing Religious Order Candidates for HIV

by James F. Keenan, S.J.

Simon, a 29-year-old man who has recently tested positive for HIV, applies to enter a major Roman Catholic religious order known for its apostolic work. Aside from the applicant's HIV status, the man's health and psychological status are fine, his reasons for entering the religious order are fundamentally ministerial, and his prayer life over the past few years has consistently evidenced a vocation to the priesthood in this particular religious order. The admissions committee for the religious order is faced with one major issue, whether to reject the man singularly on the grounds of his HIV status.

When I first heard about cases like this, I soon learned that though there were such policies, few were known. In 1992, Jay O'Connor said that of the 181 dioceses, there was an even split between those who do testing and those who do not.[1] I have no idea what those figures are today, though I am told that nearly all dioceses and men's religious orders do test. For instance, in two of the largest religious orders in the United States, testing is required for all candidates in all provinces. It occurs at the earlier stages of application. However, in terms of outcome, the vocation director of one province stated that any candidate who tests positive is automatically excluded but another man from another province claimed that the exclusion was not automatic. Thus existing policies seem to differ even among provinces, but we have no available record of those policies. And, not surprisingly, there has been little written about the topic.[2]

Moreover, though this case focuses on a Catholic order, the policies are not exclusively a Roman Catholic phenomenon. In an ecumenical collection of essays entitled *The Church with AIDS,* one author remained anonymous:

> John is in the process of seeking ordination and look-ing for a job; therefore he has decided not to use his full name. His sexual orientation, about which he is fairly open, may well prevent him from being hired by a parish. If his HIV status were made known, it is virtually certain he would be regarded as unemploy-able even by the most "liberal" churches. In another situation, he might be inclined to make an issue of it, but he needs a church job and the insurance coverage is too much to take that risk.[3]

I present three issues—for and against testing; minimal ethi-cal standards that must be employed by those who do require test-ing; and, my own assessment of the issue.

Reasons For and Against the Testing

Among the reasons that support testing, the first pertains to suitability for service. Because most members of religious orders are apostolically engaged, candidates are routinely required to undergo some physical examination to ascertain their physical ability to carry out future apostolic work. This insight is sup-ported in the Code of Canon Law (1029, 1051). Moreover, because a candidate faces many years of preparation for ministry, "chronic diseases and life threatening illnesses" are considered severe liabilities.

Second, unlike any other form of contemporary life, incorporation into a religious order means that the order assumes almost all care for the individual. Each novice goes from being an outsider to becoming a brother, from being a stranger to becoming a family member. For this reason, if an order were to dismiss an already accepted member because he was HIV positive, his religious brothers would be appalled. Of course, not all religious orders are the same, nor are all provinces; yet the standard is, for the most part, that religious orders do care fully for their own members. This happens to some degree in diocesan life as well.

Our case, however, is not about a member who tests positive but rather about a candidate who does. If an order were to accept such a candidate, then it is bringing in someone whose health needs will tap the emotional, psychological, and physical resources of a group of men who use those resources for apostolic purposes. Thus, several superiors have said that with diminished manpower, they fear that in an apostolic community, the care for a member who developed AIDS would eventually fall singularly to the already overburdened superior. Similarly, they argued that if an HIV positive member were to develop AIDS during his formation, that too would change significantly the small community's formation agenda.

Third, there are financial considerations. Certainly the cost of caring for a person who develops serious HIV-related diseases is, though considerable, not exceptional for serious illness. Religious orders often assume these costs. But when many religious orders are already strapped financially, to admit a candidate with a known condition challenges the order's financial stewardship.

Fourth, most religious orders consider entrance into formation as probationary. At times a person in formation is judged unsuitable for ministry and is dismissed. Would superiors have the freedom to evaluate members in formation if they knew a man to be HIV positive? If, after two years in the novitiate, a man were considered not suitable not because he was HIV positive but for some other issue, would mercy or some other disposition compromise the probationary function of formation?

The arguments against testing candidates are five. First, the American hierarchy has argued against any blanket discrimination of persons who are HIV positive. In the "Many Faces of AIDS," the bishops wrote, "We oppose the use of HIV antibody testing for strictly discriminatory purposes . . . It is critical that persons with AIDS continue to be employed as long as it is appropriate. The Catholic Church in the United States accepts its responsibility to give good example in this matter."[4] Later, in "Called to Compassion and Responsibility," the bishops describe an individual with HIV as "handicapped" and recall an earlier statement they made: "Defense of the right to life . . . implies the defense of other rights which enable the handicapped individual to achieve the fullest measure of personal development of which he or she is capable."[5] Notwithstanding these assertions, in "Called to Compassion and Responsibility," they write in a footnote: "It may be appropriate for seminaries and religious communities to screen for the HIV antibody . . . The point here is not to automatically exclude a candidate who is HIV positive; but rather to discern carefully this person's present health situations as well as future health prospects; and thus to make an overall moral assessment of an individual's capacity to carry out ministerial responsibilities."[6] Thus, though they admit the possibility of testing candidates, they argue that this can only be a contributing but not a determining factor in considering a candidate's admissibility.

Second, these applicants can be tested because they are not, by virtue of the separation of church and state, protected by federal law. In fact, only prisoners and military employees can be legally screened for HIV in the United States.[7] The bishops' written statements, then, are a challenge not for society's standards but for the church's own practices. The bishops have set their words and not the diocesan and religious orders' policies as the moral norm and that norm basically contradicts the exclusionary policies.

Third, as Al Jonsen notes, "The public language . . . of AIDS is as important as the science."[8] On account of public language, we understand HIV/AIDS as that with which someone lives as opposed to that from which someone dies. The insight delivers, nourishes, and sustains the right of people who are HIV positive or who have AIDS to continue to work and live and not to be dismissed and discriminated against. Moreover, that insight has pushed the medical and pharmaceutical industries to find better methods for fighting the infection. In short, the notion of living with the infection has empowered not simply the HIV-positive person, but our entire society. The decision to exclude candidates, then, substantially places itself at loggerheads with this social construction. In particular, the routine exclusion of anyone testing positive virtually contradicts the metaphor.

Fourth, in making it an absolute condition, the orders are pressuring a candidate to examine something he may believe is against his interests to know. In cases where the test is used simply to exclude, there is a double jeopardy. If the candidate finds out that he is positive, not only does he learn that he is not accepted into priestly ministry, but he also learns that he is infected. Canon lawyer Calvo writes:

> Because testing opens a wide window of vulnerability—psychological, social, economic—for an individual against which the seminary and diocese can guarantee only limited protection . . . the need for a seminary to screen out HIV infected persons is not compelling enough to outweigh the established right of a person to protection against potentially damaging intrusion of privacy.[9]

Fifth, if testing HIV positive is not absolutely predictive of AIDS, if persons who are infected are known now to have greater longevity, and if we can reasonably assume that therapeutic interventions in the even near future ought to alter the overall prognosis of persons testing positive, then a person testing positive has a chronic illness or disease. Does a chronic illness constitute grounds for exclusion when other chronic conditions like obesity, smoking, and heart disease are not? In short, do the orders significantly understand the nature of HIV or are they selective in their interests in weeding out those with this particular chronic condition?

These reasons for and against testing suggest that the decision to test or not to test is not an easy one. There are compelling interests on either side. The problem of course is that many orders (and dioceses) do test, though we do not know why they test, or what their reasoning and consultation process was, or even what their final policy is. Moreover, it seems that they have not subjected their own original decisions to any critical inquiry beyond a narrow consultation with an ad hoc committee that was probably constituted of superiors, lawyers, and treasurers but not necessarily physicians and ethicists. Finally, despite requests, provincials have not considered reexamining their policies, ten years after they put them into effect.

Basic Ethical Standards

Because many orders require testing, a number of issues must be considered to assure that this practice observes minimal ethical standards. First, if testing positive is automatic grounds for exclusion, then it must be done early in the application process. When I asked one vocation director whether or not by testing he felt that he was leaving the candidate extraordinarily vulnerable, he remarked that the entire process usually involves opening several of Pandora's boxes; he pointed expressly to a variety of psychological and emotional self-discoveries that may arise in the application process. All the more reason, then, that the candidate ought not to be exposed to other vulnerable information, especially when the community has no intention of accepting him.

Second, a religious community offends justice and does itself harm when it decides to require testing only for those whose interviews suggest that they may have been exposed. Justice demands that applicants be treated fairly. To target certain individuals suggests that the testing is for screening purposes other than health-related. It also implies that interviewers are able to prognosticate about HIV.

Third, whether the religious community uses the testing to exclude automatically or simply to assess the candidate's overall health, it must clearly warn the candidate of the risks of testing positive with regards to health and life insurance, as well as employment and housing. Likewise, it should consider its responsibility toward the candidate who tests positive, particularly helping him to live with the news.

Fourth, confidentiality must be absolutely respected.

The decisions of religious orders to enforce these policies have substantially changed the relationship between applicant and order. Though an order supports a member after acceptance, prior to admissions, it generally considers itself free of responsibilities to care for the applicant. The applicant is after all seeking admissions; the responsibilities for caring for him are still singularly his. But many orders and dioceses now require him to ascertain his HIV status, not in most cases for his welfare but for their apostolate. (As I noted, a few orders and dioceses may require testing for the candidate's own welfare; in those instances, the testing is not to exclude, but rather to help the candidate live with his chronic condition.)

This requirement is much different from psychological testing which is required for two reasons: To protect both the people of God from persons who could do them harm and the candidate himself from the pressures associated with priestly work. But in the HIV testing, the candidate is not being tested to protect either his own or others' physical and/or psychological well-being. The order is asking the candidate to make himself vulnerable solely to protect the resources it uses for ministering. The HIV testing no longer allows us, then, to think of the candidate as simply one who is knocking, seeking, and asking. The candidate is now submitting himself to a very problematic test, for the sake of the order.

My Own Assessment: Virtue Questions

The reasons for and against testing and the minimal standards stated above are only general positions. In order to ascertain what is morally required, we must descend from the general to the specific and consider individual circumstances. For instance, those who oppose testing that routinely excludes all persons testing positive assert that there is no person whose HIV status is typical.[10] A universal policy of exclusion ignores too many circumstances attendant to medical health and moral logic.

But what other circumstances should be engaged in order to determine a morally right policy with regard to testing? The circumstances are too numerous to mention here, but I will offer three only to illustrate that we should not expect all orders, dioceses, and provinces to have the same policies. First, who are the people that the order or diocese serves? Given, for instance, the percentage of persons infected in some parts of Africa, could such a group of priests seek being purely HIV negative? Second, what about an order, like my own, that in its early years identified itself in caring for victims of the plague?[11] Certainly other dioceses or orders may have similar legacies: Does not that original decision to go to the margins of society suggest that one's own boundaries should not be so firmly shut? Third, what financial and manpower resources does an order have to support persons with chronic diseases? These three questions highlight the importance of circumstances.

They also prompt us to face three groups of persons involved in this case: The order, the actual candidates, and the people we serve. Indeed, as superiors decided on their policies, they seemed to focus more on the candidates and the people they serve, and not on themselves. But virtue ethics reminds us: It is the order's policy; they are the ones most directly affected by the decision they make. This can be seen by several considerations; I will mention two.

First, several writers argued that because orders don't test for other chronic illnesses, why should they test for HIV? They were raising the fairness question: Why test for one disease and not another? I kept thinking the opposite: If orders keep testing for HIV, when will they begin the next exclusionary test? Orders test for HIV because they can! When they can test for another serious illness, they will!

Furthermore, by making the decision to test for HIV they entered new territory regarding screening: By instituting the HIV test they have begun an implicit policy of excluding candidates who may have other conditions that, with some probability, will develop into a very costly disease. They have established something new here—they are excluding on predictive health grounds. In perhaps a decade the human genome project will supply us with such a wealth of information that we will be able to predict other illnesses. Should orders begin pursuing a policy of excluding people not who *are* ill but who probably *will be* ill?

Just recently the federal government ruled that businesses cannot use this information to discriminate in hiring.[12] But will religious orders and dioceses turn to genetic testing in order to exclude when the rest of society will not, by law, be allowed to discriminate? Orders have begun going in that direction with HIV testing and, if DNA proves to be as reductive as it seems to be, we may decide that other predictable illnesses (and even dispositions) ought to be screened. What will religious orders become if they begin to deny people access to realizing their vocation on grounds of predictive physical conditions?

Orders did once discriminate against those with epilepsy. While they discriminated against people suffering from this illness, they also contributed to the unjust exclusion of those people from full participation in society by insisting that such people were not capable of assuming all social responsibilities. They also contributed to the terribly unjust social stigma attached to that disease. They reversed themselves from that wrongful policy, but only (again) after society had already instituted laws that protected those with epilepsy from discrimination. Has the mindset that gave us the ban on epilepsy returned? Is it operative again in this ban on HIV positive candidates? Will it be operative even more so in testing for genetic diseases in the future?

Second, purity issues concern the fact that groups and organizations, in order to maintain identity, establish a set of identifiable standards to include or exclude members.[13] Mary Douglas notes that these standards are usually set in corporeal practices: The Jews have circumcision and dietary laws; Roman Catholic religious have virginity and celibacy; the Protestant Reformers have married clergy.

Yet the Scripture scholar Jerome Neyrey[14] finds that Jesus, through his own practices, reformed contemporary purity laws and provided a new hermeneutics for determining membership in the community. Similarly, Majella Franzmann[15] sees in the eating practices of Jesus another way of understanding how Jesus set normative standards for the believing community. The universal invitation to approach the table and eat the body of Christ is rooted in the eating practices of Jesus himself who broke down the purity standards that kept so many on the fringe. These scholars show how significantly Jesus used his body to break down barriers.[16]

In this light, exclusion on grounds of purity compromises the very mission of a religious order. If orders act out of purity interests, how can they be bearers of the Gospels? Thus, we need to ask: How much are orders excluding these candidates because of purity interests? I believe that an unspoken reason for excluding a candidate who tests positive is because orders are concerned with how the people of God will perceive the priesthood if yet another priest develops AIDS. Is the testing, in part, over concern about the purity of the priesthood?

Questions of sexuality, chastity, and celibacy are influential in this testing question. There is, however, a terrible double irony here. First, if a candidate tests positive, then the candidate did not contract the illness while having religious vows. Second, that same purity issue which I think inhibits discussion about testing decisions similarly inhibits many seminarians, religious, and priests from ever discussing their fears, their desires, or their actual concerns about their sexuality and their health. These purity issues both keep out some candidates and inhibit many within. The issue of testing, then, may be more the purity problem than the disease.

How can we conclude? Questions regarding policies must address the reasons I mentioned earlier, both for and against testing. Moreover, whatever policy a particular order adopts ought to observe at least minimal ethical standards, ought to consider the particular circumstances of the order as well as the specific candidates, and ought to find ways of sharing these policy decisions and the methods of arriving at them.

These questions and these decisions are, however, historical ones. And, the history that we are presently living in is, as Enda McDonagh and Kevin Kelly remind us, a time of AIDS.[17] Acknowledging our historical context means, then, that there are good reasons to reexamine those decisions made ten years ago. After all, there is new data. Persons who are HIV positive are living with it and they are living better and longer than ten years ago. The people of God have gotten used to learning that "Father" has AIDS. Some insurance companies have been forced to face supporting healthcare claims of policyholders. Many members of religious orders are opposed to the blanket discrimination. And most of us have been mysteriously, graciously bettered by encountering people who have tested positive. These people have taught us much about life, love, and integrity.

Hopefully religious orders who at present hold these policies to exclude may learn from those candidates who test positive that for Christians a particular moment in time is not trapped in the past but tied to the future. Tied to that future, religious orders must ask themselves what type of people they intend to become. From the case of Simon we see that the applicant knows who he wants to become. As they meet, the admissions committee must no less face the question of who they will become by the decisions they make.

1. Jay O'Connor, "HIV Testing of Applicants," *Clergy and Religious and the AIDS Epidemic* (Chicago: National Federation of Priests' Councils, 1994), 77.

2. The most important work appeared in 1994: Jon Fuller, "HIV/AIDS: An Overview," in *Clergy and Religious and the AIDS Epidemic*, 3–50. In that same collection, see Fuller, "HIV-Considerations for Religious Orders and Dioceses," 57–76; James Schexnayder, "HIV/AIDS Policy Department," 83–86; Diocese of Oakland HIV Policy Committee, "Policy Statement," 87–93. In canon law see, R.R. Calvo, "Admission to the Seminary and HIV Testing," *Roman Replies and CLSA Advisory Opinions 1991* (Washington: Canon Law Society of America, 1991), 72–75; and R. Gibbons, "Admission to the Seminary and HIV Testing," ibid., 76–77. Jack Anderson, "How Healthy is Healthy Enough? Canon Law Considerations in Matters of Health and HIV-AIDS Testing Policies," *Horizon,* Winter (1993): 8–18. See also James F. Keenan, "HIV Testing of Seminary and Religious-Order Candidates," *Review for Religious* 55 (1996), 297–314. Much of this essay reflects my earlier essay.

3. Letty Russell, ed., *The Church with AIDS* (Louisville: Westminster/John Knox Press, 1990), 17.

4. Administrative Board of the USCC, "The Many Faces of AIDS: A Gospel Response," *Origins* 17 (1987): 482–89.

5. From the "Pastoral Statement of the U.S. Catholic Bishops on Handicapped People," Nov. 15,1978, in NCCB, "Called to Compassion and Responsibility," *Origins* 19 (1989): 421–36.

6. Ibid., footnote 45.

7. L. Gostin, "The AIDS Litigation Project," *JAMA* 263 (1990): 2086–93.

8. Albert Jonsen, "Foreword," *The Meaning of AIDS*, eds. Eric Juengst and Barbara Koenig (New York: Praeger Publishers, 1989).

9. R.R. Calvo, "Admission to the Seminary."

10. Richard McCormick, "AIDS: The Shape of the Ethical Challenge," *The Critical Calling* (Washington: Georgetown University Press, 1989), 315–28.

11. John O'Malley, *The First Jesuits* (Cambridge: Harvard University Press, 1993), 171.

12. Warren Leary, "Using Gene Tests to Deny Jobs Is Ruled Illegal," *New York Times* (April 8, 1995), a7.

13. See Mary Douglas, *Purity and Danger* (London: Routledge and Kegan Paul, 1966).

14. Jerome Neyrey, "The Idea of Purity in Mark's Gospel," *Semeia* 35 (1986): 91–128; see also "Body Language in 1 Corinthians," 129–70, at 158.

15. Majella Franzmann, "Of Food, Bodies, and the Boundless Reign of God in the Synoptic Gospels," *Pacifica* 5 (1992): 17–31.

16. Louis William Countryman, "For the Clean or the Unclean," *The Gospel Imperative in the Midst of AIDS,* ed. Robert Iles (Wilton: Morehouse Publishing, 1989), 33–50, see also Patricia Wilson-Kastner, "Realm of the Pure and the Impure," 59–68; Richard Smith, *AIDS, Gays and the American Catholic Church* (Cleveland: Pilgrim Press, 1994), 64ff.

17. Kevin T. Kelly, *New Directions in Sexual Ethics: Moral Theology and the Challenge of AIDS* (London: Geoffrey Chapman, 1998); Enda McDonagh, "Theology in a Time of AIDS," *Irish Theological Quarterly* 60 (1994): 81–99.

B. Ordination, Marriage, and Pastoral Assignments

Chapter Three
Ordination and Immigration

by Carlos Piar

Pedro Rodriguez arrived from Guatemala to assume the pas-
torate of Puerta del Cielo Christian Church, a small Spanish-
speaking congregation in Los Angeles established under the
auspices of a mainline Protestant denomination. Because the
denomination has a congregational polity, the local church was
free to call Mr. Rodriguez as pastor even though he was unfamil-
iar with the denomination and even though Mr. Rodriguez had
completed only the U.S. equivalent of junior high or middle
school. He was called to be the pastor because of his abilities,
pastoral experience, and character. As for theological education,
Mr. Rodriguez had taken some courses at a Pentecostal Bible
institute and through Theological Education by Extension in
Guatemala. Upon assuming the pastorate in California, the
Commission on the Ministry (the denomination's regional body
in charge of pastoral oversight) granted Mr. Rodriguez a preach-
ing license. A year after Mr. Rodriguez was installed as pastor,
the congregation, in accordance with the denomination's polity,
submitted a request to the Commission on the Ministry, that Mr.
Rodriguez be ordained.

Should the leadership of the denomination consent to ordain
Mr. Rodriguez?

The issue illustrated by Mr. Rodriguez's case is one that is aris-
ing for increasing numbers of denominations, especially as the
immigrant population from Latin America grows and the need for
church leaders increases proportionately. Besides the ministerial
ethics of taking a pastorate with a denomination about which a
candidate is uninformed or perhaps even at odds with theologically, Mr. Rodriguez's case also raises questions about social justice that impinge on the meaning and purpose of ordination.
Similar social justice questions concerning ordination have been
raised by women and homosexuals, but little attention has been
given to the ordination of Third World immigrants in First World
churches. To deal with this case we will need to consider the values at stake and demonstrate how an ethics of virtue can best
address the issues involved.

The Ethical Values Involved

The main value that is at issue in this case is that of distributive justice. Is it just that the title "Reverend" and the privileges
attendant to it be granted to someone who has not met the necessary prerequisites, namely a university and seminary education?
On the other hand, is it just that the title "Reverend" and the privileges attendant to it be granted only to those whose historic privileges (being born and raised in the United States, being able to
afford a college and seminary education) give them a better
opportunity to obtain ordination?

Because Mr. Rodriguez has completed only a junior high
school education, the regional leadership finds itself conflicted:
To ordain Mr. Rodriguez, they feel, is to lower the standards of
ordination and to cheapen the efforts of those who labor in seminary for years so that they might be ordained to the ministry. On
the other hand, to refuse to ordain Mr. Rodriguez is to consign
him and the vast majority of Spanish-speaking ministerial candidates (who have no reasonable opportunity to enter into a state-

accredited seminary) to a second-class status within the denomination. Only native-born Americans would be ordained, while Third World immigrants could not be ordained given their inadequate or suspect credentials.

Issues of authority, power, and prestige are also at play here.

Virtue Ethics and Ordination

How can an ethics of virtue best address this problem? A look at the history of ordination reveals that ordination has been a contested arena in church history precisely because ordination imparts to the recipient authority, power, and prestige that he or she would not otherwise have; and yet, there are structures of power within ecclesial institutions that determine who should or should not be a recipient of such authority, power, and prestige. Ordination designates the recipient as worthy of being a holder of such power and prestige.

In light of these observations, we need to recall that an ethics of virtue is concerned with the development of character. As Joseph Kotva has noted about virtue ethics: "There is, however, a certain priority or primacy of character, a special concern for the kind of people we become. . . . [B]efore we can concern ourselves with analyzing particular actions, we need to concern ourselves with becoming the right sort."[1] The most important criterion to be considered in ordination for the ministry, therefore, should not be how much knowledge (measured in university degrees) candidates have, but what kind of people they have become and are becoming; are they now and are they continuing to become the right sort of person? The latter is important to consider because virtue is not an end but a process.

In assessing the character of the moral agents we must examine their habits, dispositions, and attitudes. Included in dispositions and attitudes are the motivations for action. Are those motivations worthy? As Marjorie Warkentin argues, the only worthy motive for ordination is service:

> The authority of any one member of the believing
> community is not an independent authority, but exists
> only in its relationship to the authority held by the
> members in common. The purpose of such authority
> is service, *diakonia* . . . Only if ordination facilitates
> the legitimate use of authority in the church is it a
> valid form.[2]

Thus, to request or grant ordination simply to fit an individual within a power structure is not a worthy motive. Both Mr. Rodriguez and the Commission on the Ministry must inquire into their respective motivations for requesting and granting or denying ordination. For Mr. Rodriguez to request ordination simply because he wants to be called "Reverend," for example, or does not want to be the only pastor without it in the region he serves, would not be a weighty enough reason. On the other hand, for the Commission on the Ministry to consent to ordain Mr. Rodriguez because the Commission fears charges of racism, or it fears creating feelings of animosity and resentment on the part of Mr. Rodriguez's congregation towards the regional leadership, would be to allow the process of ordination to be politicized and racialized and the worthiness of the individual ignored. Still, the Commission needs to be equally attentive to its moral reasons for denying ordination, recognizing that its members might be motivated by racist attitudes or other irrelevant biases. To deny Mr. Rodriguez ordination because he does not have a Master of Divinity degree might be unwise, unjust, and unloving if the denominational leadership fails to take into account the full spectrum of factors in all their complexity, that may make Mr. Rodriguez a worthy candidate for ordination.

Beyond worthy motives on the part of all the parties involved, there must also be worthy standards or criteria for ordination. These must be prioritized, for some will clearly be more important than others. Let me suggest a set of criteria and their order of importance:

1. Evidence of Christian faith
2. Evidence of Christian character
3. Evidence of ministerial abilities
4. Evidence of intellectual development

Because an ethics of virtue is concerned with someone being and becoming the right sort of person, then the criteria for ordination should be such that they help assess a person's present and future spiritual, moral, and intellectual development.

Evidence of Christian faith should be obvious in one seeking ordination to the Christian ministry, but it is not something that should be taken for granted by those making the decision to ordain or not. It is possible that someone in the course of their studies (or lack thereof) might have become so alienated from their faith, that he or she could just as easily call himself or herself agnostic as Christian or to have developed such tortured interpretations of Christian doctrines that their beliefs could not justly be construed as Christian. In the case of Latin American immigrants seeking ordination, the committee deciding to approve or disapprove the ordination must assess the influence of such syncretic religions as Santería, Curanderismo, or Spiritism on the candidate's beliefs.

Evidence of Christian character is the second criterion, but it is as important as the first in considering ordination because profession of faith is not enough. The candidate must give evidence that he or she is making progress in becoming more Christ-like. This is more difficult to assess; those doing the assessment must recognize that "Christ-likeness" is a process. No one reaches that goal in this life, as the apostle Paul made clear in Philippians 3:13–14, "forgetting what lies behind and straining forward to what lies ahead, I press on toward the goal for the prize of the heavenly call of God in Christ Jesus."

Moreover, "Christ-likeness" or Christian character encompasses a host of virtues and attitudes that may be difficult to enumerate. The lists given in the Pastoral Epistles (1 Tim 3:1–13; Titus 1:7–9) as well as those dealing with Christian character

(Rom 12:9–13, 14; 1 Cor 13; Gal 5:19–23; Eph 5:1–12; Col 3:5–17) may help in this regard. Whatever list is used, however, it must be recognized that a candidate may be mature in many areas, but immature in others. The assessment of a candidate's character will require delving into the candidate's past and carefully weighing a candidate's self-description as well as the testimony of associates, acquaintances, and friends. Whether someone is of mature Christian character can only be known in light of their history, for only so can a person's constancy in the practice and pursuit of Christian virtues and fidelity to Christian values be assessed.

The third criterion for ordination is ministerial abilities. Besides the conviction of being "called" by God, does the candidate have the abilities that will make him or her a competent minister? Here, of course, candidates will vary in their abilities; some will have preaching ability, others will have organizational skills, and others will have counseling expertise, for example. No one individual will possess all the necessary abilities to the same degree. Some may be especially gifted, while others may just be average. But these will be qualities that, educated or not, the candidate will have demonstrated in the service of a believing community.

The fourth criterion is intellectual development. It is here where education will be a most important consideration. Is the candidate in the process of honing his or her critical thinking skills? Is the candidate developing his or her exegetical skills? Is he or she increasing in his or her understanding of the history of Christianity and of his or her particular denomination? Is he or she reading a wide spectrum of theological viewpoints? It is important that the ordinand be able to show that he or she is continuing to grow in knowledge, for it is thus that he or she will (1) acquire a sense of denominational identity, (2) be able to give a defense of the faith to those that ask it of him or her, and (3) be able to relate the faith to the issues and concerns of the modern world.

For the immigrant candidate, whether from Latin America or elsewhere, such intellectual development should include English acquisition. Competence in English will enable a minister to communicate with denominational leadership, hospital personnel, and city authorities; in short, a bilingual minister will be in a better position to meet the needs of his or her congregation than one who speaks limited English. An ethics of virtue with its perfectionism, its emphasis on the pursuit of excellence, would envision ordination candidates well disposed to make every effort to learn English. But it would also envision the candidate as one who seeks to improve himself or herself in every area, to educate himself or herself if more formal learning opportunities are absent.

Should Mr. Rodriguez be ordained? The answer will depend on the assessment of Mr. Rodriguez's character: His constancy in the Christian virtues, his record of faithful and fruitful service to the church, his disposition to persevere in a process of personal and intellectual development, his disposition to be accountable to his congregation and to the denominational leadership for this process of development. Specific, attainable benchmarks should be set by which Mr. Rodriguez's progress can be measured, and only after reaching some of these benchmarks should ordination be granted.

Virtue and the Ordaining Community

In addition to the character of the ordination candidate, virtue ethics would assess the ordaining community's collective character and decision-making process. The ordaining entity, the denomination or church, needs to examine itself to see if it embodies in its practices, processes, and organizations or institutions the requisite virtues for creating true community and assuring that immigrant candidates are treated justly.

One institutional reason for ordination is that it helps the denomination or church to screen out those who are theologically, morally, or psychologically unfit for formal ministry. Religious organizations have histories and traditions that they have a legitimate right to maintain; they have values that they want to sustain and enact in relation to the broader society. The process of ordination makes it possible for a religious organization, on the one hand, to preserve and maintain its historic identity and, on the other hand, to expand its coterie of leaders and ensure its continuance into the future. There is, therefore, a legitimate basis for exclusion and/or disqualification by a religious organization; it cannot ordain all comers. Ordination is a means by which the trustees of churches or denominations maintain organizational boundaries.

There can be, however, illegitimate, unjust bases for excluding and/or disqualifying potential ordinands, especially when the trustees of churches or denominations apply criteria or values that contradict the organization's professed values. When the Ku Klux Klan excludes African Americans or Hispanics because of their race, one can at least say that they are being consistent with their professed values, however horrible those values are. But when a Christian church or denomination excludes any person from membership or leadership because of their race, ethnicity, or country of origin, for example, then any objective observer would judge that church or denomination to be inconsistent with its professed Christian values of universal inclusion, equality under God, justice, and love as mutual regard (i.e., servanthood).

But is the level of educational attainment a legitimate or an illegitimate basis for excluding someone from the ranks of the ordained? It is not an irrelevant consideration particularly as trustees (e.g., an ordination committee) seek to safeguard their denomination's distinctive tradition and as they seek to shape the church into a community of service. In considering education as a criterion for ordination, as in Mr. Rodriguez's case, an ordination committee must assess the value of formal education in light of the overall vision of the church or denomination as a community that serves God and neighbor.

Servanthood should not only be the vision or mission that a church hopes to realize in relation to its own membership and in relation to society as a whole, but it should also be its working principle of leadership. As Jesus said:

> You know that among the Gentiles those whom they
> recognize as their rulers lord it over them, and their
> great ones are tyrants over them. But it is not so
> among you; but whoever wishes to become great
> among you must be your servant, and whoever wishes
> to be first among you must be slave of all. For the Son
> of Man came not to be served but to serve, and to give
> his life a ransom for many. (Mk 10:42–45)

The fulfillment of this vision of servant leadership will be possible only as those who oversee ministry put into practice the virtues they expect from potential ordinands. Mr. Rodriguez must be able to rely upon the denomination and its leadership's collective character. Are they, in Stanley Hauerwas's words, a "community of character?" Do they embody the virtues that they expect of Mr. Rodriguez?

The members of a ministerial committee are more than keepers of the gate into ordained ministry. They provide leadership to ordained ministers and potential ordinands. In shaping the church into a community of virtue, its leaders must play the role of pacesetters and thus be servants.

In order to carry out this leadership role of servanthood, a ministerial or ordination committee needs to develop self- and other-regarding virtues, suggested by the following questions:

First, self-regarding virtues:

Does the committee have a clear vision of what the church should become? What is the church's mission?

Does it have a clear understanding of its role and duties within the church or denomination? Is it cognizant of its capabilities and limitations?

Is it self-critical? Is it honest in assessing its shortcomings? Does it question itself critically about its objectives, motives, methods, rules, processes, attitudes, and choices?

Is it diligent in the pursuit of excellence? Is it seeking to become the best that it can be?

Is it spiritual? Do committee members inspire one another and potential ordinands in its care to greater spiritual and personal growth?

Does it seek to build consensus among its members? Does the committee operate democratically and persuasively, rather than autocratically and coercively?

Do the committee members complement each other's strengths and build upon them?

Are the committee members accountable to each other?

Second, other-regarding virtues:

Is it just? Is it fair? Is the ministerial committee even-handed in its treatment of ordination candidates?

Is the ministerial committee reasonable? Are the expectations it has of candidates attainable?

Is it supportive? Does the committee make available to the potential ordinand the resources of the church or denomination, or provide the means (institutional, financial) for the realization of objectives or expectations?

Is it trustworthy? Sincere? Transparent? Without hidden agendas?

Is it responsible? Is it serious in the discharge of its duties? Does it discharge its duties in a timely fashion?

Is it (at least) respectful of differences? Is it (at best) appreciative of differences?

Immigration, Ordination, and Justice

If denominations or churches are going to reach out to immigrant populations because they envision themselves as communities of virtue and service, then they must be prepared to practice justice towards these immigrant populations. To say to them, "We want to include you in our faith community, but we will not ordain any of your spiritual leaders unless he or she graduates from one of our seminaries" is unjust and undercuts the aim of being/becoming a community of service and of virtue. We cannot

invite immigrants to come and then marginalize them. The practice of communitarian justice requires that churches or denominations make a good faith effort to facilitate the full participation
of its immigrant constituents in every one of its organizations and
institutions.

To clarify how justice is applicable in this issue, I rely on
Philip Selznick's listing of principles of justice:

> [A theory of justice] should take its departure from
> principles that have received recurrent recognition.
> These include: *entitlement*—claims of right must be
> based on what has already been granted by law or
> custom; *justification*—when deprivations are
> imposed, reasons must be given or tacitly understood,
> and some form of consent is presumed; *equality*—at
> a minimum, like cases must be treated alike, and the
> intrinsic worth of every member must be recognized;
> *impartiality*—bias and self-interest must be excluded
> from rule-making and administration; *proportional-
> ity*—relevant differences must be considered when
> allocating benefits and burdens; *reciprocity*—a bal-
> ance of giving and taking must be maintained, espe-
> cially in determining mutual obligations;
> *rectification*—injured parties must be compensated
> for the losses they have suffered; *need*—allocations
> must be based on what people are thought to require
> for survival or for a minimally acceptable standard of
> existence; *desert*—comparative worth, merit, or
> blame must be weighted; and *participation*—every
> person must be recognized as a member of the com-
> munity, especially in respect to basic rights and hav-
> ing a voice in decisions that affect vital interests.[3]

Although Selznick's purpose is to expound a theory of justice
for civil society as a whole, many of the principles he enumerates
are clearly relevant to Mr. Rodriguez's case, and to the issue of

ordaining immigrants. For example, the principles of *need* and *participation* suggest that it is not enough for a denomination simply to demand of men and women like Mr. Rodriguez that they improve their education. The denomination must also change its institutions and its organizational rules to enable immigrant candidates to be *entitled* and *deserving* of ordination. In seeking to be or become a just community, a church or denomination will also practice *reciprocity:* It will ask that immigrant candidates get better educated, but it will furnish the means and opportunities to make that possible.

Denominational structures, especially seminaries, should lead by providing educational opportunities appropriate to the needs of immigrant faith communities—they should not expect immigrants to enter existing degree programs with their unattainable admission requirements as well as high costs. Denomi-nations must recognize that the target population is poor, not well-educated, and cannot afford the time or money to take three years of full-time study to complete a Master of Divinity. The attainment of an M. Div. by a Latino immigrant is possible in the best of all possible worlds; but reality often flies in the face of these expectations. New models of theological education need to be devised and implemented. Already some models, like Bible institutes and Theological Education by Extension modules, are appearing and a few seminaries are now establishing innovative degree programs for Spanish-speaking immigrants.[4] Denomi-nations and churches, however, need to be more proactive in their cooperation with seminaries in developing and providing appropriate courses for the spiritual leaders of these immigrant communities.

The presence of immigrant communities poses a challenge to the leadership of churches and denominations in the United States, a challenge to grow in virtue by doing justice. Religious organizations can pass resolutions, publish press releases, and march down Main Street denouncing xenophobic policies proposed by politicians, but they need to look a little closer to home and see where they are falling short in serving and including as equals their own immigrant co-religionists.

1. Joseph Kotva, Jr., *The Christian Case for Virtue Ethics* (Washington, D.C.: Georgetown University Press, 1996), 30.

2. Marjorie Warkentin, *Ordination: A Biblical-Historical View* (Grand Rapids: William B. Eerdmans, 1982), 183.

3. Philip Selznick, *The Moral Commonwealth: Social Theory and the Promise of Community* (Berkeley: University of California Press, 1992), 431–32.

4. Seminaries like San Francisco Theological and Fuller Theological in California offer alternative degree programs for Latino pastors. The Association for Hispanic Theological Education (AETH) in Decatur, Georgia provides financial and educational resources to Latino pastors and Bible Institutes. The Hispanic Theological Initiative provides scholarships and grants. The Latin American Faculty of Theological Education (FLET) provides theological education through the module model in the U.S.

Chapter Four

Married Clergy and the Acceptance of Appointments

by Gilbert Meilaender

Luther Martin graduated from seminary at age 26 and served for seven years as pastor of a small rural congregation. He then accepted a call to serve as pastor of Holy Trinity Lutheran Church in Elyria, Ohio, where he has served for sixteen years. Pastor Martin married his wife, Kate, before his last year of seminary. They have three children: 22-year-old Beth, who will soon enter medical school; 20-year-old Paul, who is in college; and 18-year-old Margaret, who will graduate from high school in a few months.

Kate was trained as a nurse and was, in fact, working as a nurse when she and Luther married. After Beth was born, she stopped working for a time, but she has been working full-time again for the past ten years. Initially, she returned to work largely in order to supplement their family's income. Luther's salary has always been adequate for their needs, but it has certainly never been more than adequate. Gradually, however, Kate has devoted herself more and more to her work as a nurse in an intensive care unit. She has worked at the same hospital for seven years, is the most experienced ICU nurse there, and finds the work constantly challenging. Moreover, her salary is now almost $20,000 more per year than Luther is paid.

Two weeks ago Luther received a call to a large but struggling parish in a suburb of Detroit. The parish was ill served by its previous pastor, who left the congregation deeply divided between his detractors and his supporters. The congregation needs a capable, experienced pastor—which is precisely what Luther is. His talents and interests seem to fit the congregation's needs well, and he is at a point in his ministry when he might well undertake the challenges this call presents. Indeed, as he has pondered and prayed over this matter, he has gradually come to think that the call from this congregation to him truly is God's call, mediated through the congregation.

Over the past decade Luther had received and declined three calls to other congregations. In part, he did not think—as he does of this call—that the fit between his gifts and those congregations was particularly close. In part, he took into consideration the need of his children for stability during their years in school. Now, however, he faces a new complication. Kate is very reluctant to move. She would be happy to spend the rest of her life in Elyria, where they have many friends and acquaintances. And more important still, if they move she will have to give up her work—and the income that work provides. No doubt with her skills and experience she could find another job, but there is no guarantee that she would enjoy it as much or find the work as challenging and satisfying. Kate is willing to move if Luther decides to accept the call, but she does not find the prospect in any way appealing. Clearly, if the decision were hers, they would not move.

Luther is genuinely uncertain not just about what he ought to do but even about how he ought to think through this decision. He does not think of his ministry simply as a job. He takes his vow of ordination seriously and, over the years, has allowed it to shape his identity in countless ways. Yet, of course, he also takes his marriage vow seriously, and it too has shaped him profoundly. The claims of both ministry and marriage weigh heavily upon him.

I begin by setting the boundaries within which I will consider this case. First, and most important, I will consider it from a particular angle of vision: The Lutheran tradition, to which Pastor Martin belongs. For all its differences from Roman Catholicism, and despite the animus that accompanied the break with Rome in the sixteenth century, that tradition has nevertheless understood the pastoral office in ways deeply continuous with the Catholic tradition. It has held that ordination sets a man apart to occupy an office established by God as the foundation of the church.[1] Indeed, in the Lutheran Confessional writings "[t]he term 'sacrament' is applicable both to the sacred ministry itself and to ordination by the laying on of hands" and was understood "as something over and above a mere calling."[2] Obviously, for a Protestant body without any concept of "holy orders" this case might appear somewhat different, but Lutheranism is not that sort of tradition. The case as set forth above also presumes a setting quite common in this country, in which congregations, with the aid and direction of the larger synods to which they belong, extend a "call" to a pastor, to be accepted or declined by the pastor.

Second, a word is in order about "virtue ethics." An emphasis on character rather than obligation, an emphasis on creating discerning moral agents rather than rules to guide conduct, has been quite strong over the past several decades of philosophical and theological ethics. This move toward virtue ethics was often presented as an alternative to "quandary ethics," which focused attention on dilemmas pitting one obligation against another. Obviously, however, Pastor Martin finds himself in a bit of a quandary. Moreover, it may well be that his decision and conduct in this case ought to be governed by certain rules (as, for example, to keep the promises he has made). It would be a mistake to suppose that a "virtue ethic" relieves us of the necessity to think about obligations and rules. What it should do, at least in the case under consideration, is remind us that character develops and expresses itself within communities. Ethics was for Aristotle a branch of politics precisely because only the person who had been brought up properly within a well-ordered society could have the kind of character needed to make moral choices and discern appropriate action. That indeed will be the chief thrust of my commentary. Only if certain things have been established in advance, not simply by Luther and Kate, but by some larger communities, will they be in a position to deal with his call in ways that do not seem to fail either his ministerial or his marital commitment.

I

We can begin not strictly with theology but with the meaning of well-ordered love for one's spouse (or, in fact, any human being). If Luther's love for Kate (and hers for him) is not placed within, and indeed subordinate to, some larger commitment, their love for each other will not be well ordered. When Ken Burns produced his much acclaimed series of public television shows on the Civil War, one of the most powerful moments for many listeners was the reading of a letter written by Major Sullivan Ballou of the 2nd Rhode Island regiment of the Union Army to his wife, Sarah. Believing that his regiment would engage in battle within a few days, he reckoned with the fact that he might not return alive. "The memories of the blissful moments I have spent with you come creeping over me, and I feel most gratified to God and to you that I have enjoyed them so long. And hard it is for me to give them up and burn to ashes the hopes of future years, when, God willing, we might still have lived and loved together. . . . If I do not [return], my dear Sarah, never forget how much I love you, and when my last breath escapes me on the battle field, it will whisper your name." One could hardly ask for a more steadfast love. Yet, what gives it such nobility is precisely that it is not Ballou's only love, perhaps not even the love that most strongly claims him at this moment. Thus, he can write: "Sarah, my love for you is deathless, it seems to bind me with mighty cables that nothing but Omnipotence could break; and yet my love of Country comes over me like a strong wind and bears me unresistably on with all these chains to the battle field." His love for Sarah has grandeur and honor because he does not make everything of it. There are other powerful claims upon him, and he must honor them as well. He cannot desert those other claims simply in the name of their love. To rest the whole weight of the heart in one's beloved is to ask too much—more than any of us can or should give.

Nor is Sullivan Ballou's sentiment idiosyncratic or unusual. "To Lucasta, Going to the Wars," by the well known Cavalier poet Richard Lovelace (1618–57), expresses (also in the context of going into battle) essentially the same relation between passionate devotion and its limit:

> Tell me not, sweet, I am unkind,
>   that from the nunnery
> Of thy chaste breast and quiet mind
>   To war and arms I fly.
>
> True, a new mistress now I chase,
>   The first foe in the field;
> And with a stronger faith embrace
>   A sword, a horse, a shield.
> Yet this inconstancy is such
>   As you too shall adore;
> I could not love thee, dear, so much,
>   Loved I not honor more.

Commenting on the last lines of the poem, C. S. Lewis writes: "There are women to whom the plea would be meaningless. . . . Lovelace can use it with confidence because his lady is a Cavalier lady who already admits, as he does, the claims of Honour. . . . They have agreed and understood each other on this matter long before. The task of converting her to a belief in Honour is not now—now, when the decision is upon them—to be undertaken."[3]

Lewis here makes the crucial point: The "quandary" is insuperable—even for the most virtuous of people—unless there has been agreement "on this matter long before." Lovelace and his lady, along with other Cavaliers, belong to a community that has formed and shaped them. Their loves have been ordered in advance of potential conflict. In *The Four Loves,* Lewis had in mind not precisely the kind of vocational conflict faced by Pastor Martin but a more general conflict that any husband and wife might encounter. We might face what looks to be a choice between faithful obedience to God and loyalty to the beloved.

> It is too late, when the crisis comes, to begin telling a wife or husband or mother or friend, that your love all along had a secret reservation—"under God" or "so far as a higher Love permits." They ought to have been warned; not, to be sure, explicitly, but by the implication of a thousand talks, by the principle revealed in a hundred decisions upon small matters. Indeed, a real disagreement on this issue should make itself felt early enough to prevent a marriage or a Friendship from existing at all.[4]

Without such prior agreement on the relative order of our commitments, we cannot possibly hope to do justice to the several loyalties that press upon us.

II

If we now try to think about the case within the particular ecclesial context that claims Pastor Martin's loyalty, we will see that a similar point emerges.[5] In the Catholic tradition out of which Lutheranism emerged, it was generally held that the demands of marriage and of ordination were each too heavy for one person reasonably to carry both of them; hence, clerical celibacy came to be required. The demands were heavy not simply because they required a good bit of time but because of the way they claimed the person's devotion and loyalty.

When, then, Lutheran churches broke with the requirement of clerical celibacy, they did not intend anyone to suppose that a pastor's marriage was merely a happenstance, of no particular significance for his ministry. On the contrary, "Luther regarded his marriage as by no means adventitious to his status as ordained, but as a decisive act to reform ordained Ministry, carried out in fulfillment of his responsibility as ordained. It was precisely a new churchly and social entity, the evangelical pastoral family, which he intentionally created."[6] The marriage vow, like the ordination vow, becomes integral to the identity of the one who makes it. Both vows are, in Robert Jenson's words, "totalitarian in the lives of those who enter them."

> It is thus not surprising that marriage and ordination together have usually been thought [in the Catholic tradition with which the Lutheran Reformers wanted to maintain continuity] to be simply too much for one person to bear. And when the reformation decided it was nevertheless right and necessary to join marriage and ordination, it was understood that in the nature of the cases this could not be done with integrity and without destructive conflict, except by truly joining them, by interleaving the two totalitarian commitments in the structure of a new churchly and social unit created to contain them, the pastoral family.[7]

Jenson's point is crucial for our understanding of the case with which we began. If Pastor Martin thinks that he must consider this decision out of his own resources alone, or out of the resources he and his wife jointly bring to it, he can only be impaled on the horns of a dilemma. They must understand their marriage in terms the churchly community gives them—as part of the way by which the church most effectively carries out its ministry and most effectively nourishes and sustains the pastors whose office centrally constitutes that ministry. Hence, Pastor Martin's commitment to his ministry and his commitment to his marriage are not really—within the context of the understanding provided by the churchly community—two different and potentially competing commitments. On the contrary, together they are "one complex commitment."[8]

Of course, if the church fails to supply such an understanding, it leaves Pastor Martin and others like him without the support they need to face such decisions. And the church's failure is often patent. Moreover, I know of occasions when Lutheran seminarians have been told that their marriage comes first, the duties of their ministry second. They are told this, I am sure, as part of a laudable effort to shore up the many weak and threatened clergy marriages of our time. But it is the wrong advice. A serious return to clerical celibacy would be far better if we cannot—in the face of cultural pressures to the contrary—conceive of "the pastoral family" as a union with only "one complex commitment."

As with the Cavalier poet and his lady, Luther and Kate need to have been agreed in advance upon certain things, namely, that he could not love her so much, loved he not his ordination vow more. But, of course, it will never work if this is just their private understanding. Any private understanding is unlikely to be able to withstand the stresses and strains that life brings. However virtuous Luther and Kate may be, they require support, which will take the form of rules and requirements, from the churchly community they serve.

What sort of rules? Ones that, in fact, are quite obvious. The church must decline to ordain to the pastoral office any man whose wife cannot or will not understand that their marital union is, as a union, to be committed in service of that ordination vow.[9] Likewise, an already ordained man who wishes to marry cannot be permitted to continue as a public minister of the church unless the woman whom he intends to marry understands and accepts that his continuation in the pastoral office is decisive for the meaning of their marriage.

Something like this is what a Lutheran church that took both marriage and ministry with full seriousness would have to say. None of it, of course, would "solve" Pastor Martin's quandary.

He would still, in serious conversation with his wife, have to consider the several claims upon them. There is no single decision which would be the sole "right" one in such circumstances, although we can say that Kate's job must not by itself be the decisive factor. But only a community that takes seriously its responsibility to shape the conditions under which such decisions are made has really understood that virtue is always communal and never merely private.

1. Among the Lutheran Confessional Writings cf. Article XIV of the Augsburg Confession: "It is taught among us that nobody should publicly teach or preach or administer the sacraments in the church without a regular call." Also, Article V: "To obtain such faith God instituted the office of the ministry, that is, provided the Gospel and the sacraments." Also par. 25, 27 of the Treatise on the Power and Primacy of the Pope: "As to the statement, 'On this rock I will build my church' (Matt. 16:18), it is certain that the church is not built on the authority of a man but on the ministry of the confession which Peter made when he declared Jesus to be the Christ, the Son of God. . . . Nor is this ministry valid because of any individual's authority but because of the Word given by Christ."

2. Arthur Carl Piepkorn, "The Sacred Ministry and Holy Ordination in the Symbolical Books of the Lutheran Church," in *The Church: Selected Writings of Arthur Carl Piepkorn,* eds. Michael P. Plekon and William S. Wiecher (Delhi, NY: ALPB Books, 1993), 53–75, at 61 and 62.

3. C. S. Lewis, *The Four Loves* (New York: Harcourt Brace Jovanovich, 1960), 173.

4. Ibid., 173–74.

5. For what follows, my thinking has been especially influenced by Robert W. Jenson, "Marriage and Ministry," *Lutheran Forum* 31 (Winter, 1997): 20–22.

6. Ibid., 20.

7. Ibid., 22.

8.   Ibid., 22.

9.   And, of course, in those branches of Lutheranism that have departed from the Catholic tradition also in that they ordain women, the church would have to decline to ordain any woman whose husband cannot or will not understand the decisive change ordination means for their marriage.

SECTION TWO

The Way Pastors Live

Introduction

*B*ecause virtue ethics reflects on the character of the moral agents, its first task is to invite agents to self-understanding. Prudence, arguably one of the most important virtues, is not simply the virtue that helps us decide what conduct will get us from one point to another. Rather, it also helps agents to understand what conduct they personally are capable of. When applied to self-understanding, prudence is the virtue that helps agents to know themselves, their limits, and their contexts. Prudence, a dynamic, personal, future-oriented virtue, helps agents know how they can concretely move forward.

In ministry, prudence is especially important. Because pastors' roles are enmeshed in a variety of relationships, pastors need to be expert in the prudence of right relations. The first expertise they need is that of knowing where they are vulnerable and where they are strong. To know how to lead their congregation forward, pastors need to know their own personal histories. For pastors to have the freedom to know and acknowledge their own humanity, they need, in turn, friends whom they can trust and with whom they can confide. As Richard Gula and the other moral theologians acknowledge, the selection of those friends cannot be from among those whom pastors counsel, confess, guide, and serve;

pastors need support from their peers. But, pastors also need support from their congregations. The congregation must prudently temper their expectations of the pastor with the virtue of what Paul Wadell calls in his essay, "a gracious realism." With that virtue pastor and congregation acknowledge the limited humanity of each other.

Still, none of these insights are lived out in a vacuum. We humans create our histories by the characters we become, the actions we perform, and the relationships we establish. Through those histories we develop institutions and cultures which, in turn, shape the stories we tell and the people we become. As both Judith Kay and Samuel Roberts make clear respectively, the humanness of these institutions and these cultures cannot be overlooked. Prudent pastors must be attentive to the particular and all-too-human environment in which they find themselves. Aware of their context, prudent pastors can serve and be the pastors that they wish to become.

As Joseph Kotva writes, pastors grow by their friendships. Kotva notes that Aristotle developed a large segment of his virtue ethics precisely on the virtue of friendship. If a virtue is a practice that forms our character, then the virtue of friendship is both an ordinary and an important one. In worthy friends we discover those who give us joy, who allow us into intimate sharing, and who define us by their own selves. And, as Kotva shows us from his own experience, we can learn about becoming better people by emulating in our lives the gifts and virtues we see in theirs.

Like prayer, friendship is something that pastors need to establish as a priority, not as a task but as a virtuous activity, that is, as something that provides them with an opportunity for their own flourishment. In the highly duty-and-task oriented life of pastors, the virtue of friendship brings pastors into a deeper contact with their humanity, not to show them their limits but to show them the possibilities of happiness that come with being human.

Richard Gula leads the reader to see that pastors who overlook their need for friendship might begin to have those needs fulfilled by persons whom pastors elected to serve. In the light of recent movements that challenge the legitimacy or even relevance of boundaries, Gula examines the topic from the perspective of a woman who has become an inappropriate surrogate for a pastor's needs. From her perspective, Gula is able to describe the evident power inequities that people in power rarely experience. Then, because of the Christian call to the virtue of justice, Gula outlines proper relational conduct that is attentive to those inequities, so that both pastor and congregation can relate well with one another.

Sondra Wheeler develops these insights in two concrete directions. First, she analyzes the relational lives of pastors, specifically from a sexual viewpoint; second, she provides a set of virtues for the right growth of a pastor as a sexual person. She begins by turning to the classic cardinal virtues, starting with prudence, reminding the reader of the words of Aquinas who saw "unchastity as the first enemy of prudence." But because these virtues are invoked for the formation of pastors, she turns to the context of their lives and proposes two practices that are constitutive supports for right pastoral conduct—prayer and "stable and trustworthy contexts of accountability."

An awareness of context is precisely the underlying theme of the next two essays. In the environment of death-row ministry, Judith Kay provides a virtue approach to support a chaplain ministering courageously and with integrity in an atmosphere of profound moral compromise. Whereas this essay reflects on a ministry that is oriented not toward a community but to an individual, in many ways it parallels the concerns later raised by Samuel Roberts, that is, where the context of a pastor's service could seriously compromise the pastor's service. By her focus, Kay offers a model of virtuous practices that include self-knowledge, a docile spirit willing to learn from prisoners about their humanity when no others are interested, and an integrity and courage that mutually define each other. Readers will find in Kay's essay an apt model not only for those who work in prisons but also for others whose ministry to individuals places them in potentially compromising situations.

Samuel Roberts's essay brings us into the humanity of one's own people. He explains the culture of deference for the preacher living within the African American communities of faith. Through his case, Roberts explores the vulnerabilities of both pastor and congregation and invokes the virtue of discernment. Discernment enables the pastor to appreciate the depth and breadth of those vulnerabilities and to find the proper virtuous or middle course in addressing those whose well-being the pastor serves.

Along with discernment, Roberts discusses the virtues of justice and courage, defining the latter in terms of "a quiet confidence in one's ability to do the right." Roberts brings us into the life of the community where the ethical solutions are found in the wonderfully human relationships that mingle all about. Like Judith Kay's essay, this one calls us to recognize that good virtue ethics for ministerial cases must really attend to the variety of persons and to the multitudinous ways those persons look to one another with love and expectation.

A. The Pastor and Personal Relationships

Chapter Five
Seeking Out Good Friends[1]

by Joseph Kotva, Jr.

Several years ago, North Church—our small, fledgling, urban congregation—called a new minister: Pastor Sam. Sam quickly became more than my minister; he also became my friend. We had attended the same seminary, although at different times, and now Sam was the pastor of the church I attended while I sought further theological education. Sam and I are close in age; our mutual interests range from sports to music; our theological convictions are similar; and we are both deeply committed to our denomination. It is only because Sam became a good friend that he has shown me so much about the pastoral virtue of presence.

Presence concerns being with people in a way that communicates the church's support and God's presence in the midst of their confusion and pain. Presence has as much to do with body posture and the tone of one's voice as it does with the words that one chooses. It is a skill of knowing when to hold another's hand, when to offer prayer or to read Scripture, when to simply sit with others in their pain, and when to leave them alone. This virtue cannot be learned from a book or acquired quickly. It cannot be mimicked or parroted and still be the virtue of presence. Instead, presence must be modeled and creatively emulated.

Because Sam and I are friends and share a similar commitment to the church, I noticed that his life embodied pastoral virtues, such as presence, that I found lacking in myself.[2]

Moreover, our friendship meant that we were together enough for me to see those virtues manifest in a variety of settings. This variety allowed me to begin to understand and analogically "copy" those virtues in my own life. Although neither of us still lives in that city, Sam and I are still friends, and he continues to teach me what it is to minister well.

This case concerns two friends, and it reminds us that who we are and who we become is in part the consequence of the friendships we cultivate. Friendship is a major theme in most accounts of virtue. Aristotle devoted nearly one-fifth of the *Nicomachean Ethics* (books VIII–IX) to friendship, and friendship is a major component in the current, renewed interest in virtue.[3] In referring to friendship, virtue ethics does not mean those superficial acquaintances that we sometimes mistakenly label as "friends," although these too might have some character-shaping effect. Virtue ethics is instead particularly interested in those friends whose values we share and whose company we treasure.

Why is friendship so important in virtue ethics? The short answer is that friendships are both intrinsic components of, and necessary instrumental means to, the best kind of human life.[4] Friendships have more than instrumental or utilitarian value. Good friendships involve intimacy, trust, mutual concern, shared commitments, and a recognition of both similarities and differences between the friends.[5] We find such relationships intrinsically valuable and worthwhile. These friendships enrich and enliven our lives in ways that are hard to specify, but we know that we would be the poorer without them. To delight in our friends, to do good to them, to have them do good to us, to share experiences and commitments—such things are of immense value.[6]

Friendships are intrinsically valuable and are to be prized, but they also have the instrumental value of being morally formative. Indeed, virtue ethics sees friendship as perhaps "the primary adult context for the development of moral judgment and character."[7] Good friendships provide a kind of mutual moral tutoring that is vital to the formation and maintenance of adult character.

There are several interrelated mechanisms for this mutual moral influence. First, consider the role our friends play in moral discernment. It is among our friends that we are most likely to seek advice and to expose our judgments to correction. Even when we seek additional advice from others besides our friends, it is the counsel of those whom we have come to love and trust that usually most influences us.[8] Friends also offer a listening ear. Sometimes what our moral discernment most needs is simply to bring to voice the issue with which we are struggling. At such times, friends do not advise or critique; they listen. By listening, they provide a forum wherein we gain some distance from the issue and can think it through.

Second, friendship often serves as an invitation to values and activities. If your friend, whom you love and value, loves and values certain commitments or activities, you will be inclined to accept those commitments and activities as worthwhile simply because they are important to your friend. Moreover, because we want to spend time with our friends, there is a strong inclination to spend time sharing in those things that are important to our friends. And because we love our friends and want to share in their activities, there is strong motivation to cultivate our tastes and abilities in the direction of those activities.[9]

This kind of invitation happens all the time in human friendships. To choose a mundane example, I learned to love jazz not because I grew up in a family that cared about jazz (they did not) but because one of my best friends, Jerry, loved jazz. I accepted jazz as meriting attention because Jerry viewed it as worthy. I spent time listening to and talking about jazz as an intrinsic part of how I spent time with my friend. In the process, I found a passion for the music, which I have similarly transmitted to other friends. Friends implicitly invite us into activities and values that we might not otherwise consider.

Other mechanisms of friendship's moral influence rely on good friends being both similar to and different from each other.

In our similarity, our friends provide us with a kind of moral mirror.[10] We see our values and virtues (and perhaps our vices) embodied in another self. We thus come to better self-understanding because we can see ourselves in our friends. But our friends are not identical to us, and the differences are also important to self-knowledge. Sometimes it is in recognizing our differences that I learn of a virtue that I lack or a vice that I have avoided. Such differences are revelatory, however, because we share enough that the differences stand out.[11] Differences can also occasion imitation and emulation. When we respect and admire our friends, we often want to be more like them. Learning to be more like our friends involves a kind of analogical, imaginative enrichment, not crude mimicking. In being with, observing, and listening to our friends, we can imaginatively "copy" some of their characteristics in our own lives.

This type of imitation is apparent in the case that opened this essay. From Sam I learned of a pastoral virtue, presence, that I lacked, and I began to imitate what I saw in him. Yet, my need for this virtue became apparent only because we shared so much in common in the first place. Because we spent time together, because we both valued ministry, because we had similar theological commitments, Sam's greater embodiment of the virtue and its impact on ministry showed in bold relief. Had we not been so similar, it is unlikely that I would have learned from this particular difference.

Friends' differences are vital to moral formation in other ways as well. Friends come together with at least somewhat separate histories and experiences, and therefore different perspectives. This means, of course, that my friend may see things about a given situation that I do not. It also suggests that by collaborating on projects, sharing experiences, and listening to each other's stories, we may learn how to look at things from the other's perspective; we may "learn different ways of reading a situation and different questions to pose."[12] Indeed, sometimes we learn to know our friends so well that we almost literally learn "to see as our friends see, to hear as they hear, and to feel as they feel."[13] Thus, because our friends differ from us, and because they are our friends, we gain access to a range of experiences beyond our own.[14]

Ruth, a colleague in ministry, tells of learning from a friend to understand and experience images—both visual and verbal—in a new manner. In talking with an African American friend about the sermon that Ruth had preached that day, they discussed together Psalm 51:7, "Purge me with hyssop, and I shall be clean; wash me, and I shall be whiter than snow." Through their conversation, Ruth came to see that her friend did not experience white snow as a helpful image of being cleansed from sin. In a racist environment, the image merely reinforces implicit stereotypes about the spiritual superiority of whiteness. As their conversation continued, Ruth began to look differently at her church's many visual depictions of Jesus, which she suddenly realized were all very Caucasian. Hence, through her friend, Ruth began to ask new questions about their worship service and began to spot ways in which their service unwittingly reinforced the racism of the surrounding culture. Friends can teach us to ask new questions and to see new things.

Another mechanism of friendship's moral influence derives from the satisfaction that accompanies shared activity. The enjoyment and pleasure that come from working alongside or with our friends draws us to that shared activity, making it more continuous and protecting us from boredom and burnout. We give more energy to those things that we share and, no matter how significant the project, we eventually grow weary of it if we cannot share it with others who also value its significance. Companionship makes the activity more desirable, and the fact that our friends value the activity or project confirms its worth for us.[15]

This need for companionship is visible in everything from research papers to yard work. I often find it difficult to sustain a writing project if I allow my pastoral schedule to cut me off from the people who are most interested in the project. Similarly, people in my congregation commonly remark that it is easier to help friends with their yard work than it is to stay at home and do one's own. What is true of research papers and yard work is true of the moral life more generally. Striving to become more just, compassionate, generous, and so on is more alluring when we have companions with whom we share those goals. Lacking such companions, it is difficult to sustain that striving.

Friendship's moral significance also reaches to our self-image and identity. As Paul Wadell observes:

> Some of our identity comes from our recognition of another, but a lot of it comes from how we are recognized by them. So much of who we are is a measure of the attention we have received, so much of how we think of ourselves, our appreciation of self, our self-image and identity is other-bestowed. It is exactly this reciprocity that makes friendship so morally important to securing identity.[16]

We accept ourselves and know who we are, at least in part, by how we are accepted and perceived by our friends.

Virtues such as integrity and self-care or self-esteem are therefore friendship-dependent.[17] Integrity, which I define as a combination of consistency, honesty, and honor, relies on a strong sense of self, and this sense of self is, in part, friend-bestowed. Similarly, the care and respect for oneself that conjoins with our love of God and others are, in part, friend-bestowed. We learn to care for and respect ourselves, because we are cared for and respected by others whom we love and admire.

In short, friendships are vital to the moral life. From a virtue perspective, good friendships are both intrinsically valuable and instrumentally essential to our moral formation. Friends advise and correct us, invite us into their values and commitments, serve as moral mirrors, occasion imitation and emulation, provide windows into other ways of seeing and experiencing the world, protect us from boredom and burnout, and shape our self-image and self-understanding.

Those concerned with ethics in ministry are thus well advised to give greater attention to friendship. Consider, for example, the

need for pastoral self-identity. Several recent works point to confused pastoral identity in explaining why there is a need for
renewed attention to clergy ethics.[18] The assumption here is that
reflection on ethics will help clarify pastoral identity. There is
truth in this assumption, but if pastoral ministry really is "a per-
plexed profession,"[19] then attention to the who, what, where, and
how of friendship should be included in those reflections.
Pastoral identity is not secured solely by providing codes of conduct or images of ministry. Also required are friends who remind
us of ministry's value and goals, exhibit a strong sense of pastoral
identity, and can struggle with us when we confront conflicting
images of what ministry is about.

Similar claims can be made regarding integrity. Joe Trull and
James Carter discuss clergy ethics in terms of an "ethics of
integrity." They argue that the elements of character, conduct,
and moral vision must be united in a "life of moral integrity" that
is shaped by the "life and teachings of Jesus Christ."[20] Compara-
ble claims about the importance of integrity to ministry are made
by Stanley Hauerwas, Walter Wiest and Elwyn Smith, and Karen
Lebacqz.[21] These authors recognize the high level of consistency
and trustworthiness necessary to ministering well.

What these authors could say more fully, however, is that this
life of integrity requires good friends. Pastoral ministry contains
many threats to integrity: Society's depreciation of our role,
parishioners who are always critical, parishioners who place us
on a pedestal, the constant pressure to compromise the truth for
the sake of efficiency or "peace" or "pastoral care." Few can
maintain the self-identity and steadfastness necessary to navigate
these threats without good friends to help them stay on course.

There are, of course, various kinds of friendships. Friendships among members of the clergy will differ in important ways
from friendships between clergy and their parishioners, or
between clergy and those outside the church. The general sketch
of friendship's moral importance offered here is most applicable
to friendships between clergy or between clergy and others similarly located in church leadership. Such peer-friendships usually

include a shared focus on the good of the church and a relative equality of power and social status.

My outlining of some of friendship's moral significance is meant in part simply to encourage clergy to seek out good friends. Congregational or parish life is often so consuming that there is little time, energy, encouragement, or opportunity for pastors to develop quality friendships. Yet, if virtue ethics is correct, this does not bode well for clergy. Clergy are admitted into the intimacies of people's lives; they are called to mediate meaning in times of great sorrow and joy; they are expected to be theologically competent and yet pastorally sensitive; and they are to remain steadfast to the truth of the gospel in the midst of life's ambiguities. This is a nearly impossible task without good friends to advise and correct us, to serve as mirrors of our virtues and commitments, to help us understand when our vision is distorted, and to serve as role models to be admired and emulated.

1. Much of this essay is taken from my article, "The Formation of Pastors, Parishioners, and Problems: A Virtue Reframing of Clergy Ethics," *Annual of the Society of Christian Ethics* 17 (1997): 271–90.

2. I first realized that Sam's life exhibited this virtue, which I still lacked, during a funeral sermon. The sermon itself was a kind of testimony to the virtue of presence. Sam gave the sermon at the funeral of a man whose drug addiction brought him a life of pain and an early death. Sam talked about God's walk with this man. The words were well chosen and the tone of delivery fit the occasion. But what made the sermon especially fitting was Sam's own presence to this man and his mother for several months preceding the man's death. Sam's own presence throughout that period lent authenticity to his words in the sermon about God's presence.

3. William C. Spohn, "The Return of Virtue Ethics," *Theological Studies* 53 (1992): 73.

4. For example, Martha C. Nussbaum, *The Fragility of Goodness: Luck and Ethics in Greek Tragedy and Philosophy* (New York: Cambridge University Press, 1986), 345.

5. Marilyn Friedman, "Friendship and Moral Growth," *Journal of Value Inquiry* 23 (March 1989): 3, 8; Nussbaum, *Fragility of Goodness*, 354–55; Rose Mary Volbrecht, "Friendship: Mutual Apprenticeship in Moral Development," *The Journal of Value Inquiry* 24 (October 1990): 305; Paul J. Wadell, *Friendship and the Moral Life* (Notre Dame: University of Notre Dame Press, 1989), 130–33, 137.

6. On the intrinsic value of friendship, see especially Nancy Sherman, *The Fabric of Character: Aristotle's Theory of Virtue* (Oxford: Clarendon Press, 1989), 124–28.

7. Volbrecht, "Friendship: Mutual Apprenticeship," 308; cf. Wadell, *Friendship and the Moral Life*, xiii.

8. Nussbaum, *Fragility of Goodness*, 363; Sherman, *Fabric of Character*, 139.

9. Friedman, "Friendship and Moral Growth," 4–5; Nussbaum, *Fragility of Goodness*, 363.

10. Nussbaum, *Fragility of Goodness*, 364; L. Gregory Jones, *Transformed Judgment: Toward a Trinitarian Account of the Moral Life* (Notre Dame: University of Notre Dame Press, 1990), 83; Stanley Hauerwas, "Part III: Companions on the Way: The Necessity of Friendship," *Asbury Theological Journal* 45:1 (1990): 36.

11. Sherman, *Fabric of Character*, 142; Volbrecht, "Friendship: Mutual Apprenticeship," 309.

12. Sherman, *Fabric of Character*, 30.

13. Volbrecht, "Friendship: Mutual Apprenticeship," 309.

14. Friedman, "Friendship and Moral Growth," 7.

15. Wadell, *Friendship and the Moral Life*, 59–60; Nussbaum, *Fragility of Goodness*, 363.

16. Wadell, *Friendship and the Moral Life*, 157.

17. On integrity, cf. Stanley Hauerwas, "Constancy and Forgiveness: The Novel as a School for Virtue," in *Dispatches from the Front* (Durham: Duke University Press, 1994), 31–57; Alasdair MacIntyre, *After Virtue*, 2nd ed. (Notre Dame: University of Notre Dame Press, 1984), 203, 242–43. On self-care, cf. James F. Keenan, "Proposing Cardinal Virtues," *Theological Studies* 56 (1995): 726–28.

18. Richard Bondi, *Leading God's People: Ethics for the Practice of Ministry* (Nashville: Abingdon Press, 1989), 7–8; Gaylord Noyce, *Pastoral Ethics: Professional Responsibilities of the Clergy* (Nashville: Abingdon Press, 1988), 11; Karen Lebacqz, *Professional Ethics: Power and Paradox* (Nashville: Abingdon Press, 1985), 140–46.

19. H. Richard Niebuhr, *The Purpose of the Church and Its Ministry* (New York: Harper, 1956), 48ff, quoted in Joseph L. Allen, "Recent Books on Ministerial Ethics," *Interpretation* 45 (October 1991): 406, and Noyce, *Pastoral Ethics*, 11.

20. Joe E. Trull and James E. Carter, *Ministerial Ethics: Being a Good Minister in a Not-So-Good World* (Nashville: Broadman & Holman Publishers, 1993), 63, 62 respectively.

21. Stanley M. Hauerwas, "Clerical Character," in *Christian Existence Today: Essays on Church, World and Living in Between* (Durham: The Labyrinth Press, 1988), 143; Walter E. Wiest and Elwyn A. Smith, *Ethics in Ministry: A Guide for the Professional* (Minneapolis: Fortress Press, 1990), 23, 28–30, 57; Lebacqz, *Professional Ethics*, 73–75, 89.

Chapter Six

The Wisdom of Boundaries
Power and Vulnerability in Ministry

by Richard M. Gula, SS

*I*n recent years, an increasing number of victims of sexual abuse
by professionals have come forth to tell their stories. Out of concern to protect vulnerable persons, desire to hold professionals
accountable, and fear of legal liability, business corporations,
government, schools, and churches have tried to clarify their professional ethics. A common concern of professional ethics is the
right use of power in the professional relationship and the boundaries that are necessary to safeguard the vulnerability of those
seeking a professional service. Pastoral ministers have more to
gain than to lose by attending to the wisdom of boundaries that
professional ethics enshrines to guide the right use of power. The
wisdom of boundaries in ministry is fundamentally about the
minister using power to safeguard trust in the pastoral relationship and to protect the vulnerability of the one seeking a pastoral
service. To live by this wisdom requires that a minister be pre-
disposed to care in ways that are trustworthy, prudent, and just.

To explore the wisdom of boundaries, I will begin with a
hypothetical case in spiritual direction that will serve as a particular expression of pastoral ministry to which we can apply the
theoretical analysis that follows. In light of this case, I will first
examine the nature of boundaries and some forces in society and
church that can undermine their importance. Second, I will

examine the nature of power and dual relationships. Third and finally, I will offer some criteria for evaluating the right use of power.

John is now in his second month as the associate director of a spiritual life center run by his religious community. His first assignment after ordination was for five years as an associate pastor in a nearby suburban parish.

He was considered a good associate pastor. Parishioners were fond of him. He was as a minister should be—caring, sensitive, kind. He worked hard and for long hours, often late into the night. While at the parish, he established a reputation as a good spiritual director, even though he had never received any formal training in this ministry. He was sought out not only by his own parishioners but also by those from the neighboring parish. Because his ministry as a spiritual director had grown so large, he applied for and got a position on the staff of the spiritual life center. As a member of the staff, he is subject to ongoing supervision for his direction and is paid for each session according to a sliding scale.

John's own family background was not a happy one. His parents were both alcoholics and divorced when John was in high school. He demonstrated typical co-dependent behavior towards his mother in his attempts to rescue her from his abusive father. He feels good about himself when he can take care of people. John himself gets depressed easily, but his involvement with others keeps his depressive tendencies at bay so that they do not pull him down.

Before he left the parish, Jane, a recently divorced woman, began to see him for spiritual direction. It means a lot to her that John gives his time. She is further reassured when he shares with her that he knows the pain of divorce from his experience of his mother. This is not the first time a divorced woman has sought John for counsel. While at the parish, his full schedule buffered him from any feelings he might have towards the women who came to see him. He was unaware of being sexually attracted to any of his parishioners or directees. Because he was so well-liked, seemed to be so effective, and interacted with his parishioners in so many different contexts, he was unsure where his limits should be with parishioners who are also directees.

Now that John is at the spiritual life center, Jane continues to see him for direction. She knows that John likes art films, so she invites him to take in a movie that portrays some of the issues they are pursuing in spiritual direction. She suggests that they see the movie and then, as part of spiritual direction, discuss it at the coffee shop across the street from the theater. She makes this her treat, as it is an opportunity to thank John for the time he is giving her.

John has been so busy with his transition to a new ministerial setting that he has not yet established any bonds with other members of his staff. Jane is the only person who represents continuity and stability for him at this time. John enjoys his sessions with Jane and has a good, relaxed rapport with her. Before and after their meetings, the two share a hug and a light kiss. Taking in the movie together and going to the coffee shop seem like an extended part of their spiritual direction relationship.

Meeting for a movie, coffee, and "direction" at the coffee shop goes on once a month for three months. Then these meetings taper off as John becomes settled into his new position and with his new community at the spiritual life center. Jane notices that John is less available to her for these "social" meetings. She becomes confused. This is the first time she has really felt safe with a man and felt a real mutuality in the relationship. She wonders what is going wrong. John tells her that meeting as they have been doing has interfered with their spiritual direction relationship. He gives her the name of another director she might want to see and says that he is sorry that the relationship has gotten so confusing.

If you were Jane, how would you feel? If you were John, how would you explain what happened? These are two adults. Who is responsible for the boundaries, and why?

Boundaries

Boundaries set limits. They separate me from you, my space from your space, what's mine from what's yours. We recognize them as necessary and helpful on the highway as guardrails that keep us from falling over a cliff, or as the white lines that divide driving lanes. We know them in baseball as the foul line, and in football as the sideline. To step across the line is to be declared out of bounds. In life, we can cross the line by the way we speak to and about others, by the way we touch them, or by the way we look at them. We can also cross the boundary by throwing things at them, by sending messages (even e-mail), by giving gifts, or by postings on the billboard or bathroom stalls. In sports and in life, boundaries are for safety and fair play in reaching one's goal.

In ministry, some often resist any talk of boundaries because of the negative connotations associated with them, such as barriers or walls that divide or exclude. Boundaries in this sense only undermine the spirit of ministry which aims to liberate and to nurture one's growing in the Spirit and in accepting God's love.

Although boundaries do separate, they need not alienate, especially when they are established out of the virtue of hospitality in the minister. Boundaries can be the means by which we set the limits that create a hospitable space wherein others can come in and feel safe with someone who makes room for them and accepts them. In spiritual direction, for example, directees make themselves vulnerable to a director by expressing their needs, their experiences, their fears. They trust that the director is trustworthy and will not take advantage of them. Boundaries safeguard this trust and protect the vulnerability of directees. In the safe space created by clear boundaries, directees will be able to focus on their own needs, experiences, and fears without having to deal with those of the director.

All relationships have boundaries, but these boundaries differ according to the nature of the relationship. In personal relationships, such as a friendship where two people seek to meet the needs of each other, boundaries are flexible. Each party shares mutually in the responsibility to maintain them. But in a pastoral relationship, such as the case of spiritual direction, the boundaries must be more clearly defined and the minister/director has the greater burden of responsibility to define and maintain clear boundaries. Establishing boundaries and respecting them is an act of love and justice towards the other. In the hypothetical case, if John would have set clear boundaries, Jane would have had greater freedom to recognize and respond to the movements of God in her life rather than to confuse them with John's needs to be caring and to find companionship.

Common Boundaries

Some of the most common boundaries that a director, like any other minister, must establish and maintain are of time, space, and person.

Time

Boundaries of time give the security and safety of respecting the other and being committed to the other's interest by starting and stopping meetings on time, by setting enough time to complete a project, and by taking on a limited amount of projects that will honor one's emotional, mental, spiritual, and physical health. John seems to have crossed this boundary often in his habit of working long hours and often late into the night. He also seems to have taken on a great number of directees while still serving primarily as associate pastor. To be faithful and just in his ministry as a director, John needs to monitor his workload, stay within the limits of reasonable hours of a workday, and limit his number of directees so that he can be present to them with more physical, emotional, and spiritual energy.

Space

Boundaries of space respect limits on where ministry occurs. Changing the setting or the environment can confuse, threaten, or distract the one seeking a pastoral service. Such is the case for John when he changed the setting from the spiritual life center to the coffee shop. Place is an important way to clarify one's role and the purpose of the relationship. For John to be trustworthy as a director, he needs to establish a place for direction that clearly supports the objectives of spiritual direction and does not confuse, or give the appearance of confusing, spiritual direction with other kinds of relationships.

Person

Boundaries that respect the person also help to secure a safe haven wherein one seeking pastoral service can be vulnerable without fear of being exploited. This safe space includes such things as how physically close we stand or sit to another, how we use touch as a gesture of pastoral concern, what we do with gifts, whether we can keep secrets and not gossip about another, and whether we can avoid dual relationships that confuse roles. John violated personal boundaries with his hug and kiss before and after each session, by socializing with Jane, and by letting her treat him to the movies and coffee. To be faithful to Jane as her director and to sustain a trustworthy relationship, John must take care of his needs for companionship outside his spiritual direction relationships and also monitor his relationship with Jane through supervision.

Forces Undermining Boundaries

The importance of establishing and maintaining boundaries of time, space, and person can easily be undermined by some prominent forces at work in society and in the church. These are the ethos of postmodernism, the feminist movement, the reactionary defensiveness to a litigious environment, and a new ecclesiology.

First, the ethos of *postmodernism* resists any suggestion that we must put limits on our behavior or that we ought to abide by standards in professional relationships. Boundaries only interfere with exercising free choice. We find evidence of this ethos in some modern advertisements. A Ralph Lauren advertisement declares: "Your world should know no boundaries." A promotion for Don Q rum proclaims: "When you have a passion for living, nothing is merely accepted. Nothing is taboo. . . . Break all the rules." The epitome of a no-boundaries theme are the Calvin Klein advertisement that says, "I don't know where I end and you begin" and the Cadillac ad which asks, "Isn't it time to live without limits?" These ads catch a pervading spirit that refuses to believe that we can live with limits and still be free, or that relationships that respect limits can ennoble and build up personal and social life.

Second, in the *feminist movement,* some feminists argue that boundaries are a vestige of patriarchal practices that shut out the possibility of realizing some of the prized feminist values of mutuality, vulnerability, and friendship. One such feminist view holds that no relationship should be prevented from becoming mutual.[1] It wants to make "friendship" the primary analog of the right use of power and the best expression of the kind of mutuality that ministry ought to seek.[2] Other feminists, however, recognize that relationships that do not enjoy mutuality are not necessarily oppressive and abusive. Power in relationships does not have to be mutual for its use to be ethical. Denying the differences of power in the pastoral relationship only leads to avoiding the difficult challenge of using power appropriately.[3]

Third, the *reactionary defensiveness* that some feel we must assume in our highly litigious environment is the opposite extreme of the other two forces. It is reflected in the attitude of Tom Sanders in Michael Crichton's novel, *Disclosure.* Commenting on the changing social climate, the narrator lists some of the "new rules" that now operate for men:

> Don't smile at a child on the street, unless you're with
> your wife. Don't ever touch a strange child. Don't
> ever be alone with someone else's child, even for a
> moment. If a child invites you into his or her room,
> don't go unless another adult, preferably a woman, is
> also present. At a party, don't let a little girl sit on
> your lap. If she tries, gently push her aside. If you
> ever have occasion to see a naked boy or girl, look
> quickly away. Better yet, leave.[4]

And when talking about the changing practices in the business
world, he says:

> Sanders knew men who would not take a business trip
> with a woman, who would not sit next to a female
> colleague on an airplane, who would not meet a
> woman for a drink in a bar unless someone else was
> also present. Sanders had always thought such cau-
> tion was extreme, even paranoid. But now, he was not
> so sure.[5]

Such absolute avoidance of all connection is an overly reactionary stance that avoids the complexities of boundaries, power,
and vulnerability. Ministry of any sort cannot survive with such
aloofness and disinterest. Ministers are just as wrong to withhold
authentic emotional connection as they are to touch another in a
way that is experienced as confusing or abusive. Genuine connection with people is essential in ministry. But it requires not the
paranoia of avoidance but the prudential sense of what the other
will experience as affirming, supportive, and loving.

A fourth force is a *new ecclesiology* at work in the church.
Two models of the church seem to be in tension when it comes to
boundaries in ministry. One is the hierarchical model that establishes clear lines of how we ought to organize ourselves and
where the power lies. The other is the model of the spirit-filled
community where everyone is "one in Christ" and so enjoys the

evangelical equality of the baptized. This ecclesiology without proper nuance can easily obscure the boundaries that must exist between those who have power and those who are vulnerable in their pastoral needs. For all the good this model of the church has done to affirm and to call forth the baptismal dignity of each person and to nurture diverse gifts in the church, we cannot forget that there are real differences of power between those who minister and those who seek pastoral service. To insist on the importance of boundaries is not a vestige of the clericalism that treats the laity as children and keeps them in their place. Boundaries can get blurred or lost in the name of evangelical equality and when promoting shared ministry. But the church should be a place where boundaries are predictable and reliable so that people will not be harmed or exploited.

Heeding the wisdom of boundaries is one of the most significant professional challenges ministers in every ministry have to face. The challenge is to maintain pastoral relationships with boundaries that are neither too fuzzy nor too rigid in order to shape the kind of relationship that will provide appropriate pastoral service while protecting the vulnerable from exploitation. Only prudence can meet this challenge. The challenge comes from at least two fronts: The inevitable inequality of power and vulnerability in the pastoral relationship, and the dual relationships ministers often maintain. To each of these I want to turn now for a fuller appreciation of the wisdom of boundaries.

Power

In her novel, *The Robber Bride,* Margaret Atwood describes the experience of Tony, a college professor:

> She unlocks her office door, then locks it behind her to disguise the fact that she's in there. It's not her office hours but the students take advantage. They can smell her out, like sniffer dogs; they'll seize any opportunity to suck up to her or whine, or attempt to

impress her, or foist on her their versions of sulky
defiance. I'm just a human being, Tony wants to say
to them. But of course, she isn't. She's a human being
with power. There isn't much of it, but it's power all
the same.[6]

Whether as a college professor or a minister, we bear the blessing and the burden of power in relation to those whom we serve.
If we resonate with Tony's feeling that "there isn't much of it,"
we can easily fail to recognize that "it's power all the same."
Whether we feel powerful or not is irrelevant. The fact is, in pastoral relationships, the minister has the greater power and must
use it in the right way.

The Nature of Power

Power is ambiguous. It is often a despised or feared reality
arousing more suspicion and defensiveness than acceptance. It is
hard for some ministers to acknowledge that they have any power
because the very notion evokes so many negative images — corruption, power-tripping, one-upmanship, coercion, and exploitation, to name a few. This dark side of power is associated with a
controlling and dominating style of leadership, wielding the
heavy hand of intimidation and oppression. It reduces people *for*
whom and *with* whom we are to work to people *over* whom we
have control. This kind of negative power opposes who we want
to be as people for and with others. But power has another side.
It can also be liberating by releasing the goodness in another and
allowing it to flourish. Love and power are not necessarily oppo-
sites. This bright, positive side of power is the expression of
power more compatible with our professional commitment. It
deserves a hearing.

Social scientists commonly define power as the capacity to
influence others. Power and vulnerability are relative to resources
such as role, gender, personality, competence, social status, financial security, emotional stability, age, physical size, and others.

Power describes having resources the other person needs. Vulnerability describes a lack of these resources. Power and vulnerability are always a matter of more or less, because they are relative to the resources we have in a particular context. We feel our power or vulnerability in the interplay of the differing needs and strengths in the relationship. In the hypothetical case, John has the power of his role, competence, gender, personality, and security, as well as power from the projections and transference Jane makes towards him. He also has "numinous" power that comes from being a representative and mediator of things holy. Jane is vulnerable in her gender, social status, and emotional turmoil after the divorce.

Inequality of Power and the Fiduciary Obligation

Because of the inequality of power between them, John has the obligation to establish boundaries that will give Jane confidence that her vulnerability will not be exploited to satisfy his own needs. Jane's action of entrusting her vulnerability to John and his accepting her entrustment by taking on the responsibilities of being her spiritual director commit him to a special moral responsibility known as a *fiduciary obligation*, a defining characteristic of a professional. It means that John has the duty to exercise his power and authority in ways that will serve Jane's need for seeking spiritual direction, that he will not exploit her vulnerability, and that he will give greater preference to her best interest over his own when there is a real or possible conflict of interest between them.

The fiduciary obligation also entails the duty to avoid creating conflicts of interest and even the appearance of a conflict lest trust be jeopardized. John will be able to fulfill his fiduciary obligation if he is both cognitively committed to being a fiduciary agent and emotionally committed to caring for Jane as a directee. The cognitive commitment and emotional altruism foster other habits of feeling and acting in her best interest. Habits of care, altruism, trustworthiness, justice, and prudence are core virtues of a spiritual director. John will show that he is virtuous in these ways by establishing and maintaining boundaries that manage the inequality of power in the spiritual direction relationship.

Clear boundaries create a safe space for Jane to focus on her own experiences of God rather than on John's needs and conflicts. Even though Jane may try to manipulate the situation and is responsible for that behavior, nonetheless, John is obligated to maintain appropriate boundaries because, as spiritual director, he has the greater power. In his early relationship with Jane, he does not seem to be aware of his feelings and of how much Jane is influenced simply by him being a symbolic representative of God, the church, and a religious or spiritual tradition. Moreover, John is very busy, perhaps overly committed. He seems unaware of the transference and countertransference going on in his relationship with women generally, and with Jane in particular.

Marilyn Peterson's provocative book, *At Personal Risk,* makes the point that when, for whatever reasons, professionals lose sight of the power gap between them and those seeking their professional service, they pave the way for exploiting their clients. She documents convincingly that professionals are most at risk of unethical behavior when they minimize the significance of the relationship and refuse to accept the authority that comes with their role, ignore the magnitude of their power, or are unaware of their own needs[7] Her work shows that the person in the best position to help others is the very person in a powerful position to hurt them. Once hurt, people trust again only with reluctance. This is evident in the testimony of one victim of sexual abuse by her pastor who was asked, "What do you struggle with today?" She said, "Well, it's very hard to regain the sense of trust, not only trust in pastors but also trust in people and trust in the goodness of the universe."[8]

In the hypothetical case, John must first acknowledge and own the power that he has. The first step in preventing boundary violations is to do a critical self-examination that will bring self-knowledge. Then John must be sufficiently self-disciplined so as to restrain from using his spiritual direction relationships to satisfy his needs for companionship, acceptance, pleasure, or profit. In order for John to be faithful to Jane as her director and to maintain a trusting relationship, he will have to take care of himself better.

Appropriate self-care is often the neglected side of pastoral care. The case also suggests that John must learn how to take care of himself outside his spiritual direction relationships by taking time for friends and colleagues away from his ministry in order to satisfy his needs for intimacy. He would do well to acknowledge his sexual feelings to himself and a trusted friend, spiritual director, or supervisor, for he seems unaware of the countertransference that is interfering with his serving Jane as a spiritual director. John could also avoid meeting with her in settings that only confuse the expectations of his relationship with her. Perhaps it is time for John to refer Jane to another director, if he is becoming too strongly attracted to her sexually.

The Lure of the Friendship Model

One of the great temptations to minimize or ignore the inequality of power in the pastoral relationship is to treat it as if it were a friendship. This is what happened to John when he began to socialize with Jane. Trying to make spiritual direction a personal, peer relationship only falsifies its real nature, confuses roles, and puts the director at greater risk of unethical behavior.

In her analysis of different styles of pastoral leadership, Martha Ellen Stortz shows that several of the facets of friendship conflict with what ministry demands. She shows, for example, that pastoral relationships do not enjoy the equality of friends or the mutual self-disclosure that creates the emotional bond of intimacy in a friendship.[9] I find Stortz's analysis to be very helpful for clarifying the difficulties of using the paradigm of friendship for pastoral relationships in general and spiritual direction in particular. The demands of self-disclosure and trust made upon the directee conflict with the mutual demands of the personal relationship of a friendship.

Dual Relationships

The above discussion about mixing pastoral relationships and friendships falls squarely within the domain of dual relationships in ministry.[10] When we interact with another person in more than one capacity, we form a dual relationship. This happens, for example, when, as teachers, we become the spiritual director of one of our students; or as pastors, we become long-term counselors to someone on our staff; or as youth ministers, we date someone from the youth group; or as spiritual directors, we develop a friendship with one of our directees.

The strict prohibition of dual relationships is a well-established principle in the helping professions. The wisdom enshrined in this restriction warns helping-professionals about the great potential for harm in mixing roles with the same person. Dual relationships can be inappropriate and even wrong because they are fertile ground for impairing judgment, harboring potential conflicts of interest, and exploiting the trust and dependency of the vulnerable.

But spiritual directors are not exactly parallel to other helping-professionals, even though they share many of the same skills and objectives. Spiritual directors in some settings, such as seminaries and schools of theology, interact with their directees in many different aspects of life, not just in the specifically religious sector. Those for whom spiritual direction is a specialized ministry, and who work out of a spiritual life center, as in John's case, can avoid mixing roles with their directees more easily than spiritual directors who are also teachers of their directees in seminaries and schools of theology.

As a general rule, spiritual directors ought to avoid mixing roles with their directees as much as possible. But in some settings, they will know only an inevitable overlapping of roles. For example, sometimes out of necessity, a spiritual director is the teacher and director of the same student, or a pastor will be a director for an employee of the parish. In small towns, spiritual directors have few options for professional services. In such contexts, certain kinds of dual relationships are inevitable. Even though it is a good rule to avoid dual relationships insofar as possible, spiritual directors cannot always do so, and they are not necessarily wrong in having them in those instances where they can fairly easily avoid conflicts of duties or loyalties.

Dual relationships become problems when roles get confused, transference and countertransference prevail, and professional boundaries are crossed. But they do not have to become problems if the minister is:

- being honest with himself or herself,
- paying attention to his or her own needs,
- satisfying his or her personal needs beyond the limits of the pastoral relationship,
- keeping the role of spiritual director as the primary one in the relationship, and
- monitoring the development of this relationship, such as through therapy, supervision and/or spiritual direction.

By following such guidelines, some pastoral ministers have not let inevitable dual relationships become a hindrance to effective ministry. So, to insist only on rigid boundaries in all instances would be as crippling of ministry as allowing flexible boundaries to prevail. But because the inevitable inequality of power in spiritual direction demands well-established boundaries, the greater burden of responsibility falls on the director to keep the boundaries in sight and sharply focused. Although all dual relationships are not automatically wrong, they do need to be carefully evaluated, and the director has the professional duty to make this evaluation.

Dual relationships can become a problem when we are not satisfying our needs appropriately and so take advantage of another's trust. This seems to be the case with John. He is more vulnerable than usual because of the stress of making a transition to a new ministry and a new community. Times of transition are ripe for boundary violations. He was not meeting his needs for acceptance and companionship adequately outside his ministry. Often the people we meet in our ministry are the most accessible and attractive ones to whom we turn in seeking to satisfy personal and social needs. We can easily end up using them more than ministering to them. That is what John seems to have done.

Marilyn Peterson's observation about professionals violating boundaries is instructive here:

> Most of the time, professionals find that their misuse of the client did not grow out of some malicious intent or unresolved psychological issue. Rather, the violation happened because they were unaware of their needs and the client was convenient. Using him or her made their life easier. Within this reality, professionals begin to grasp how they used their greater power in the relationship to cross the boundary and take what they needed from the client.[11]

Peterson goes on to say that to understand why we cross boundaries, we have to examine the rationalizations we use to disregard limits. Perhaps we believe that our behavior is not really interfering with the goals of the relationship or, because we are both adults, each can take care of himself or herself, or that we are doing what other directors would do.

Such rationalization avoids the responsibility we have to find acceptable options for meeting personal needs. Peterson argues that what really leads to crossing boundaries is that we have "either minimized the relationship or equalized the power differential."[12] Making use of ongoing supervision is one way to monitor and to check our rationalizations and the dynamics of transference and countertransference going on in the dual relationship. John, of the hypothetical case, is contributing to transference and countertransference by socializing with Jane and meeting in a nonprofessional setting. He does not seem to be making the best use of his opportunity for supervision of this relationship in order to notice the relational shift going on and the importance of confronting it as gently as possible.

The reality of dual relationships in spiritual direction is one of those instances of an ambiguous situation that calls, in the end, not for extensive rules in a code of ethics but for keen moral sensitivity, prudential discernment, and a virtuous character that can strike the balance between serving self-interest and the interest of the other.

Assessing the Use of Power

If the nature of spiritual direction is marked by a difference of power between us and those seeking direction, then the pressing ethical question is "How do we use our power?" Our moral criterion for the right use of power must be one that protects and promotes the dignity of the person made in the image of God. Karen Lebacqz holds up the criterion of justice through liberation as the proper measuring rod for relationships that have an inequality of power as their central dynamic.[13] To assess our use of power, we can ask, "Is liberation happening here?" Power is used rightly when it enables the other to become increasingly free. The perspective that determines whether power is enabling or disabling, empowering or oppressing, belongs not to us who hold greater power but to the one who is vulnerable, as long as he or she is being reasonable about this judgment.

Our power as spiritual directors, then, is used rightly when we enhance the directee's freedom. We do not fulfill our professional commitment to serve the interests of others by doing for them or giving to them in ways that keep them passive and dependent on us. Rather, we serve by enabling and empowering them to recognize their potential, and then we encourage and guide them to develop it. This is using power as service and not as lording it over others.

The ministry of Jesus is a model of the right use of power. He rejected the use of power that dominates or promotes oneself over others in favor of power that serves others by empowering them. Several scenes in the Gospels give us examples of Jesus insisting that those who share his values must reimagine power and its use in human relationships. Perhaps no episode in the Gospels illustrates better the character of a minister and the style of what ministry ought to be like than the foot-washing scene at the Last Supper. This story from John 13:6–10, which captures the dynamics of the fuller character and style of Jesus, is used as the Gospel reading on Holy Thursday in conjunction with the Pauline text of the institution of the Eucharist (1 Cor 11:23–26). When taken in that context, coupled with our understanding that it takes the place of the institution narrative of the Eucharist in the Gospel of John, the action of Jesus in washing feet highlights even more what the character and style of a minister in a eucharistic community ought to be like. In this scene, when Peter sees Jesus, the master, acting like a servant, he knows something is wrong. This is not the picture Peter has of how power works. So Peter resists being washed. He realizes that if he complies with this washing, he would be accepting a radical reversal of the use of power for domination. When Jesus deliberately reverses social positions by becoming the servant, he witnesses to a new order of relationships in the community and to a new use of power where domination has no place in its ministers.[14]

Jesus further demonstrates that power is for service, particularly the service that liberates, in his healing the crippled woman in Luke 13:10–17. There Jesus calls to a woman who has been bent over by an evil spirit for eighteen years. First, Jesus addresses her as a "daughter of Abraham" to show that she is equal in dignity to the "sons of Abraham." Then he places his hands on her and she stands up straight. She who was once weak is now strong. Friends of Jesus rejoice over her liberation, but the religious officials who rule over the community are angered by this deed. The power that liberates by making the weak strong is too challenging to them. The power of control wants to keep some weak while others remain strong. But the power Jesus expresses challenges behavior that seeks to dominate.

In spiritual direction, the use of power is the key moral issue. We inevitably have power over those seeking direction because we have something they need. Our fiduciary responsibility protects their vulnerability for it obliges us to maintain clear boundaries and to subordinate self-interests to serving their best interest. The ministry of Jesus models for us a power that need not be oppressive but liberating. He demonstrated justice through liberation in the way he set people free. As disciples, we are called to go and do likewise.

1. Such a view is advocated by Carter Heyward, *When Boundaries Betray Us* (New York: HarperCollins, 1993).

2. A "friendship" model for ministry is advocated by Lynn N. Rhodes, *Co-Creating: A Feminist Vision of Ministry* (Philadelphia: Westminster Press, 1987).

3. See, for example, the perspectives advocated by Marie Fortune, "The Joy of Boundaries," and Karen Lebacqz and Ronald G. Barton, "Boundaries, Mutuality, and Professional Ethics," *Boundary Wars,* ed., Katherine Hancock Ragsdale (Cleveland: The Pilgrim Press, 1996), 78–95, and 96–110.

4. Michael Crichton, *Disclosure* (New York: Alfred A. Knopf, 1993), 218.

5. Ibid.

6. Margaret Atwood, *The Robber Bride* (New York: Bantam Books, 1993), 24.

7. Marilyn R. Peterson, *At Personal Risk: Boundary Violations in Professional-Client Relationships* (New York: W.W. Norton & Company, 1992).

8. Taken from the videotape *Choosing the Light: Victims of Clergy Sexual Misconduct Share Their Stories* (Milwaukee: The Greater Milwaukee Synod of the ELCA, May 22, 1990).

9.   Martha Ellen Stortz, *PastorPower* (Nashville: Abingdon Press, 1993), 117–19.

10.   For a psychological perspective on boundaries and dual relationships in ministry, see Donna J. Markham and Fran A. Repka, "Personal Development and Boundaries Shape Ministry," *Human Development* 18 (Spring 1997): 33–45.

11.   Peterson, *At Personal Risk,* 154.

12.   Ibid., 155.

13.   Karen Lebacqz, *Professional Ethics: Power and Paradox* (Nashville: Abingdon Press, 1985), 128–29.

14.   For an elaboration of this interpretation of the foot-washing scene, see Sandra Schneiders, "The Foot Washing (John 13:1–20): An Experiment in Hermeneutics," *Catholic Biblical Quarterly* 43 (January 1981): 76–92; see esp., 80–88.

Chapter Seven
Virtue Ethics and the Sexual Formation of Clergy

by Sondra Ely Wheeler

A minister has been functioning well as an associate with a large and vital congregation in a suburban town for five years. The associate's particular gifts and training make him an especially good pastoral counselor. Over time he has established many warm personal connections with parishioners, both male and female, through counseling relationships or shared work in church leadership. During this entire period, he has been struggling with a problematic and painful marriage, which finally ends in divorce after fifteen years, in his sixth year of ministry with this congregation. Colleagues and parishioners alike are supportive and offer many expressions of care and affection in the weeks following his letter apprising them of his situation.

In later months, several members of the congregation and members of the community he has met through his work indicate in ways direct and indirect their interest in a romantic and/or sexual relationship. His own moral and professional judgment tell him that these would be ill advised due to the obligations of his role. In any case, he regards a serious relationship as premature at this time in view of his own need to finish grieving over the failure of his marriage. However, his own loneliness is acute, and his need for personal affection and affirmation in a difficult time is deep and compelling. He is uncertain about how to remain genuine and emotionally present to his parishioners without

Who we are

sending confusing signals to those who have expressed a desire for a sexual relationship. He also worries about the risk of distorting or abusing his pastoral role due to his own unmet needs, which he recognizes make him morally as well as emotionally vulnerable.

The case presented above may appear to some not to constitute a "case" at all: No concrete dilemma is presented, no misconduct is alleged, no wrongdoing is contemplated, no actual conflict exists. If this were a movie, it wouldn't have much of a plot. From the point of view of virtue-based approaches to ethics, that is what makes it interesting. Here the question is not how one should make a forced choice from a set of undesirable alternatives. It is not a matter of how we should respond when a person violates some moral norm or fails in some positive duty. The question is, how does a person who intends to fulfill a set of delicate and difficult moral obligations equip himself to do so? Moreover, how does he prepare to do so reliably over an extended period of time in which the personal challenges of his professional role may be foreseen to be very great? This is the very stuff of virtue, for virtue ethics focuses not on the decisions we make or the rules we adhere to but on who we are as we make those decisions or abide by those rules. In particular, virtue theory concerns itself with the skills, dispositions, and habits that enable us to behave rightly under pressure, and with how they are to be cultivated.

There are two kinds of help that virtue ethics can give us. First, it gives us a language for and a description of those central features of character we need. This is the fruit of long experience and reflection on the capacities that equip us to live well. Traditionally divided into discussions of the four cardinal virtues of prudence, temperance, justice, and fortitude, this body of material gives us a richly textured account of the fundamental skills that enable us to behave morally. It fleshes out what we are seeking as we try to become persons who can both embrace and discipline our own sexuality for the sake of just and faithful service to others. The second kind of help virtue ethics can give us is in its understanding of the integral relation between character and action, between what we do and who we become. Virtue ethics insists upon a truth that all logic resists and all experience confirms: You cannot act virtuously without possessing virtue, and you cannot develop virtue without acting virtuously. This insight, frustrating as it may be, leads to an indispensable account of the centrality of *practice,* in both senses of the word.

In beginning to address the character of the actor prior to the act, a virtue approach offers one additional benefit: It corresponds to the experience of many counselors and church leaders who have found that it is usually too late to prevent harm, often grave harm, if they wait to address the moral problems of sexual life until they present themselves in the form of an illicit relationship, whether actual or only contemplated. It is therefore especially unfortunate that most of the church's address to the issue of sexual ethics for clergy has come in reaction to reported cases of sexual misconduct, particularly to those that have proceeded to litigation. Inevitably, the institutional response has been self-protective and juridical, as denominational bodies have tried to establish rules of conduct, lines of responsibility, and policies for dealing with violations when they occur. Even as this work must be done, from a moral and theological point of view, such a response by itself will always be both too little and too late.

Because sexuality is grounded so deeply in who we are, rooted in our most basic needs, and entwined in all of our experiences of care and well-being, we cannot begin with rules for sexual conduct, nor can we finish by developing procedures for adjudicating charges of sexual abuse by clergy. If we hope to develop ministers who not only know what is required but have the capacity to act accordingly even when it is difficult to do so, we must begin to think and speak much earlier and much more seriously about sexual formation. This formation is integrally moral and spiritual, and its reach is very broad, including what we teach about dealing with loneliness, about forming genuine relationships with God and with other people, and about the conditions for sustaining a life of discipleship. In fact, the natural place to begin the process of sexual formation is in seminary, where moral, intellectual, and spiritual formation can be integrated and built into the life and study of the community. This requires the support, participation, and influence of a faculty committed to the comprehensive task of forming and equipping women and men for ministry. Where these are present, the disciplines that deepen and sustain moral life can be developed and can become part of the lives of those to whom we entrust the ministries of the church. It is the genius of virtue approaches to ethics that they are concerned explicitly with forming who we are—what we see, and love, and hope for, and fear. They aim to shape what we desire as well as what we do. In addressing anything that goes as deeply into our most basic needs and longings as the mystery of sexuality, it is here that we must begin.

Presuppositions

Any discussion of virtue in sexual life presumes that there is such a thing as right or wrong sexual conduct, and that norms for sexual behavior are neither arbitrary nor simply expressions of private choice. I want to identify the basic assumptions about sexual behavior that underlie the following discussion. They are, naturally, debatable, but those debates are not my subject here.

First, the human union that sex expresses and fosters is aimed at deep, honest, and complete sharing between the partners at every level. Such comprehensive communion requires the stability and safety of committed relationships where a unique degree of mutual knowledge and trust can be sustained, and where any children born of the union can be nurtured and protected. Conversely, I assume that sexual intimacy without such commitment debases and harms the partners, particularly when the need for secrecy entangles them in systematic deception.

My second and more specific assumption is that sexual relationships between ministers and their parishioners are irresponsible and abusive, a misuse of the authority of ordained ministry. I assume that they are at least potentially dangerous to parishioners, threaten the well-being of congregations, and violate the trust the community places in its clergy to use their pastoral power for the good of the congregants and not simply as a means to fulfill their own needs and desires. Even where there is relative parity between the partners, and where neither violates an existing commitment in entering into a sexual relationship, the mingling of pastoral responsibility and erotic attachment confuses and compromises the minister's role. Thus it is a threat to his or her integrity as a leader and caregiver in the church.

The Challenge of Pastoral Sexual Ethics

For those who accept such an account, the moral challenges are formidable. Unlike many other helping professionals, clergy cannot protect themselves and those they serve from the risks of sexual attraction and response by retreating to a safe emotional distance. Within their congregations, ministers must be prepared to acknowledge their own vulnerability and human neediness, and to give and receive affection, affirmation, and care. In particular, the concrete tasks of ministry require them to be with people made vulnerable by illness, fear, grief, and confusion. But the risks associated with pastoral ministry are not merely a matter of proximity to those in crisis. The heart of the pastoral role is addressing congregants' spiritual needs for communion with God, which are closely tied to the basic human longings for mutuality, security, and fundamental acceptance. These are needs often channeled through sexuality. Moreover, the connection between spirituality and sexual attraction, however problematic it may be, is more than accidental. It is the very fact that sex is linked so closely to other aspects of human experience that enables it to be a means and expression of deep human union at all levels.

As Christian theologians and pastors, we must find ways to be aware of and careful about the connection between sexuality and spirituality, and yet to celebrate that this is the way we are made. For in a deep and broad sense, it is good news that there is a profound relationship between the emotional, spiritual, and physical dimensions of our lives: Good news that we are embodied beings who need "somebody with skin on" fully to experience the grace and presence of God. It remains good news even when faithfulness to God and one another stringently requires that we not let a relationship of spiritual care shade over into one of sexual intimacy. But the complexity of setting and maintaining appropriate boundaries in such a context is very great. More difficult still is the work of maintaining our inner balance, the balance of moral clarity, critical self-awareness, and compassionate self-acceptance that will allow us to live within the boundaries we must set without distorting who and what we are. If we are to sustain our lives as ministers and caregivers in the church, we must learn to discipline our sexuality without trying simply to ignore or suppress it. Virtue ethics directs us to the work of becoming persons who can not only maintain such a discipline but flourish under it, and in that work it proves our strongest ally.

Accordingly, I want to offer a sketch of the relevance of prudence, temperance, justice, and fortitude in forming sexual conduct. I will follow with a brief discussion of the place of practice in moral development, and a few concrete suggestions about some practical disciplines that might be of help to the pastor of our case. Finally, I will close with reflections about the implications of all of this for seminary education.

Virtue and the Virtues

Prudence

Prudence is at its root the capacity to see the world truthfully, and thus to act in accord with things as they really are. Spoken of most narrowly as skill in fitting means to ends, it embraces as well the larger vision that enables us to see what ends are worth pursuing, and why. In this way it is tied to the fundamental convictions and loyalties by which we make sense of our lives, closely related to the theological virtues of faith, hope, and charity. It is at once a practical application of reason, and a moral discipline requiring that we maintain a clear view of reality, undistorted by our fears or our desires. This helps to illuminate the connection of prudence to the other moral virtues, which deal directly with ordering our passions, our partiality, and our fears so that they do not overwhelm our capacity to chose rightly and ultimately to become the persons we wish to be. Prudence is what keeps our eyes, our heads, and ultimately our hearts clear of illusions and self-deceptions so that we can move through the world as it is, rather than as we wish it were or as we are afraid it might be.

With this in view, it is possible to understand why Aquinas held that "unchastity is the first enemy of prudence" (*S.T.,* II–II, 53.6), because in the grip of sexual desire we are tempted to be selective in what we attend to, both in the situations we confront and in our assessment of our own motives and actions. This is more and not less the case if the desire is genuine and serious, a desire for real intimacy with another human being, rather than merely the physical impulse of sexual frustration looking for an outlet. The more deeply a desire is rooted and the more a person is taken up in it, the more compelling and potentially dangerous it will be. The answer cannot be to suppress such longings, but rather to maintain a view of the overarching goods that order our lives and the lives of those for whom we care. The response to such a desire is to take the reality of the self and of the one whom we desire more seriously, not less so. This requires us to be ruthlessly honest about whether what we propose as love will help or harm the one we say we love, to consider whether the acts we desire to embody our union will express or distort the truth about how we can genuinely be given and received in this relationship. A cynic has observed, "In real love you want the other person's good. In romantic love, you just want the other person." The virtue of prudence teaches us to ask what real love requires, and enables us to see and embrace it.

Temperance

Temperance is that ordering and direction of natural enjoyments and appetites which keeps them in proper relation to the central goals of human life. It is important to understand that temperance is aimed not at the denial of these appetites but at their harmonious fulfillment. With regard to eating, for example, the expression of temperance is no more self-starvation than it is gluttony; it is the balanced use and enjoyment of food in the service of health and well-being. Similarly, in the realm of sexual pleasure, temperance is what enables us to order and govern our delight in sexual touch so that it fosters and does not destroy the human union and fruitfulness toward which sex is directed.

At the same time, all of the natural appetites that are the subject of temperance are relativized even as they are affirmed. Their enjoyments are legitimate and good, but in two different senses, they are not ultimate. First, they exist not for themselves but for the sake of something beyond themselves which they serve: Health in the case of eating, human communion and the continuation of life in the case of sex. Second, the goods these appetites are directed to may be overridden by other more ultimate goods and ends. For example, there may be a circumstance (say, absolute scarcity) in which love for the neighbor would lead one to deny oneself even necessary food for the sake of feeding another. Similarly, both the New Testament and the practices of many ecclesial communions envision that some will forgo the goods and enjoyments of sexual expression for the sake of unhindered devotion to the gospel. In such cases, the natural goods are not denied or demeaned, but they are subordinated to the pursuit of other, higher goods.

There is a vital relationship between temperance and prudence. The clarity afforded by prudence can enable us to see when our desire for some satisfaction cannot be fulfilled without harm to ourselves or others. However, only those who are temperate and so in control of their desires can act on that insight, or even remain clearheaded about it. In the absence of temperance, the judgments of prudence may be overcome by rationalization, as we entertain specious arguments for how we can have what we are unwilling to forgo without forfeiting our integrity.

Justice

The virtue of justice empowers us to give all persons what is due to them. It rests upon a kind of impartiality, the capacity to give each person's claims their proper weight, whether they are our own or others', whether they concern friends or enemies. Justice is what enables us to recognize and have regard for the otherness of the other, her or his needs and interests apart from our own, at the same time that we recognize an essential symmetry: This other has needs and interests and claims quite as real and significant as our own. It is thus linked to both prudence and temperance, in that it depends upon a clear-sighted appreciation of the actual case, and on the restraint of those desires that may tempt us to subvert the interests of others.

Even brief reflection will show that the failure of justice is a basic feature of sexual misconduct, particularly among clergy. Because the pastor occupies a position of special and even sacred trust, and is invested with the moral and spiritual authority that goes with leadership in the church, he or she exercises a significant degree of power within the community. When a minister initiates or allows himself or herself to be drawn into a sexual relationship with a parishioner, this power is abused and the claims and interests of others are devalued and sacrificed to the pastor's own desires and needs. This is evidently true when the other party is married and has a spouse who is injured; but it is true even when what is violated is simply the parishioner's claim to the disinterested care, love, and attention of the pastor. Also ignored are the interests and well-being of the congregation as a whole, which are threatened by such a relationship and by the deception that attends it. The virtue of justice is simply the steady refusal to give priority to the self, or to make an exception in one's own case to the obligations of morality. It stands as a fundamental barrier against exploitation and self-indulgence in sexual life.

Fortitude

Fortitude is the courage that nerves us to face injury or loss for the sake of the good that is to be realized. It is not, therefore, mere physical courage, much less is it the lack of fear which may arise from an inadequate understanding of the real danger or an inadequate appreciation for the goods that are threatened. It has nothing to do with contempt for the life or well-being or happiness that is placed at risk. In fact, fortitude is absent unless goods that are rightly prized are knowingly risked for the sake of some greater good. More properly, fortitude is the *willingness* to risk or sacrifice lesser goods for greater, including the good of life for the sake of fidelity to God, and it may be possessed as a virtue by those who are never actually placed in peril.

The discussion of fortitude in the classical and medieval literature leans heavily toward daring the physical risks of battle or persecution and the capacity to face martyrdom rather than renounce the faith. Even though this remains in a sense the prototype for fortitude, the virtue extends to moral courage and the daily, unspectacular courage of simple endurance. Indeed, it has been truly said that courage is the form of *every* virtue at its testing point. In the realm of sexual life, the minister of our case may require, more than anything else, simply the courage to go on: To face his own loneliness and grief and to do the hard work of coming to understanding and peace without burying his aloneness in the arms of a lover. When such a temptation *is* yielded to, it is often as much a failure of nerve as of self-control.

Even so brief a sketch suggests something of how this tradition might deepen and clarify our moral reflection. However, if it is also to discipline our practice, we must turn from how we understand the virtues to how we foster them.

The Practices of the Faith:
Developing Virtue in Christian Life

One of the enduring features of virtue ethics is a degree of circularity. On the one hand, the tradition asserts that it is the presence of actual virtue—the stable disposition to do what is right that springs from the apprehension of its rightness—that makes an act virtuous. On the other hand, the tradition is unanimous that virtue must be trained and inculcated, developed in the person over time by conformity to the right norms of conduct. It is a little like learning to play the piano; one must learn how in order to play it, and one must play it in order to learn how. In the former case as in the latter, the key transition is *practice*. Virtue must be practiced until its habits and inclinations are woven into who we are, how we see and think and feel. Only then will it reliably shape what we do.

This explains why the classical moralists are so concerned about the upbringing of children. It is crucial that the young receive the proper moral formation, the training that shapes their affections and perceptions and judgments, what they praise and blame, as well as their behavior. If we begin with the observation that most of us have been very badly brought up in regard to sex by the culture we inhabit, the character of what we need becomes clear. We have to be re-formed—transformed by instruction and example and disciplined practice—into people who rightly understand the goods and purposes of sexuality and have the skills to order our lives accordingly.

Perhaps it is already obvious that such transformation is simply a particular aspect of what Christian tradition calls *sanctification*. Here, by instruction (by Scripture and tradition and the Holy Spirit) and example (the saints living and dead) and practice (of the perfectly ordinary "means of grace"), we offer ourselves to be reshaped in understanding and passion and conduct, "transformed by the renewing of our minds" into persons who can see and embrace the truth of the gospel and the life that embodies it. Thus the practices that sustain virtuous sexual life are simply the disciplines that nurture holiness. They include Scripture reading and prayer, confession and silence, corporate worship and Communion as the means by which we nurture and deepen our relationship with God, who is the source of all goodness. They also include the practices that give concrete form to the body of Christ and open us to the support, the insight, and the admonition of those with whom we live in mutual care and accountability. Space will not permit discussion of all of these disciplines of Christian life, but I want to emphasize two of them in particular as crucial for the pastor who confronts the challenges of ministry in a period of loneliness and grief.

The first of these is the regular practice of prayer. The most essential foundation and support for genuine chastity is here, in the utter intimacy and honesty of our self-presentation before God. Here we can name our desires and our fears baldly and without pretense. Here we can acknowledge even our worst impulses and the void in the center of ourselves that drives us when we yield to them, and often haunts us even when we do not. In this sanctuary, laid bare by God's knowledge and made safe by God's love, we can face the truth about ourselves. It is not repression but self-knowledge, not rejection of our sexuality but grateful acceptance of it in the presence of its Author and Sovereign, that enables us to govern it well. Perhaps the most dangerous of the many deprivations common to pastoral life is the loss of time for a serious and consistent prayer life. If the minister of our story does not have such a life, he can no longer afford to do without it.

Almost as essential is the creation of stable and trustworthy contexts for accountability, places in which we can speak the truth about our lives and will be called upon to do so by people who are prepared to love and forgive us rather than to tolerate and excuse us. Discipleship is not a private matter, and we need the word of God's judgment and grace spoken and embodied for us by others, or we risk fatal self-deception. Such a context may be sought through spiritual direction or pastoral counseling, in peer discipleship groups or in serious and intentional spiritual friend-ships. Whatever form it takes, it is a crucial arena for guarding against the illusions and distortions that may creep into moral life under the pressure of unfulfilled desire, corrupting both judgment and conduct. These relationships also provide the emotional safety and human intimacy that ministers as human beings need to thrive, and in turn to nurture those in their care. For our pastor, some regular and disciplined form of community support and admonition will be an invaluable help in remaining both faithful and effective in his ministry.

All of the foregoing can do no more than suggest what the tradition of virtue has to contribute to the church's wrestling with the problem of clergy sexual ethics. If it serves only to display the deep dependence of Christian conscience and conduct upon the whole of spiritual life, it will have enriched the conversation. To do even this much, however, is to highlight a critical omission in the process by which we currently educate and prepare men and women for the moral challenges of ministry. In general, seminary courses in ethics are intended as an introduction to the discipline and stress the content or the methodology or the history of Christian ethics as a field. In some institutions, such basic courses are supplemented by courses in clergy or professional ethics, which address the actual moral issues that arise in the practice of ministry. Even here, however, the focus is on explor-ing what norms ought to be applied and why, rather than on pro-viding the nurture that would enable students to abide by whatever norms are proposed.

This is not a defect in such courses, but simply highlights the need for much more serious attention to the task of moral forma-tion for ministry. If, as I have proposed, this is just a special appli-cation of the need to form Christians in holiness by the disciplines of Christian practice, it implies that seminary education in ethics is truncated and detached from its vital roots when academic instruction is severed from worship and devotional practice, from prayer and the lived life of charity. In particular, we cannot hope to equip ministers to live according to the dictates of what has become a "countercultural" understanding of the aims and the character of sexual life unless we begin to form them as members of an alternative community. To do this requires that we incorporate both the private and the communal practices of Christian faith into seminary life as an integral part of preparation for ministry.

There are many possible structures for doing this, and a range of forms it might take that are rooted in the richness and diversity of Christian traditions. I will offer one model simply because it is the one with which I have some experience, as it is a required part of the curriculum in the United Methodist seminary where I teach. It is based in the historic forms of Methodism, derived from the system of Class Meetings within which eighteen followers of John Wesley gathered "to watch over one another in love" and to foster growth in faith and holiness. The contemporary form of this discipline is the Covenant Discipleship group, in which small groups of students gather weekly for one year to share their successes and failures in four areas of Christian practice—public worship, private devotion, acts of compassion, and acts of justice. These areas are further specified in a covenant drawn up by consensus within the group, in which members agree to particular acts and practices by which to incorporate these aspects of discipleship into their shared lives. Both the agreed-upon disciplines, which stress the integrated and balanced character of Christian life, and the habit of community support and accountability, aim to form church leaders as disciples who recognize their vulnerability and their need for sustained nurture and care within the community of faith. Some such process is indispensable if our formation of prospective pastors is to move beyond the articulation and defense of institutional policy regarding sexual conduct to the deeper and more serious work of "equipping the saints for the work of ministry" (Eph 4:12).

B. Context Affecting Self-Understanding

Chapter Eight

In the Shadow of the Execution Chamber
Affirming Wholeness in a Broken Place

by Judith W. Kay

Rev. Kearney has been engaged in ministry with prisoners for nearly twenty years. On his own initiative and without compensation, he offers pastoral care to men on death row.[1] Rev. Kearney believes this volunteer work to be his true calling. In order to sustain his ministry, he works in other pastoral settings for pay, though without paid benefits. At his personal expense he must drive extensive distances to reach the prison. He has never received financial assistance from his denominational conference.

After about ten years among this congregation, Rev. Kearney was informed that the state had set an execution date for Max, one of "his" advisees. Max selected Rev. Kearney, not the prison chaplain, to be his spiritual adviser. On the eve of Max's execution, Rev. Kearney was strip-searched, was denied access to water or bathroom for the many hours he was with Max, and was separated from Max during the final hour of his life. This scenario has been repeated in subsequent executions.

The Setting and Its Moral Dangers

Rev. Kearney's moral struggle centers on whether his close involvement in executions renders him complicit with the killing apparatus of the state. What are the virtues that help ensure that his work is a witness to the Divine, not a practice of evil? As Rev.

Kearney asked: "In fifty years will I be seen as part of the execution team?"[2]

Rev. Kearney persists with his ministry out of his faith that ultimately, the condemned might glimpse the face of God in the midst of suffering. Sister Helen Prejean helps Rev. Kearney articulate the purposes of such work. "Our goal for the soon-to-be-killed," she asserts, "is to help him endure, to help him hold Jesus' hand, to help him have a sense of his dignity, to help him have a sense of love and care, and to give him dignity and respect." She quotes a prison warden as stating: "I want this person to be as close to his God as he can be. Anybody who helps him do this, I'm for."[3] By representing a community that cares about them, the spiritual adviser ushers prisoners out of their profound isolation and abandonment. When Rev. Kearney works with others to commute the death sentence, the prisoner, perhaps for the first time, understands what it means to be a member of community. Good spiritual advisers embody particular virtues and avoid the temptations to which this practice and its institutional setting make them especially vulnerable.

When clergy accept employment with a prison, they face a moral quagmire about whose good and what goods they should protect. Prisons are authorized by the state to wield destructive power—to punish and at times kill. The same budget that buys the electric chair or the bullets for the firing squad also pays the prison chaplain's salary. Some chaplains live on the prison grounds in free housing and profit from the incarceration of men. Chaplains' long-term professional self-interest—being employed—can collide with a biblical vision—liberating the captive. Rev. Kearney has avoided serious moral dilemmas by working independently of the state. Nevertheless, "independent" advisers such as Rev. Kearney face the risk of succumbing to the moral logic of the execution house.

Rev. Kearney works in constant moral, spiritual, and physical danger. Solidarity with the prisoners might cost him support of his religious colleagues or his access to his flock; solidarity with the prison might cost him his soul. Protestant and Catholic state-employed chaplains signed a declaration that prisoners should not have the freedom to choose their spiritual adviser. The custody staff denied him visitation rights for months at a time—effectively laying him off. When Rev. Kearney made a three-hour trip to be with a grieving prisoner whose best friend in the prison committed suicide, the custody staff refused him entrance. Though the prisoners are ultimately the ones who suffer from such acts, the adviser can also be enveloped by this atmosphere of degradation.

Which virtues can assist Rev. Kearney to avoid character deformation and complicity with evil while in an institution that wields oppressive power? Four virtues seem most important to maintaining wholeness and preventing co-optation: self-knowledge, teachableness, integrity, and courage.

Self-Knowledge

Rev. Kearney identified self-knowledge as a chief virtue needed to withstand the deforming pressures of his work and to protect the prisoner. The adviser needs self-knowledge about his motivations, about those vulnerabilities potentially exacerbated by the prison setting, and about the necessary strategies to handle himself within that setting.

Rev. Kearney believes his motivation comes from a calling, from his sense that "despite the pain, I can do no other." His primary motive is to serve God, who calls him to tend to the prisoner's spiritual well-being. But, as James Keenan has observed: "We humans don't have pure motivations but can deceive ourselves into thinking that we do."[4] Each of us has chronic habits of mind and heart that can derail us from our course.[5] Although consciously an adviser might feel motivated by love for the oppressed, his unconscious motivation may be an old habit of thinking his survival depends on helping others. Such habits may not render an adviser's stated motivations questionable, but they do make him vulnerable to misconduct if he does not engage the virtue of self-knowledge.

How does Rev. Kearney learn about motives that might be rooted in habits? Through spiritual retreats, work with a spiritual adviser, and journal-writing, Rev. Kearney has come to understand what it means for him to be with abused and abusing men, to be "needed," and to be near death. Rev. Kearney has also observed how some prison chaplains seem to have "gone astray," apparently motivated by voyeurism or desire for attention or power. He has explored with a trusted counselor his feelings about being in the limelight and has identified the sources of his work's satisfaction and frustration. Rev. Kearney believes that the work itself has clarified his motivations. Knowing how indescribably painful it is to watch a man he loves being killed, Rev. Kearney concludes that no one could ever desire to do this work.[6] But when asked by a prisoner to be with him, he says "yes," trusting that God's grace will carry him through.

Advisers need knowledge about their own history with dehumanization in order to avoid complicity with oppressive power. Albert Camus argued that we must refuse to legitimize murder and we do so by becoming neither victims nor executioners.[7] Part of the broken logic of death row is that usually only two paths are possible—one must be either victim or victimizer. In order to forge a third path, Rev. Kearney needs self-knowledge about any habits he has acquired as a result of dehumanization or violence in his own life. Otherwise he remains vulnerable to falling into the logic of the death house and becoming a possible accomplice to murder.

How has Rev. Kearney learned about his buttons that the prison setting pushes? Prayer, Bible study, and work with a spiritual adviser have helped Rev. Kearney discern the reality of God's love and the goodness of God's creation. Illumined against this background, the contours of his habits have become discernible. Their misinformation and rigidity and persistence in his life make them readily identifiable. Rev. Kearney came to understand that anytime he operated within a habit, he had become its victim. Yet "getting his buttons pushed" and going on the offensive could be just as harmful. With self-knowledge about the kind of insult most likely to "push his buttons," Rev. Kearney can know in advance about which direction to take when brutalized. With self-knowledge, Rev. Kearney is able to walk a different path.

When his buttons have been pushed, Rev. Kearney remembers that his feelings stem from his personal history and are not appropriate to the current situation. He knows that his habits may feel overwhelmingly real and true to him and may confuse him. Self-knowledge enables Rev. Kearney to chart a course that keeps him firmly grounded in the reality of God's love, allowing him to keep his attention on the prisoner and away from his own habits. Self-knowledge enables him to be attentive to the current moment, helping to create a sacred space open to love and grace.

When Rev. Kearney has remained completely present in the moment—with all its horror and redemptive possibilities—the unhealed hurt at the core of his habits still clamors for attention. Once safely outside the prison, Rev. Kearney has sought to dismantle his habits. His exercise of self-knowledge involves keeping his attention away from his habits, functioning outside of them and, later, healing their underlying wounds.

The adviser's self-knowledge, thus, involves distinguishing true from habitual motivations and knowing his personal history. This virtue entails understanding how the prison environment may "push his buttons" and developing strategies to act free of them. Self-knowledge helps the adviser serve the prisoner's well-being by walking a path of freedom that defies the prison's moral code, which makes one either victim or victimizer.

Teachableness

The virtue of teachableness involves a willingness to learn from the prisoners, to have previous learning surpassed, and to learn about oppressive systems.

Many Americans view men on death row as sub-human. Because their actions appear to have placed them forever outside the sphere of the normatively human, they deserve to die. Killing sub-humans is not equivalent to killing the fully human. Some life is unworthy of life. Rev. Kearney has cultivated the virtue of teachableness in order to learn from the prisoners. From them he has learned that this dominant American view is inaccurate and simplistic. Prisoners are more than their evil habits; their vices never replace but only obscure their inherent nature. He has learned to see prisoners as human like himself—lovable and worthy, vulnerable to acting monstrously, and capable of choosing not to do so.

Having previously accompanied people through the dying process and having served as a spiritual adviser, Rev. Kearney assumed, when he first began this work, that it would require an extension of wisdom acquired in other settings. He soon learned that previous insights needed reevaluation. While in seminary he had explored at length his willingness to lay down his life for another. Rev. Kearney later found most of this preparation unrealistic because of the limited choices on death row. As he asked: "What happens when the evil cannot be stopped in this moment, you do not have the opportunity to substitute yourself for the person being oppressed, and you cannot mount the resistance that every cell in your body is screaming for you to make?" He expounded further:

> Unless my work in the community wins a commutation of the sentence, I am to accompany this man while he is being legally killed. My commitment does not require that I sit in the electric chair. The theological insight I finally gleaned came from my meditation upon Jesus' execution. Mother Mary's gift to Jesus was that she did not abandon him. I slowly understood that if Mary could have gotten to Jesus and been able to hold his hand, she would have. I do have the opportunity to hold the condemned's hand, a luxury Mary did not have. Nothing in my seminary training prepared me for the challenge of holding together two stances in the death house: I don't concur with this death and I can't outwardly resist it.

Aided by teachableness, the adviser is able to hold multiple truths in one moment.

Rev. Kearney also needed to come to know and be teachable with regard to systems of oppression. Being teachable meant asking why underclass men and men of color, in particular, are targeted for destruction by the state. Whose interests does this destruction serve? Why does the prison system appear to be a tool in the dehumanization of men? What in men's social conditioning instills the habits that lead to disconnection and violence? What does "liberating the captive" mean in this context? Teachableness has helped Rev. Kearney avoid complicity with evil by increasing his understanding of it.[8]

Executions involve a curious blend of order and brutality. A parody of normalcy is maintained while preparations are made for the premeditated killing of a defenseless man. As Sister Helen Prejean notes throughout her work, the ritual of execution is carried out with an extreme attention to protocol, so that the execution team is inoculated against the horror of what it is doing.[9] The atmosphere is sterile, but ordinary. Coffee pots percolate, computers whir. The prisoner is prepared as is a patient before major surgery—washed, shaved, and put into hospital-like clothing. This has always been the case. As an Auschwitz prisoner-doctor recounts of murder within a concentration camp: "It was very much like a medical ceremony. . . .They were so careful to keep the full precision of a medical process—but with the aim of killing. That was what was so shocking."[10] Part of that protocol is a detoxification of language. Killing is not referred to directly. The pseudo-normalcy surrounding an execution contributes to the self-deception that nothing evil is taking place, that people are just doing their jobs.

The death house can function only if there is personal fragmentation, where humans operate inside their habits and are disconnected from their feelings, bodies, and selves. Execution protocol encourages numbness. Music is prohibited because it arouses the emotions; touch is discouraged.

> The [executioner's] self depended upon radically diminished feelings, upon one's not experiencing psychologically what one was doing. I have called that state "psychic numbing," a general category of diminished capacity or inclination to feel . . . . Psychic numbing varies greatly in degree, from everyday blocking of excessive stimuli to extreme manifestations in response to death-saturated environments. But it is probably impossible to kill another human being without numbing oneself toward that victim.[11]

Extreme emotional blunting is a form of going passive, of letting a habit of anonymity take over.

The custody staff begin numbing themselves toward the prisoner long before an execution date is set. The guards yell "dead man walking" to each other when a death row prisoner is released from his cell on the block. By making the prisoner seem already dead, it becomes easier to treat him like a thing. The depersonalized role expected of the prisoner requires that he be passive and unemotional. Breaking out of his role near the execution—fighting back or emotionally breaking down—is a form of resistance that reveals the true horror of what is happening. Guards who witness a prisoner breaking out of his role often say that they cannot execute again.

Depersonalization is also imposed on the custody staff who must activate habits of passivity or disconnection. The custody staff becomes remote in its physical contact with the prisoner, doing the required procedures with antiseptic detachment. Staff prefer the electric chair over lethal injection because the former is more distanced than having to place a needle in a vein.

Suspending one's humanity from a depersonalized role and adhering to a strict division of labor mute any sense of responsibility. Through these means the prison ensures that no human integrity complicates the execution ritual.

Disconnection from self and others is the breeding ground of violence. Large and small forms of hostility are allowed to occur in this setting. A prison psychiatrist's voyeurism may prompt a visit a few hours before the execution. The state-appointed chaplain may visit one last time and challenge the prisoner about his choice of spiritual adviser. The state's legal team may file a last-minute court motion trying to deny the adviser access to prison by attacking his character. The custody staff may learn that there has been a stay of the execution, but strip and search the adviser and then send him and the family away without informing them.

Teachableness includes learning new ways of expressing love in this oppressive environment and being attuned to new expressions of God's grace when what has been known is denied. With this virtue Rev. Kearney has learned that the smallest gesture of humanness can create a sacred moment of fellowship, such as a prisoner secretly sharing his last meal with Rev. Kearney (who is not allowed to have food) by passing morsels of food through the bars. Once Rev. Kearney sang songs from "Sesame Street" to a mentally retarded prisoner who could not understand the Scriptures. Aided by the virtue of teachableness, Rev. Kearney has learned how to witness to the sacred in the shadow of the execution chamber.

Integrity and Courage

Integrity and courage are needed to counter the depersonalization and numbing protocol that have the potential of rendering Rev. Kearney complicit with the execution. Mark Halfon has suggested that integrity is the commitment to do "what is best" in the face of adversity.[12] Rev. Kearney believes that "what is best" is a commitment to remain whole, helping the prisoner do the same. Integrity—the commitment to wholeness in a broken place—prevents Rev. Kearney's complicity with the compromising rituals of a state-sanctioned murder. Courage is needed to sustain this commitment in the face of great evil masked as normalcy.

In an atmosphere of depersonalization, Rev. Kearney uses courage and integrity to reach for everyone's humanity in the execution house and hopes to enable the prisoner to do the same. Keenan describes courage: "These two stances, standing firm and reaching out, seem to be complementary expressions of the same reality: the courageous person is unwilling to abandon the person. . . endangered. True courage is the virtue of one who refuses to abandon in the face of threat."[13] Courage helps Rev. Kearney refuse to abandon the human in either the prisoner or others involved. Yet integrity prevents the adviser from becoming a naive romantic. Rev. Kearney holds those "abused-turned-abusers" responsible for their actions because they can act differently than they were treated. It takes courage to believe that humans can still be reached, even though they may have killed or are about to kill, and then act on that commitment. Rev. Kearney hopes to inspire the prisoner to have the courage to see the humanity of his executioners and the victim's family who may be clamoring for his death, so that he faces death with integrity, not as a victim.

Rev. Kearney exercises integrity and courage by resisting self-deception about the horror that is occurring. By naming killing as killing, he can face the execution as real, not as something that happens "on another planet." The execution chamber is not a separate moral reality where different norms apply, where depersonalization and killing are permissible. Rev. Kearney refuses to be deceived that it is morally permissible for the state to target people for destruction. Integrity involves keeping his moral focus on the "end" at which the numbing protocol aims: killing a man. Integrity prevents him from being seduced by the ritual that normalizes the "means," tempting him to be satisfied with a job "well done," blind to the immorality of its purpose.

Integrity and courage prevent the adviser from seeking moral immunity by suspending his humanity and retreating into a depersonalized role. Rev. Kearney observes that some chaplains delude themselves in believing that by being "men of the cloth" they can do no harm even while being so close to evil. As Lifton notes about Nazi chaplains: "One reason the chaplain . . .was so susceptible to. . .doubling was his misplaced confidence in his profession and his professional self: his assumption that, as a member of a healing profession, whatever he did healed."[14] Rev. Kearney resists this mechanism of disconnection by having the courage to be present fully, knowing that his role as adviser is no protection against wrong-doing.

Rev. Kearney's integrity and courage help him to remain embodied and to encourage the prisoner to remain embodied. Being embodied means keeping feelings alive—remaining whole. Being embodied creates a sacred space that helps the adviser and the prisoner avoid the temptation to retreat to the numbed "comfort" of depersonalization.

Expressing feelings at the appropriate time with the appropriate person takes courage and maintains integrity. (Additionally, being appropriately emotional prevents Rev. Kearney from getting "out of control" and becoming the center of attention, making the prisoner take care of him. Indeed Rev. Kearney's love and laughter may help the prisoner shed his tears and terror.) Jesus wept in the garden and thereby summoned the courage to be fully human facing imminent death. Rev. Kearney and the prisoner remain embodied, personal, and whole by embracing their contradictory feelings of anger, fear, sorrow, and love and granting them physical expression through trembling, laughing, or weeping. Integrity and courage help Rev. Kearney remain connected, so as to assist the prisoner to face his death embodied, present, and receptive to God's grace.

The adviser's reduction of the prisoner's exposure to hostility by taking some of it on himself is a gift given to the condemned. It is also a test of the adviser's courage and integrity. The emotional strains of an execution provoke expressions of hostility by almost everyone. For instance, a prisoner may refuse to see his family, and Rev. Kearney may become the target of the family's consequent confusion, rage, and guilt. Rev. Kearney courageously deflects hostility away from the prisoner and onto himself so that both can remain focused on the prisoner's spiritual well-being. Keenan observes: ". . .[T]he courageous one believes that he specifically is capable of keeping the situation from worsening; otherwise, he would be reckless."[15] Rev. Kearney knows that he should not be in the death house if he makes the situation worse for the prisoner by responding to other's hostility inappropriately. Courage ensures that the prisoner will find in the adviser a person of integrity, someone to be trusted even in the most threatening circumstances.

Summary

Persevering in these virtues, Rev. Kearney hopes to avoid complicity with the death house and ensure that his work does not serve evil, but instead, freely opens the door to God's grace. By practicing self-knowledge, he purifies his motivations and becomes adept at taking on hostility without becoming victim or victimizer, enabling him better to serve the prisoner. Teachableness helps him learn the humanity of murderers, be they prisoners or guards. Integrity and courage help him resist depersonalization. With integrity and courage he and, hopefully, the prisoner embrace their own humanity and affirm the humanity of those in the death house. Engaging these virtues, the adviser helps the prisoner through a process of re-personalization, bringing him freedom as he prepares for death.

1. Because Rev. Kearney works exclusively with male prisoners, I use the male pronoun with cognizance that there are women on the row.

2. Forty years after the Holocaust, a Nazi doctor realized that his presence "at that moment [of involuntary euthanasia] was used to calm the mentally ill and camouflage the killing process." Robert Jay Lifton, *The Nazi Doctors: Medical Killing and the Psychology of Genocide* (New York: Basic Books, 1986), 73.

3. From private correspondence.

4. James F. Keenan, S.J., *Virtues for Ordinary Christians* (Kansas City: Sheed & Ward, 1996), 49.

5. Habits are in contradistinction to virtue because they lack flexibility, a commitment to the good, and appropriate passion. See Judith W. Kay, "Getting Egypt out of the People: Aquinas's Contributions to Liberation," in *Aquinas and Empowerment: Classical Ethics for Ordinary Lives,* ed. G. Simon Harak, S.J. (Washington, D.C.: Georgetown University Press, 1996), 7–28.

6. Voyeurism and morbid fascination motivate some people to want to watch executions.

7. Albert Camus, *Neither Victims nor Executioners,* trans. Dwight MacDonald (Chicago: World Without War Publications, 1972), 55.

8. I am indebted to Professor Joy Kroegger-Mappes at Frostburg State University for this insight.

9. Helen Prejean, C.S.J., *Dead Man Walking: An Eyewitness Account of the Death Penalty in the United States* (New York: Random House, 1993).

10. This former prisoner was quoted in Lifton, *Nazi Doctors,* 254.

11. Ibid., 442.

12. Mark S. Halfon, *Integrity: A Philosophical Inquiry* (Philadelphia: Temple University Press, 1989), 56.

13. Keenan, *Virtues for Ordinary Christians,* 85.

14. Lifton, *Nazi Doctors,* 464.

15. Keenan, *Virtues for Ordinary Christians,* 85.

Chapter Nine

Virtue Ethics and the Problem of African American Clergy Ethics in the Culture of Deference

by Samuel K. Roberts

The preacher is the most unique personality developed by the Negro on American soil. A leader, a
politician, an orator, a "boss," an intriguer, an ideal-
ist—all these he is, and ever, too, the centre of a group
of men, now twenty, now a thousand.
—W. E. B. DuBois,
The Souls of Black Folk, 1904

*Rev. Carlton Billingsley has been the pastor of Mt. Moriah
Baptist Church, a large African American congregation, for 32
years. Over the years pastor Billingsley has earned the trust and
confidence of the vast majority of the parishioners. He has baptized and nurtured into Christian discipleship virtually all of the
members of the congregation. Among the younger members of the
congregation he is regarded as a father figure, reassuring in
demeanor and presence. Among those in his age group he is a
trusted confidant. Among those who are older he is regarded as a
faithful son. In short he cuts a larger-than-life figure in this congregation, long noted for its history of strong charismatic preachers and leaders.*

*Ironically, the high regard in which the congregation has
placed Rev. Billingsley has engendered in him a disquieting sense*

of uneasiness. Three elderly persons have let him know that they wish to include him in their wills. Although in his mid-fifties, Rev. Billingsley still cuts a dashing figure and has been told so by several female parishioners, who have also hinted that they would be willing to explore a deeper emotional relationship with him. A subcommittee of the church constitution committee has been debating the merits of having a position of church moderator among the officers in the church. This person would preside at all official church meetings and the monthly meeting of the church council. A slim majority of members of the subcommittee feels that such a move would betray their time-honored custom of deferring to Rev. Billingsley as presiding officer and the center of political power in the church.

This culture of deference leaves Rev. Billingsley with a palpable degree of ambiguity and uneasiness. He does not want to risk alienating the older members of the congregation by spurning their proffered bequests. He freely admits the feeling of rejuvenation when younger women in the church give him admiring glances. He has grown accustomed to power and has learned how to use it effectively within the church.

How might virtue ethics inform his response to the issues raised in this case?

The Cultural Context

The above case presumes a cultural phenomenon, which I have termed a "culture of deference." By this I refer to the historically grounded tendency within the African American culture to accord to the preacher relatively higher normative status and authority than other professionals. Recognized by eminent observers of African American life such as W. E. B. DuBois (in the above epigraph) and the historian Carter G. Woodson, this culture of deference had its roots in slavery and in the post-Reconstruction period.[1]

The slave system presumed that virtually all aspects of the slave's life should be determined by the will and interests of slaveholders. Politically, the enslaved were powerless.

Economically, their labor was not their own, although a few slaves managed to "hire out their own time," that is to say, derive some compensation for their labor away from their principal place of bondage. Slaves had no access to any formal educational system; for a slave to seek learning or to be taught by someone was a punishable act by law throughout much of the antebellum South.

It was only in the area of religion that slaves managed to forge a definable cultural space that lay beyond the controlling reach of slaveholders. Secret prayer and praise services could be held beyond the prying eyes of white scrutiny. Having achieved a level of relative autonomy from white control during slavery, and even a greater degree after slavery, it is not surprising that the acknowledged leader of the religious dimension of African American life—the preacher—would be accorded deference within that culture.

In all other aspects of African American life, the effects of racism limited black people from having access to leadership in other professions and, even when allowed access to those professions, the practice in them was limited to contexts governed by racial segregation.

Thus relatively free from white oversight, the black preacher exerted a near monopolistic hold on leadership in the black community. After emancipation, he (in virtually all cases, *he*) was perhaps the most widely recognized leader among black people. Consequently, for virtually two generations after the end of slavery, the most certain route a young black man could take toward success and prominence was through the ministry.

In a very real sense, Carlton Billingsley has inherited the mantle of leadership lavished upon him by an adoring and appreciative congregation in the tradition of this "culture of deference." While he apparently has earned the trust of the congregation, he is still aware that for many of the persons in the congregation he occupies a near iconic status. Many feel that he must be accorded a deference merely by virtue of the position he occupies as pastor of such a large and influential church.

Given now the historical background and context, the question remains, how can he solve his ethical dilemma through the guidance of virtue ethics? To the extent that Pastor Billingsley is disposed to employ virtue ethics for determining his moral posture relative to the exigencies in the case, he would examine his character—both the person he is and the person he hopes to become. Such examination includes attending to one's own history. Thus, he would be careful to remember the formative stages of his development, significant persons and mentors who sought to sensitize him to challenges of ministry occasioned by the needs of people. He would recall the small church in which he grew up, the value system inherent in that church, the special deference it paid to elderly people, the way in which trust was developed by the pastor, and the techniques he observed being used by older pastors as they negotiated the political straits of the church.

Based on these reflections on his past, he would also seek a greater level of self-knowledge and a more profound understanding of his own strengths, shortcomings, and weaknesses. Such a tempered view of his self could moderate and always hold in proper perspective the more vaunted view of the black preacher that emerges from the "culture of deference" in which he seeks to minister. Finally, he would constantly reflect on the kind of person he hopes to become, focusing on those aspects of the character of the virtuous preacher.

In the culture of deference, therefore, his knowledge of self is absolutely critical. Virtue ethics and its focus on the *person* and *character* of Rev. Billingsley would focus not on attempting to calculate how best he might reach a desired goal or effect a desired consequence or, indeed, seek to discern how his conscience might lead him. Rather he would search to see if a "match" might be made between the person he seeks to become— virtuous, just, upright, merciful, and without guile—and the acts that such a person would do in various contexts of life.

Implementing an Ethic of Virtue:
The Role of Discernment

Foundational to any action that might ensue from an ethical analysis done according to virtue ethics would be an ability to see the world and the aspects of the case in a way consistent with the vision of a virtuous person. One "sees" the world as a just, honest, upright person. Critical to "seeing" the world in a special way is a sense of *discernment,* the ability to see beyond the externals of any phenomenon into the inner workings, the reality beneath the surface of any phenomenon. As a practical matter, discerning solutions to ethical problems will, from the vantage point of virtue-oriented ethics, involve full utilization of one's *imagination* as well. Full use of the virtue of imagination means that the virtuous person is encouraged to marshal creative options in seeking solutions to ethical dilemmas. Freed from the burden of preordained rules on the one hand and, on the other hand, seeking to avoid an undisciplined antinomianism, the person of virtue proceeds to imagine and create possibilities for ethical problem solving. To be sure, such powers of imagination will be harnessed and disciplined by constraints inherent in the notion of virtue itself.

Following the virtue ethical approach, Rev. Billingsley would be concerned to always be aware how the background cultural dynamics of the case came to be; he would seek some intimate knowledge of both the reasons why the culture of deference developed and the reasons undergirding its current manifestation. He would understand the historical and sociological dynamics that might help explain why black people defer to him in this particular way. He would come to understand and discern how elderly people in the congregation might come to "transfer" on to him deep feelings of kinship and admiration eventuating in his being written into wills. Similarly, he might come to understand the powerful connection between charisma and sexuality.

The kind of person Rev. Billingsley seeks to be—a person who is caring, just, and merciful—would "see" the phenomena in the case through the peculiar lenses of a virtuous person. He would be made aware, perhaps, that common to each of the dilemmas raised in the case—the elderly, the women who have fallen under the sway of his charismatic personality, the members of the constitution committee who defer to him—is a relative position of *vulnerability.* By deferring to him, each has granted power and advantage to him. A virtue-oriented ethical posture with respect to the case would suggest that Rev. Billingsley assess the various levels of *vulnerability and power* differentially shown among the persons in the case. Moreover, he would be enjoined to ask how a virtuous person handles power, or how a virtuous person treats others who have less power than he or she has.

Viewed in this light, the questions for Billingsley then become: "What shall I do with my power over those who have become vulnerable? Shall I take advantage of them? What means are at my disposal to affirm them even in the context of their vulnerability?" Spurning the bequests from the elderly or lecturing them on the protocols of professional clergy ethics that prohibit such gifts runs a real risk of destroying the emotional ties by which they have learned to look upon him as a "son." Returning the warm glances of the young women with a scowl designed to chastise them could not only destroy their attitude toward their pastor, but could also undermine their confidence in themselves as sexually mature young women. Refusing to accept the role of moderator for fear of becoming a dictator might in fact compromise the sense of "order" that many persons in the congregation associate with the pastor fulfilling such a role. The issue, then, is discerning the appropriate action in light of the culture in which the action is required.

It might be that a way could be found to affirm the proffered bequests but have them converted in such a way that Billingsley's professional ethics would not be impugned or compromised. But to do this he will soon discover that the virtue of discernment must be supplemented by powers of imagination. However, such imaginative powers as he might bring to bear on his quest to discern the right thing to do will always be guided and controlled by virtue. Perhaps the bequest could take the form of a gift to the church in the name of Rev. Billingsley. Perhaps an endowment to one of his favorite charities or causes, such as the mentoring program in the church that has begun to employ African rites of passage formats, could be arranged. Regarding the women who are attracted to the pastor, Billingsley may discern that their unresolved grief for fathers who died untimely deaths constitutes a need for counseling. Attraction to him is only symptomatic of unresolved grief. With respect to the church council, the virtue of discernment would guide him toward understanding the peculiar nature of the political culture of *this* church, its operative myths, expectations, and values.

Implementing the Virtue of Justice

Rev. Billingsley desires to be a just person. He seeks to ensure a reliable and certain degree of justice among all of the persons with whom he comes into contact within the church, particularly those now referenced in the case. The question is posed: How can he be most just to all of the persons in the case?

The focus is on being just; being the embodiment of justice. Approached in this fashion, one might suggest that in each situation Billingsley would discover subtly different ways of being just. Justice, he will soon discover, is a matter of discerning what any person is due within the exigencies of a context. With respect to the elderly members' bequests, he will have to discover what justice is in their peculiar case. Justice for the elderly persons who intend to leave to the pastor their hard-earned life savings might mean attending to the *need* that leaving the bequests satisfies. Clearly, the elderly persons believe that the deprivation that allows them to leave the money to the pastor is worth it. In all likelihood they have a basic desire *to be remembered* for having left the funds with him. This is that which they, by their efforts, feel is their due. This for them becomes justice. On the other hand, Billingsley, by virtue of prudent planning and wise investments overseen by the church's chief financial officer, is in no danger of retiring in a state of financial peril. The just thing for him, therefore, is not access to more money, even if it were gained through the goodwill of elderly people who look upon him as a son. He would be most just if he could discern a way to ensure the ongoing memory of his older friends without enhancing his own financial gain in the process.

As Rev. Billingsley seeks to discern what the women are due who have expressed a sexual interest in him, one could remind him that the Christian view of human sexuality affirms that each person is an embodied consciousness; we are not pure spirits nor are we pure material. We are *inspirited beings*. For the Christian, sex at some point fulfills the desire to experience the sublime and transcendent reality that goes beyond the physical. If love is the complete union of that which is separated, or in this case, two inspirited beings, and if sex is the desire to unite two inspirited beings, then it follows that a necessary relationship exists between sex and love. But Rev. Billingsley has already pledged his love to his wife, with whom he enjoys a wholesome and satisfying life. Therefore, any sexual union between him and the other women is necessarily precluded. But an affirmation of the women as inspirited beings, beings whose sexuality is palpable, honest, and forthright, is his to seize with each greeting. They are therefore affirmed, but he is prevented from overstepping the boundaries that the necessary link between sex and love (of his wife) dictates. They are due affirmation, and *only* affirmation, as inspirited beings, not in this case the right to become a full sexual partner.

Seeking to be virtuous and just in this situation becomes enacted within the context of the power dynamics of congregational life as well. It is clear that as a result of the residual culture of deference, a majority of the members of the constitution committee would gladly yield a critical amount of power to Rev. Billingsley, even to the point of offering him the position of moderator. What is Billingsley to do with this proffered power? How would virtue and justice determine how he should act? How could Rev. Billingsley be just within the context of the church council and the suggestion that he be granted political advantage in the governance structure of the church?

Two critical questions may guide our analysis: What is the council due? and How can Rev. Billingsley best embody virtue within this context? Fundamentally, insofar as it seeks to serve as the governing body of the church and to interact with Rev. Billingsley, it is due a reliable and just system of governance based on regularized procedures, as much as possible, and the avoidance of whimsical and arbitrary rule of individual power, as much as possible. The system works best when *just* persons implement *just* procedures. Insofar as he is deferred to as the leader of the church, he owes the council an embodiment of the just and tempered use of power within the governance system of the church.

Assuming that policies and procedures are in place to check the intemperate use of power by the moderator, and assuming further that Billingsley would be guided by his own sense of self-restraint, then accepting the role of moderator might be an appropriate course of action. On the other hand, Billingsley has sought to nurture a sense of himself that is independent of the expectations of the "culture of deference." Therefore, accepting the post of moderator would only reinforce problematic cultural expectations. He would do well, therefore, to decline the invitation to serve as moderator and, instead, seize any opportunity to nurture a goal of shared power between pew and pulpit.

It is inevitable that Rev. Billingsley will always be accorded a modicum of *informal* political power within the context of this culture of deference. What is of concern is that in *whatever* role he plays in the governance of the church, he would do it with consistent regard for the policies and procedures that are in place. The essence of dictatorial power is its arbitrariness, not in the amount of power that is wielded. A sense of justice (a desire to ask the question: What is the just thing to do?) becomes in virtue ethics a question geared to asking, What shall be the relationships among principal characters in leadership as we attempt to govern the affairs of the church? Is Rev. Billingsley willing to develop requisite levels of trust and confidence among the church officers and members of the church council such that a dependence on raw political power would not have to be pursued as an option for acquiring legitimacy within the political circles of the church?

The Continuing Courage to Be

The title of Paul Tillich's classic work[2] somehow seems an appropriate heading as we conclude this virtue-oriented analysis of Rev. Billingsley's dilemma. Among the virtues that best connote constancy (a quiet confidence in one's ability to do the right as one is given discernment of the right) is the virtue of courage. At some point in his focus upon himself and the kind of person he seeks to be, courage will offer strength and moral ballast to Rev. Billingsley. How might focus on courage manifest itself in each of the troublesome contexts in the case?

Courage could overcome the temptation to seize upon the bequests of the elderly members and make Billingsley realize that he has the internal resources and the assured presence of God in his life to be financially sufficient for the rest of his life. He need not seize upon their vulnerability to ensure his own financial survival. He might take comfort in the knowledge that he has the resources to live quite comfortably without taking advantage of any proffered bequests or wills offered by persons who have clearly deferred to him out of a sense of parental love. He will survive! He might take quiet comfort in affirming the time-honored tenet in African American piety that "the Lord will provide." Courage in the context of affirmation of providence becomes, therefore, the foundation for his posture.

In his relations with the young women, it is clear that there is no way he or they can control the inevitable level of sexual tension that will be present in interactions, conversations, greetings, and so on. These are uncharted waters; there are no scripts available to dictate how conversations are to proceed or how greetings are to conclude. To guide him he has only his sense of integrity, the courage to believe that he will behave appropriately within the bounds of his marriage vows, and his desire to affirm their inspirited beings and sexuality.

Within the power dynamics of the church council and in the informal political exchanges that are inevitable aspects of congregational life, the virtue of courage would assure Rev. Billingsley that he need not cling desperately to office in order to wield power in the congregation if his reputation for fairness and consistency is maintained. He would come to understand that his contribution to the sense of order in the congregation is not necessarily tied to the office he holds, but to the *kind of person* he is. Therefore, it really does not matter if he is moderator or sits quietly in a pew while a layperson presides in the meeting or even if that person should develop a vigorous political following in the church. Rev. Billingsley can give up the trappings of power because of the power of his person. In this sense, he takes courage and inspiration from a venerable old African American patriarch who intoned to his family in ever so quiet but confident tones, "*Wherever* I sit is the head of the table."

Conclusion

The above case study focused on a typical ethical dilemma experienced by a contemporary African American pastor who seeks to lead and nurture a large and diverse congregation. The issues of trust, power, and sexuality were some of the more prominent issues in this case.

The fruits of a virtue-based ethical analysis were seen to be quite instructive and helpful. By going inward and focusing on character and the *kind of person* that Rev. Billingsley hoped to be, we were able to refashion the process of ethical analysis. Moreover, isolating certain virtues, namely those of discernment, justice, and courage, helped to guide us in asking different kinds of questions than would be the case in a process governed either by deontological ethics or teleological ethics. And because, therefore, the questions are different, the answers are different. To be sure the answers produced by a virtue-based approach are never

definitive or absolute. Yet, to the extent that a just person has discerned them and seeks to enact them, such solutions can enjoy a
fully acceptable level of viability.

1.   See Charles Hamilton, *The Black Preacher in America* (New York:
     Morrow, 1972), chap. 1; Carter G. Woodson, *The History of the Negro
     Church* (Washington, D.C.: The Associated Publishers, 1921), 198; and
     Samuel K. Roberts, "Sufficiency and the Holy Spirit: Theologies for the
     Black Church's Future," *Christian Ministry* (Nov./Dec., 1997): 11.

2.   Paul Tillich, *The Courage to Be* (New Haven: Yale University Press,
     1952).

PART TWO

CONGREGATIONS AND POWER

SECTION ONE
The Way Communities Worship

Introduction

*T*he defining context in which Christian communities have gathered for the last three millennia is to worship. There we stand together before God recognizing the Godship of God and the creaturehood of ourselves. But we are able to stand there by the body and blood of Christ who brings us to the altar of God. As we gather, the body and blood becomes for us, as it always has been, Life.

If virtue ethics is about transformative actions that help us to become the persons we aim to become, then after the death and resurrection of Christ, worship is emphatically the most transformative Christian action. It constitutes us as children of God and as brothers and sisters in the Lord. It is in worship, then, that we become who we most fully are.

Christian worship is constituted by three transformative actions: We remember, we celebrate, and we wait. Worship helps us *recall* in gratitude the journey made up until this point and how that journey has made us the people we are today. For Christians, that journey was made effective by Christ who led our forbearers in faith. In worship, too, we *celebrate* how it is that up to this point, we have been nourished by our providential God who promises undying covenantal fidelity. In worship, we also *wait,* for the coming of the kingdom which, though already established, is not yet fully present. In these three moments, the virtuous Christian community identifies itself in history, with its past, present, and future.

The encounter with the divine in history is what we each seek in prayer; finding oneself in the presence of God is, after all, the fruit of prayer. All pastors and communities know the power of prayer, where we experience ourselves fully in our human histories encountering the mystery of God. The intimacy of prayer transforms us, as Joseph Kotva shows, into a people who know where we stand in the eyes of God. Thus, through prayer we acquire the virtue of humility whereby we embrace our creaturehood not as limitation but as gift. Therein we look at our community members not with the eyes of judgment but with the eyes of understanding, becoming patient with ourselves and one another. And, knowing ourselves as beloved creatures, we fall into a humble solidarity with one another. In short, prayer brings us into a leadership marked by service and fed by God's love.

"Preacher, do I have to forgive a man who murdered my four sons?" So asked Betty Jane Spencer of her pastor, Pastor Lord. Lord, after six months of soul searching answered, "no." William Willimon revisits the case asking, "What type of church do we need to be for a preacher to answer 'yes' to Betty Jane Spencer?" Willimon helps us realize that the answer cannot come from the preacher alone but must arise from a community that has allowed itself to be formed through the narrative of the Gospels so that it can truthfully practice what it preaches. Our preaching at once shapes our practices and in turn is shaped by the practices of our own community of faith. To preach forgiveness is to preach what we have received and what we practice. Inasmuch as our liturgy is constituted by confession of sin, absolution, and prayers of reconciliation, we are reconciled continuously through the cross in our liturgies: We are formed by a narrative embodied in our rituals that has claimed for us our own reconciliation. The liturgy then is a training ground for us to learn how to forgive and how to answer "yes" to Betty Jane Spencer.

In this context of liturgy shaping a community's character, language is key to our communication. In Diana Fritz Cates's essay we face a typical pastoral situation where the issue of God language is divisive. Through a variety of characters, Cates explores the emotional investment each parish member has in the use of exclusively male pronouns to describe God. But Cates does not leave us to consider these characters individually; rather she explores the ways that their pastor, in faith, compassion, prudence, and courage, encounters the deeply felt beliefs and fears of his parishioners. Here, God language is not an academic or speculative exercise: It is a common but enlightened encounter with the lives of ordinary Christians who struggle to share their understanding of God. But the pastor, as in the essays by the Jungs, Kay, and Roberts, must negotiate these tender and differing viewpoints with a prudence that can move the community forward as it tries to understand and worship the very mystery of God.

Finally, in examining the question of intercommunion, Margaret Farley offers her thesis that "no one goes away hungry from the table of the Lord." In making her case, she argues for a recognition that the churches have already attained a degree of unity both in their relationships with one another as well as in their understanding of the Eucharist. Farley's essay is a classic example of what a Christian virtue ethicist can bring to the dialogue of what constitutes right theological and moral conduct in the churches. Mindful of the importance of growth from within and of the right realization of one's own gifts, she writes, "intercommunion is not merely a means to a missing unity but an unfolding and actualizing of a present unity that has a future." In order to celebrate this faithfully, she offers the virtues of prudence, patience, wisdom, courage, freedom of spirit, and faithfulness to the process wherever it leads.

In each of these essays the overriding insight is how our liturgical practices shape our community and, in turn, how our community advances those practices that leave us open to the saving and mysterious power of God. These essays are only touchstones to the more enduring question about how we as community members and as pastors allow ourselves to be formed by God's hand for the future. These are not essays about idealism or utopia. They are rather about people whose God has always led them through history.

A. Truth in Prayer and Preaching

Chapter Ten

Transformed in Prayer[1]

by Joseph Kotva, Jr.

A local pastoral team recently committed themselves to spending a week in prayer for each member of their large congregation. The congregation was divided into groups small enough so that the pastors could prayerfully focus on each individual, but the groups were large enough so that the pastors could pray through the congregation in one year. The members were told in advance which week they would be the focus of prayer and were encouraged to share prayer requests with the pastoral team.

The team did not start this process with particular expectations; it merely seemed like a good thing to do. What they discovered, however, is that they were slowly changed in the process. Pastor Ross, for example, talked about gaining patience. Before the year of prayer, he often found himself deeply frustrated with certain parishioners who evidenced little growth in their lives as Christians. Toward the year's end, he realized that he had stopped being so frustrated and had learned to wait for God's own timing with these members. Pastor Beverly similarly gained in the virtue of solidarity. Several parishioners had voiced opposition to her ministry ever since her arrival, but in spending weeklong periods praying for these parishioners (often praying for them as "enemies"), Beverly's anger was reduced and she began to have a sense of solidarity with the very people who stood against her ministry.

Pastor Steve—a young, engaging minister fresh out of semi-nary—spoke about learning humility. In routinely approaching God with his parishioners' lives in mind, Steve began to recognize that he shares many of their sins and weaknesses and that virtu-ally every parishioner has something to teach him about living the Christian life more faithfully. Moreover, in learning through prayer to confess his weaknesses and prize their strengths, Steve began to realize, with shock and dismay, that his implicit sense of superiority had undergirded the subtle manipulation of parish-ioners via his pastoral position and their deep sense of duty or guilt. Although Steve never "guided" parishioners into anything unseemly or morally inappropriate, he began to realize that the same lack of humility he discovered in himself sometimes leads clergy to grievous forms of misconduct. And besides, said Steve, "my parishioners deserve better than to be subtly coerced into the forms of 'service' that I deem appropriate."

At first glance this case does not appear to have much to do with ethics. The reflections by Pastors Ross and Beverly do not grab our attention with controversial issues, nor do they concern moral quandaries or powerful actions. There is nothing particu-larly morally troubling even in Pastor Steve's comments, although we are glad that he has learned to be less manipulative. In short, this case about three pastors who pray does not seem to involve anything of great moral consequence.

Yet, one gift that a virtue perspective offers is the insight that cases like this are at the core of what ethics is about. This case reminds us that prayer is something that pastors do. But from a virtue perspective, the simple fact that pastors pray means that prayer merits moral examination. According to virtue theory, ethics is first about character, not quandaries; therefore, even rou-tine, mundane activities are morally relevant because it is in and through them that character is formed. As David Norton observes, "even our trivial desires, choices, and acts have moral meaning because they have some effect—no matter how small—

on the person we are in process of becoming."[2] Because our choices, acts, experiences, and relationships influence the kind of people we become, all but the most involuntary and accidental of human acts and relationships are susceptible to moral scrutiny. Thus, prayer merits attention precisely because it is a routine, noncontroversial activity. If prayer is a regular part of pastoral life, then we ought to attend to prayer as part of the matrix of choices, activities, and experiences that helps shape the pastor's character.

In thinking about the moral implications of prayer, I am helped by Allen Verhey's discussion of the role of prayer in medical ethics. In that context, Verhey suggests that we should understand prayer to be what Alasdair MacIntyre calls a "practice."[3] A practice, as I understand it, has three central elements: (1) It is a shared, cooperative human activity; (2) It concerns the realization of internal goods; and (3) The realization of those internal goods requires the acquisition of various skills and virtues.[4]

Verhey suggests that these three central elements of a practice are visible in prayer: (1) Prayer is a cooperative activity, for we learn how to pray from and with other Christians; (2) In learning to pray, we learn that attending to God is prayer's proper (intrinsic or internal) good. Prayer waits for God, attends to God, looks to God. Prayer is not merely a means to other external goods; it is not an instrument to wealth, health, or happiness and; (3) In learning to attend to God, in learning to pray well, we discover that we are shaped in ways appropriate to prayer. If we learn to attend to God, says Verhey, we will acquire the virtues suited to such attentiveness—reverence, humility, gratitude, care, and hope.[5]

Such characteristics or virtues are, of course, also relevant in our daily, moral living outside of prayer. We cannot, however, engage in prayer for the purpose of achieving those virtues, for then prayer would quickly cease to be prayer, cease to be attention to God and, ironically, the virtues would not be formed in us. Nevertheless, morally relevant virtues are formed in us as we learn to pray rightly.

Verhey's proposal that prayer is a "practice" is illuminating. He is right, I think, to suggest that we cannot pray in order to become morally better people. Waiting for or talking with God has an intrinsic value that is corrupted when it is turned into an instrument for attaining other goods, even the commendable good of the acquisition of character. Yet, he is also right to suggest that in learning to pray well we are shaped in ways fitting to and "partially definitive"[6] of prayer.

Consider, for example, Pastor Steve's experience of growing in humility. Humility is the virtue that enables a fitting and truthful self-appraisal in relationship to God and others.[7] Growth in this virtue often goes hand-in-hand with learning to pray well, with attending to God. In attending to God, we are reminded and learn to appreciate that we are not God.[8] We do not approach God as God's equals, but as God's cherished, loved, and sinful creation. Moreover, attention to God takes our attention off ourselves.[9] If we are attending to God, we are not absorbed with ourselves, either our accomplishments or our problems. In focusing on God, we cease to be preoccupied with ourselves, cease to be the center of reflection. We thereby begin to acquire the virtue of humility.

As Pastor Steve discovered, something similar happens in prayer during intercession, petition, and confession. Intercession teaches humility: As we learn to pray for others, we learn that they are as much God's children as are we, and that their needs, weaknesses, and strengths are not so different from our own. So too, as we approach God with our needs in petition, we are reminded of our dependence on God and others. When we pray for "our daily bread," we learn to recognize that even basic bodily sustenance comes to us as a gift. In prayers of confession, including those offered in private by the individual and those offered communally during public worship, we acknowledge our guilt to God. In doing so we learn to recognize and take responsibility for our limitations and failures.[10] We begin to grasp how often we fail to act rightly, even when we want to do what is right. We similarly begin to understand how badly things go when we assert freedom from God and others.

Humility is therefore a virtue of prayer. It is difficult to imagine learning to pray rightly—learning to attend to God, learning proper intercession, petition, and confession—without also growing in humility. It is, however, vital that we recognize that such prayer-shaped humility is not a groveling, degrading sense of inferiority or subservience. The God whom we meet in prayer is our loving Abba (Daddy or Dearest Father) who cherishes us, sacrifices for us, and created us as good.[11] Moreover, our Lord taught us to ask for things in prayer—food, forgiveness, safety— which implies that we are worthy of receiving good things from God. Hence, prayer-formed humility is not low self-esteem or continually finding the worst thing to say about oneself.[12] The humble person has "neither too high nor too low" a self image, but instead disciplines her "vision with the insight that God loves all creation."[13]

Thus, prayer teaches us true humility. It teaches us that we are not God. It takes our attention off ourselves. It helps us to recognize our limitations, failures, and needs. But prayer also teaches us that God cherishes us and that all of us are equally God's children.

While humility is a virtue of prayer, it is also relevant to ethics in ministry. This relevance is evident when we, like Pastor Steve, consider questions of power, for example. Several recent books have noted the inequality of power in the pastoral relationship. Pastors are admitted into and entrusted with the intimacies of peoples' lives, often when people are most vulnerable. Pastors are also seen by many as representing the church, sometimes even seen as representing God. These factors can cause a tremendous inequality of power between pastors and parishioners. Recent books in clergy ethics rightly wrestle with this inequality.[14]

Prayer-formed humility is seldom mentioned in this context; yet, the virtue of humility is vital if we are not to abuse this inequality. If we are to use pastoral power in ways that are redemptive rather than abusive, we need humility: We need to know that we are not the center of the universe; we need the ability to recognize our limitations, failures, and temptations; we need an appreciation for the way life comes to us as a gift; we need the awareness that others stand equally with us before God.

Freeing the pastor from an over-inflated or under-inflated self-image, prayer-formed humility enables the pastor to see his or her use of power honestly and clearly. Moreover, because prayer-formed humility releases the pastor from being overly preoccupied with his or her own agenda and teaches the pastor to recognize that he or she too is capable of terrible things, the pastor will not become scornful of parishioners and is less likely to impose his or her personal agenda on them. Conversely, because humility involves proper self-respect, there is less danger that the pastor will use parishioners to boost his or her sagging ego. Thus, although the need for humility is not the only thing that should be said about pastoral power, prayer-formed humility is desperately needed and often neglected in such discussions.

The relevance of humility is not limited to this inequality of power. Prayer-formed humility permeates virtually every aspect of pastoral life. Humility needs to be at work, for example, in the preparation and delivery of sermons and homilies. Humility helps the pastor develop sermons that are accessible and useful to the entire congregation, not just to an intellectual elite. Humility also affects delivery by challenging the pastor to remember that it is the gospel, not the pastor, that deserves center stage.

There are many other prayer-formed virtues. Here I only discuss the two other virtues mentioned in the above case: patience and solidarity. Pastor Ross discovered patience in prayer. This is not surprising, for as Michael Duffey notes, "the wait" is a powerful image of what prayer is about.[15] Often enough, when we enter prayer, we sense God's absence much more than God's presence. At such times we must learn to quiet our hearts and wait.

Yet, even when God's presence is undeniable, prayer requires a different sense of time's passage. Westerners are obsessed with speed, efficiency, and progress, but prayer requires something different:

> Prayer is the suspension of time and the adoption of a
> patient and quiet heart in order that we might be led
> into deeper communion with God. Praying requires
> stepping out of the current of activities in which we
> are caught up. . . . Prayer is first of all the intention to
> create an opening, a space where we might wait for
> the stirrings of God.[16]

Thus, learning to pray means learning to wait, learning a different sense of time's passage, learning patience.

Such prayer-formed patience is no small matter to ethics for ministry. Pastors who desire their own moral transformation, and the moral growth and transformation of their parishes or congregations, must learn patience. Patience is vital if they are to avoid despair over the slight moral progress, backsliding, and failure that are so often a part of church life. Patience is vital if they are to resist the temptation to manipulative or coercive means in the name of a just cause. Patience is vital if they are to communicate a gospel that claims that salvation comes not in frantically working for it but as a gift.

In a very difficult situation, Pastor Beverly grew through prayer in the virtue of solidarity. The prayer-formed quality of this virtue is perhaps easiest seen in the Lord's Prayer. Our Lord did not teach us to pray to *my* Father, but to *our* Father. I am not to ask for *my* daily bread but for *our* daily bread. I am to seek not only that *my* debts be forgiven, but that *our* debts be forgiven, not merely that *I* will be delivered from evil, but that *we* will be delivered.[17] As we learn to pray this prayer authentically, we gain a sense of being united with all others who call on the same divine Parent. Indeed, we gain a sense of solidarity with all humanity.[18] To learn to pray this prayer rightly is to be changed: It is to recognize that others are also God's children; it is to know that I cannot rest content when my needs are fulfilled while yours are unmet; it is to share in a mutual need for forgiveness and deliverance.

What is true of the Lord's Prayer in particular is true more generally of confession and intercession. In confession we acknowledge to God how we have failed and hurt others, not merely how we have failed God directly. In intercession we go to God with another's need, but we cannot do this honestly unless we have come to identify with that need. In intercession our neighbor's pain becomes painful for us. In intercession we learn to yearn with others, and thus learn to desire and seek their well-being.[19]

Prayer-formed solidarity is a morally significant virtue that informs many facets of church life. Solidarity is important in everything from hospital visitation to church-based community organizing. Our ability to express God's mercy and presence at the hospital bedside depends on this virtue. Many parishioners know immediately if we do not share their pain and their yearning. Similarly, solidarity is *a*, if not *the*, central virtue behind church-based community efforts such as soup kitchens, neighborhood watches, youth clubs, and interracial discussion groups.

And, as Pastor Beverly discovered, prayer-formed solidarity can even transform how we treat our adversaries. Without neglecting or dismissing the injustice with which some of her parishioners treated her, Pastor Beverly was able to treat them with grace and empathy. In some cases adversaries became supporters; in other cases they remained antagonists. In either case, Beverly's sense of solidarity enabled her to show them care and somehow freed her ministry from being immobilized by their antagonism. Previous to the yearlong effort at prayer, Beverly's ministry was nearly stymied by their antagonism, largely because she could focus on little else. In growing in solidarity, Beverly grew free to minister to her congregation, adversaries included.

Virtue ethics teaches us not to ignore "mundane" matters such as prayer, for it is in such activities that one's character is given shape. Indeed, when we look at prayer, we discover how important it is in the formation and maintenance of the kind of character necessary to sustaining ministry. Following Allen

Verhey, I argue that prayer is a practice with the internal good of attending to God. In pursuing that good, we grow in virtues such as humility, patience, and solidarity—virtues essential to ministering well.

1. Much of this essay is taken from my article, "The Formation of Pastors, Parishioners, and Problems: A Virtue Reframing of Clergy Ethics," *Annual of the Society of Christian Ethics* 17 (1997): 271–90.

2. David L. Norton, "Moral Minimalism," in *Midwest Studies in Philosophy XIII Ethical Theory: Character and Virtue,* eds. Peter A. French, Theodore E. Uehling, Jr., and Howard K. Wettstein (Notre Dame: University of Notre Dame Press, 1988), 186.

3. Allen D. Verhey, *The Practices of Piety and the Practice of Medicine: Prayer, Scripture, and Medical Ethics* (Grand Rapids: Calvin College and Seminary, 1992), 16.

4. My understanding of what constitutes a "practice" depends heavily on Alasdair MacIntyre, *After Virtue,* 2nd ed. (Notre Dame: University of Notre Dame Press, 1984), 187–203; id., "Plain Persons and Moral Philosophy: Rules, Virtues and Goods," *American Catholic Philosophical Quarterly* 66:1 (1992): 6–8; Jeffrey Stout, *Ethics After Babel: The Languages of Morals and Their Discontents* (Boston: Beacon Press, 1988), 266–76.

5. Verhey, *The Practices of Piety,* 17.

6. Cf. MacIntyre, *After Virtue,* 187.

7. For example, Helen Oppenheimer, "Humility," in *The Westminster Dictionary of Christian Ethics,* eds. James F. Childress and John Macquarrie (Philadelphia: The Westminster Press, 1986), 284; Richard Bondi, *Leading God's People: Ethics for the Practice of Ministry* (Nashville: Abingdon Press, 1989), 143–44.

8. Verhey, *The Practices of Piety,* 17.

9. Craig Dykstra, *Vision and Character: A Christian Educator's Alternative to Kohlberg* (New York: Paulist Press, 1981), 96–98.

10. Verhey, *The Practices of Piety,* 22–23.

11. Arthur Paul Boers, *Lord, Teach Us to Pray* (Scottdale: Herald Press, 1992), 34; Matthew 6:9; Galatians 4:6–7.

12. Richard J. Foster, *Prayer: Finding the Heart's True Home* (New York: HarperCollins, 1992), 61.

13. Bondi, *Leading God's People,* 143–44.

14. For example, Richard M. Gula, *Ethics in Pastoral Ministry* (New York: Paulist Press, 1996), 74–90; Karen Lebacqz, *Professional Ethics: Power and Paradox* (Nashville: Abingdon Press, 1985), 112–36.

15. Michael K. Duffey, *Be Blessed in What You Do: The Unity of Christian Ethics and Spirituality* (New York: Paulist Press, 1988), 34.

16. Ibid., 38.

17. Matthew 6:9–13; Luke 11:2–4.

18. Theodore W. Jennings, Jr., *Life as Worship: Prayer and Praise in Jesus' Name* (Grand Rapids: William B. Eerdmans, 1982), 37–39, 70–71.

19. Ibid., 73.

Chapter Eleven
The Preacher and the Virtue of Forgiveness
by William H. Willimon

Consider the case of Pastor Lord: "Do I Have to Forgive?"[1]

I was asked by Betty Jane Spencer, "Preacher, do I have to for-give a man who murdered my four sons?"

A few years earlier, a group of young men had gotten high on drugs and broken into her Indiana farmhouse and committed mass murder. Betty Jane's sons were killed. She was shot and left for dead. Since beginning his prison sentence, one of the con-victed criminals wrote to tell her he had "found Christ" and asked for her forgiveness.

When she said "Preacher," I knew she wanted more than my opinion. She wanted a statement that represented the Christian tradition. "Am I obligated as a Christian to forgive in this situa-tion? Just what does the church mean by 'forgiveness'? He did not say 'I'm sorry . . . .just 'Forgive me,'" she continued. "What am I to do?"

I told her to give me six months and I would try to give her an answer. During that time I sought out victims of violent crimes, and those whose loved ones have been shattered by crimes. I studied the Jewish tradition and looked at what the church has said. The victims who talked with me were very dis-turbed by the issue of forgiveness. They were constantly being told they must forgive, but most could not . . .

Victims' resistance to forgiveness seems to focus on two elements: Forgiveness as forgetting and forgiveness as excuse. . . . Victims of violence are deeply concerned that their loved ones not be forgotten.

Forgiving may also imply excusing. . . .Does finding Christ excuse what was done? . . . .Leaders of the prison ministry say that man should be released so he can witness for Christ. Betty Jane wonders why he can't witness for Christ in prison.

What can we learn from the Judeo-Christian tradition about forgiveness which does not imply forgetting or excusing? On Yom Kippur, sins against God are forgiven. But if you have sinned against your neighbor, you must go to him or her and seek forgiveness. Not even God forgives what you have done to another. . . .

I remembered the times I have proclaimed, "Your sins are forgiven." I now imagine a battered wife thinking to herself, "Who gave you the right to forgive the one who beats me?" I no longer say in a general or public way, "Your sins are forgiven." . . .Victims ask us not to demand that they themselves pronounce absolution. Those of us who speak on behalf of the Christian community can speak of God's mercy to the truly repentant, but we have no right to insist that the victim establish a relationship with his or her victimizer to effect a reconciliation. Even without some reconciliation with the perpetrator, most victims can gradually "let go" of their hate, anger, rage, or despair. Their negative energy becomes channeled into constructive activity such as working for victim causes or supporting other victims.

Betty Jane Spencer is open to a future without her sons. She is a prominent national leader in the victim rights movement, currently the Florida state director of Mothers Against Drunk Driving. But she is not open to a future with those who killed her children. She had no relationship with them before the murders and she desires none now. She hopes they create for themselves a positive future, but one that does not include her.

Betty Jane is quite ready to affirm that God is merciful and is hopeful that the murderers of her sons will find a genuine relationship with God. But don't ask her to be responsible for their salvation. Don't ask her to go to them and judge their hearts. Let a representative of the church assume that burden. When I saw Betty Jane six months later, I told her No.[2]

Pastor Lord presents himself as one who, confronted by a specific, suffering parishioner, empathetically struggled with her situation in a caring, compassionate way.[3] Some pastors, when asked by this woman, "Do I have to forgive?" might have quoted Scripture to her because Jesus is the one who brought Pastor Lord and Betty Jane Spencer together. Jesus certainly had much to say on the subject of forgiveness, much of which was very straightforward and specific: "And forgive us our debts, as we have also forgiven our debtors" (Mt 6:12).

Lord was too deeply concerned for this woman to quote any Jesus to her. So he went rummaging in the "Judeo-Christian tradition" for answers and, after six months, found the answer: That she really need not try to forgive the young killer who asked her forgiveness.[4] That was not her vocation as a Christian, nor was it Pastor Lord's "right" to urge her to do so.[5]

Considering how hot a topic forgiveness has been throughout the history of the church, it is interesting that Lord found little help from Scripture, the Church Fathers, or his own denomination. Now that Lord has a deeper understanding of the matter, he even finds that he can no longer speak of blanket forgiveness in his liturgical leadership of his congregation.

This episode, in which a parishioner and a pastor are confronted with the demand to forgive, is an opportunity to see how the church does not merely preach certain abstract ethical demands like, "We ought to forgive," but rather the church cultivates a whole set of virtues and practices whereby we are enabled to love others as God has loved us. Christians in no way deny the seriousness of the evil that people sometimes suffer, nor do we deny the culpability of those who commit evil acts. Rather, we seek to counteract the evil through induction into a counter-community called *church,* which, in all it does, is trying to worship the Triune God. We forgive not as a sign of weak resignation to the evils in this world but as an alternative form of power which is itself a protest against an undoing of the evils of this world.[6]

Pastor Lord represents his actions as caring and compassionate. But in our willingness to keep things private and personal, detached from ecclesial demands, we clergy have not rebelled against cultural expectations. We have acquiesced into the grip of moral practices that are inimicable to the gospel.

True morality—the ability to judge our own self-deception, the gift of seeing things in perspective, the courage to act with an imagination counter to the world's conventions—comes from practices outside those sanctioned by the system. It comes from the virtue of being forced, Sunday after Sunday, to lead and to pray the Prayer of Confession followed by the Words of Absolution. It comes from being ordered, Sunday after Sunday, to "Do this in remembrance of me." It comes from submitting our lives to the reading and preaching of Scripture. Our extravagant claim is that through obedience to these practices, Jesus gives us the character we need to be faithful disciples. And we will never know whether or not Jesus was speaking truthfully if our pastors refuse to hold us accountable to Jesus' demands. Our aim as pastors is to help people inculcate those virtues whereby we become the sort of persons whose lives will make Jesus appear to be either incredibly crazy ("Love your enemies and pray for those who persecute you"; Mt 5:44) or amazingly able to produce the sort of disciples he demands ("To you has been given . . . the kingdom"; Mk 4:11).

During a recent lunch the chair of our chemistry department noted that ministers could profit by the ethics of chemists. "The ethics of chemists?" I asked. "Sure. It is impossible to be a good chemist and a liar at the same time. The chemist's honesty about experimental results, openness with other chemists, and commitment to standard methodology would enhance the practice of ministry." This tie between the practice of chemistry and the need for certain qualities of character suggests that we don't need to be better rebels from the practices of our faith. Rather, we need to be more deeply linked to them. As Pastor Lord demonstrates, the irony is that by acting independently, thinking for ourselves, and standing on our own two feet, we have not rebelled against the system; we have capitulated into the worst aspects of it. Separated from the skills and commitments of our tradition, we are left morally exposed, victims of conventional wisdom.

The notion that we are most fully ourselves, most fully ethical, when we have freed ourselves from the demands of Scripture, tradition, and church merely demonstrates the power of the socially sanctioned story that holds us captive. In our culture, the individual is the basic unit of reality, the sole center of meaning. We are all children of modernity, that story which holds that each of us has a right, a duty, to be free of all stories save the ones we have individually chosen. This is Peter Berger's "heretical imperative," the modern conceit that we are free to determine our own destinies, that we have no fate other than the fate we choose. In earlier times, heresy was that way of thinking in which a person chose what to believe rather than believed what he or she had been told. Today, we are all fated to be heretics in that we all live under the modern presupposition that none of us should be held to commitments which we have not freely chosen. Our morality has thus made freedom of choice an absolute necessity. Freedom has become the fate of the individual. If I explain my actions on the basis of tradition, community standards, Scripture, I have obviously not thought things through (for six months, like Pastor Lord!), have not decided for myself, have not been true to myself, have not rebelled against the external imposition of a role, so I have not been moral.

As Stanley Hauerwas has shown repeatedly, this mode of thinking is but another form of deception, enslavement to a story (the Enlightenment myth of the free individual), which tells us that it is possible to choose our own stories. We have merely exchanged narrative masters. Pastor Lord has jettisoned the older, traditional story that it is my duty as an ordained leader of the church to bear the church's tradition before my congregation for a more socially acceptable one: My duty is to my individual feelings and standards in order to free my parishioners to be dutiful to their individual feelings and standards.[7]

Pastor Lord acts as if he is freeing himself and then his parishioner from an oppressive, naive, externally imposed, traditional story—that we Christians have a duty to forgive people who wrong us, even when they don't deserve it. In reality, the episode as narrated by Pastor Lord shows how difficult it is for modern liberal societies to acknowledge the subtle forms of coercion that hold them together because they derive their legitimation from the presumption that there is no moral authority more significant than the individual conscience. They do not see that what they call "individual conscience" is also an externally imposed tradition. Believing that he is free from external, social determination and that his main pastoral role is to free his church members from external, social determination, Pastor Lord is able to dismiss Scripture, Jesus, church tradition, and the liturgy of the church in favor of the freedom to do what he thinks personally to be right. The only external coercion recognized is the unacknowledged coercion that everyone must do what each of us personally thinks to be right. In other words, we have dismissed one ethical tradition for another but we are still submitting to an ethical tradition.

Pastor Lord even dismisses the feelings of his parishioner. The possibility of forgiveness, which initially troubles her so deeply that she seeks out the counsel of her pastor, is explained away in a barrage of anxious pastoral reading and reflection. There is no exploration of the possibility that perhaps Betty Jane Spencer's concern is a legitimate expression of her discipleship. How does the pastor know that she is incapable of the radical action Jesus demands? Who told the pastor that he was responsible for protecting the woman from radical action like forgiving her enemies? Not wanting to "preach" at her, he ends up preaching at her through the more subtle but nevertheless powerful techniques of counseling and therapy.

Why doesn't he at least ask her, "What does forgiveness mean to you?" Perhaps she has an inadequate notion of Christian forgiveness, thinking it to be a facile pat on the head or moral amnesia. Pastor Lord acts as if he has graciously sidestepped issues of power and authority, thrusting the issue back upon Betty Jane Spencer after reporting on his six months of research. Yet one is intrigued by the subtle but powerful ways he continues to define the situation for her. Power has been wrenched away from church tradition and Scripture and reduced to an exchange between an individual pastor and his parishioner. Nothing is more insidiously powerful than people who think they have no power.

In responding to a barrage of letters critical to his article, Lord said: "At times we do our theology standing on our biblical tradition, but at other times we do our theology standing beside those in pain . . . We must also stand with those who are hurting and let their pain define what we shall do and who we shall be. We do not define them. They define us."[8]

Aside from questions about a theology that lets "hurting" and "pain" define us and our sisters and brothers, one notes Pastor Lord's inability to see how Betty Jane Spencer's questions did not define him. He defined her.

What the pastor presents as a case of exemplary, empathetic pastoral care might be seen as an abdication of pastoral responsibility in favor of the exercise of purely personal power. Is protection and care of the woman his goal or is his own self-protection more important? Her question, "Preacher, do I have to forgive?" raises threatening questions for a pastor. Was Jesus crazy? Are the words of Jesus relevant only for Jesus who forgave his enemies (Lk 23:34), or perhaps a saint like Stephen who forgave his murderers (Acts 7:60), but not for his ordinary disciples? How does Pastor Lord know if his response arises out of his pastoral compassion or out of his participation in the modern control of people by managers who control people precisely by reassuring them that through managerial niceness they are being allowed to be individuals? By the end of the story, there is no one left in the story except Pastor Lord and Betty Jane Spencer. Mrs. Spencer, once a tragic victim of violence, continues as a victim, though now as a "national leader in the victim rights movement." She becomes a professional victim, a person defined solely by pain and hurt. This is precisely the end of the story Jesus sought to avoid with his instructions to mourners, the hungry, and the persecuted in his Sermon on the Mount. The ethic there is not to produce and perpetuate victims but to urge the means of enabling victims to be victorious over their victimizers through forgiveness, blessing, and prayer.[9]

When definitions of forgiveness are cut off from their theological sources and forgiveness is reduced to some sort of heroic act of individual conscience, Christian forgiveness appears to be absurd, even cruel. Christians don't forgive their enemies because we are trying to be nice people or because we hope to bring out the best in our enemies; rather, we forgive because we, enemies of God that we are, have been forgiven.[10]

Moreover, Christian forgiveness is not something that we do as individuals but something the church does in response to what God has done. We each experience forgiveness as a gift given to us before we launch forth to forgive anyone else. Furthermore, we are able to forgive because Christian forgiveness is part of a whole set of practices and habits that surround the worship of a Triune God. Detach the demand to forgive from the practices which make that demand intelligible, and Christian forgiveness appears to be an incredible overlooking of culpability or else an impossible ideal to which no one save some Saint Francis should aspire.

Rather than first ask, "What sort of person would I have to be to forgive?" the prior question is: "What sort of church would we need first to teach me that in Jesus Christ I have been forgiven?" Along with this we can then ask, "What sort of church would be required to have a member seriously ask, 'Preacher, do I have to forgive?'" Pastor Lord implies that he and his church are now so sensitive to the plight of battered spouses and wronged women that he now no longer works for reconciliation and forgiveness, no longer dares to ask God for reconciliation in worship. What he may mean is that our church is already so lacking in sources of power outside our own psyches, our leaders so devoid of any moral authority beyond whether or not they are nice and we happen to like them, and our worship so bereft of liturgical resources (like the Catholic Rite of Reconciliation), that we are now unable to make big, countercultural moves in our lives. We can no longer afford to have people running around loose asking, "Preacher, do I have to forgive?"

Somewhere Iris Murdoch notes that most of the really important ethical work is done long before we arrive on the scene of a decision. That is certainly true for the ethical work of the church. Because our call to forgive is rooted in our theology and therefore in our liturgical practices, training in forgiveness takes place every time the church sings or prays or recites a creed. A Christian forgives for much the same reasons that a Christian prays: To be close to the God whose nature it is to forgive. A Christian forgives for much the same reasons that a Christian intercedes to God in prayer for others: To be in communion with those whom God loves and for whom Christ has died. Training in the arts and practices of forgiveness begins long before we are wronged by someone.

One of the gifts of historical reflection, subservience to tradition, and participation in the liturgy is conversation with a *polis* outside ourselves. The tradition of the church has a way of raising the political, communal power question for the church. Rather than see Betty Jane's question as an opportunity for community soul-searching, Pastor Lord quickly assures her that this is a personal matter, nothing that might potentially involve the whole church, nothing that might require a reexamination of pastoral style and substance, but something just between the two of us. Nothing political. In the end, Betty Jane is abandoned to her hate, her hurt. Perhaps even more tragic for the baptized, the church is also abandoned to be a conglomeration of isolated individuals who muddle through as best they can, with little responsibility to the Betty Jane Spencers of the world.

What sort of pastor would I have to be to answer this woman with "Yes, I really think Jesus means for you to be the sort of person who can forgive even an enemy so great as the man who killed your sons"? What set of ecclesial practices and internal disciplines would need to be developed? What sort of preacher would I need to be to craft sermons that would give this woman the courage to be as radical as Jesus seems to demand? Without consideration of these congregational disciplines and pastoral resources, the teachings of Jesus are unintelligible and we are all abandoned by the church and its clergy to "making up our own minds" on matters as serious as forgiveness, as if our minds were all that mattered, as if we already possessed minds worth making up.

For John Wesley, founder of the Methodist movement in eighteenth-century England, a guiding text was the outrageous statement by Jesus in the Sermon on the Mount (Mt 5:48), in which Jesus tells his people to "Be perfect, therefore, as your heavenly Father is perfect." Wesley did not ask, "Did Jesus really mean these words in this way?" or "Why would a nice person like Jesus say something impossible like that to earnest people like us?" Rather, Wesley said, in effect, "What sort of church and church leaders would be required to produce people who can be perfect as their Father in heaven is perfect?" He knew that it would not be the established Church of England. It must be a church in which people knew the cost of discipleship and were encouraged to pay. It would be a church with highly developed practices of grace and forgiveness.

Wesley invented something new: Small groups of laypersons bound together for prayer, singing, accountability, mutual correction, and forgiveness. He thus made ordinary eighteenth-century English people into saints on the basis of his insight that Christian morality is inherently communal, corporate. Not as individuals, but only as a group formed by a set of practices are people able to summon the courage and the honesty to forgive.

Lacking the kind of bold, risky, practiced, political, and creativity of a John Wesley, all we can do is service the status quo, be chaplains to the present order, urge people to think deeply, feel sincerely, and make up their own minds. Clergy are thus fated to be nice. Nobody will get hurt doing that. Of course, nobody will get saved either. Nobody will get to be a saint.

So the discussion between pastor and parishioner occurs in the abstract, as if there was no church. Nothing is asked of the church, as if Pastor Lord realized that everyone in the church would see this woman's dilemma as her personal problem. There is no reaching out to the church as the sort of people who might enable ordinary people to make extraordinary moves in their lives. Surely someone in the congregation has had to learn to forgive an enemy. There is no mention that this woman is baptized, a person who is pledged to live under the sign of the cross. Nor is there any mention that she lives among the baptized, people who are pledged to provide the support necessary not for her to be happy but to be faithful, people who have been washed, are being washed of their sin and clothed in righteousness. Sentimentality is the best such ethics can deliver.

It is not necessary for Pastor Lord self-righteously to tell Betty Jane Spencer that she ought to forgive her enemies. Rather, it is necessary for those who are ordained to witness to the faith of the church that in Jesus Christ, God has forgiven us, that we are the recipients of forgiveness, and that we are commissioned to show the world that we are God's answer to what ails the world. Pastors ought never to stop being preachers. Of course, we pastors are smart enough to know that if we told someone like Betty Jane Spencer to take the teachings of Jesus seriously, she might turn and ask us when was the last time we took Jesus with such seriousness, and then where would we be?

Perhaps well on our way to a recovery of the disciplines of discipleship.

To be a Christian is to be someone who is baptized into those practices and virtues based upon the claim that in Jesus Christ God is busy saving the world, not on our terms but on God's terms. Christians claim to have a truthful account of the way the world is put together. The demand that we forgive is a gracious prod to the church to keep seeking those virtues in our life together whereby we are able to show forth, in our lives, what God is doing in the world. A church that seriously attempts to embody forgiveness will be a church that desperately needs to worship God on a regular basis, for it is only in the worship of the church that we inculcate those habits, dispositions, and practices whereby we are able to know that we are forgiven and that we can forgive.

The beautiful link between liturgical practice and ethical activity is illustrated in Jon Sobrino's account of the celebration of All Souls Day in a refugee camp in San Salvador:

> Around the altar on that day were various cards with the names of family members who were dead or murdered. People would have liked to go to the cemetery to put flowers on their graves. But as they were locked up in the refuge and could not go, they painted flowers around their names. Beside the cards with the names of dead family members there was another card with no flowers which read: "Our dead enemies. May God forgive them and convert them." At the end of the Eucharist we asked an old man what was the meaning of this last card and he told us this: "We made these cards as if we had gone to put flowers on our dead because it seemed to us they would feel we were with them. But as we are Christians, you know, we believe that our enemies should be on the altar, too. They are our brothers despite the fact that they killed us and murder us. And you know what the Bible says. It is easy to love our own but God asks us also to love those who persecute us."[11]

* * *

When we refuse to jettison our language, our peculiar way of relating to the world, by such odd practices as praying for and forgiving enemies, we thereby testify to our adoption of Jesus' quite different account of the way the world is. For the world is right in judging the truth of our convictions on the basis of the virtuous lives that the church and its preaching are able to produce.

1. I have dealt with the case of Pastor Lord previously, with different intent, in William H. Willimon, "Clergy Ethics: Getting Our Story Straight," in *Against the Grain: New Approaches to Professional Ethics,* ed., Michael Goldberg (Valley Forge, PA: Trinity Press, 1993), 161–79.

2. Richard Lord, "Do I Have to Forgive?" *Christian Century* 108:28 (October 9, 1991): 902–903, at 902.

3. Alasdair MacIntyre, in *After Virtue* (Notre Dame: University of Notre Dame Press, 1981), 72–74, demonstrated how the modern claim of expertise, combined with the illusion of value neutrality, led to professional ethics as we know it. He also showed the subtle manipulative qualities behind such detached, expert neutrality that calls itself "compassion." See also Stanley M. Hauerwas and William H. Willimon, "Ministry Is More Than a Helping Profession," *Christian Century* 106:8 (March 15, 1989), 282–84.

4. Among the many misconceptions inherent in the notion of a "Judeo-Christian tradition" is the idea that Jews and Christians have basically the same ideas about forgiveness. Here L. Gregory Jones, *Embodying Forgiveness: A Theological Analysis* (Grand Rapids: William B. Eerdmans, 1995), 101–34, is particularly lucid. When Christians forgive, it is one of the ways of demonstrating to the world that Jesus really is the hoped for Messiah and that God's kingdom really is present and is taking visible form in our ability to forgive.

5. Lord implies the often repeated notion that only those who have actually suffered a wrong can discuss whether or not to forgive the wrong. George Steiner's comments are typical: "Only those who actually passed through hell, who survived Auschwitz after seeing their parents flogged to death . . . can have the right to forgive. We do not have that right. . . . What the Nazis did in the camps and torture chambers is wholly unforgivable. . . . The best now is, perhaps, to be silent; . . . " in *Language and Silence* (New York: Atheneum, 1967), 163.

   As Christians, we do not have so much a right as a duty to encourage one another to explore the gospel promise that, even for people like us, caught in sometimes terrible circumstances of injustice, there is the good news of Jesus Christ. With the help and the prodding and support of the church, even I can be a saint.

6. I have been helped, in my reflection on forgiveness, by L. Gregory Jones's masterful treatment of the subject in *Embodying Forgiveness.*

7. This is what is amiss in Lewis Smedes's account of forgiveness in his *Forgive and Forget: Healing the Hurts We Don't Deserve* (New York: Harper and Row, 1984). Smedes tends to make forgiveness internal and private. Wrongs are merely misguided but well-intentioned acts that, for our own good, ought to be forgiven because it may make the forgiver a freer, better person (12–13). Rarely does Smedes speak of forgiveness as something others and God do for us.

8. Richard Lord, "Reply," *Christian Century* 108:34 (November 20–27, 1991): 1118.

9. I find it sad that Mrs. Spencer is left to pursue a kind of perpetual victimhood as spokesperson for victims. Forgiveness is a way of empowering victims, not of producing them. As Roberta C. Bondi has noted, "If we identify ourselves as victim, or place most of the blame for our condition outside ourselves, we also take away from ourselves our own ability to affect what happens to us"; *To Pray and To Love* (Minneapolis: Augsburg Fortress, 1991), 82.

10. "The path of forgiveness cannot be authentic unless there is truthful moral and political engagement. Of course that means, in the first instance, acknowledging the senses in which all of us have been, and to some extent still are, enemies of God. . . . it means to repent daily, to continue to unlearn the patterns of sin and evil as we seek to become holy people." Jones, *Embodying Forgiveness,* 263.

11. "Latin America: Place of Sin and Place of Forgiveness," *Concilium* 184 (1986): 50, cited in Jones, *Embodying Forgiveness,* 266.

B. Inclusive Language and Communion

Chapter Twelve
Imaging and Speaking of God

by Diana Fritz Cates

A few members of a small, relatively diverse ELCA Lutheran congregation gather on Sunday morning for an adult forum devoted to the topic of God-language. Shortly after the program begins a discussion ensues, and Anna speaks up. She tells the group that she has been wrestling hard with this issue over the past several months.

"Each Sunday, I come to church with the hope of being fed with the life-giving spirit of Christ. And each Sunday, I'm becoming more concerned that I'm not being nourished here. It's hard to explain, and I myself am puzzled about what is happening to me, but when I hear God referred to repeatedly as Father, Lord, and King, when we recite the creeds and affirm our belief in God as Father, Son, and Holy Spirit, when the risen Christ is referred to only as He, and the congregation sings praises only to Him— well, it hurts me. I hear these all-male references, and each one hits me like a slap in the face. With each slap, I notice the references even more, and before long the most prominent feature of my worship experience has become the feeling of resisting these references. I feel alone, shut out, like I don't belong."

An older woman in the group, Dorothy, speaks up immediately, partly flabbergasted, partly offended. "I don't get it! If you really feel that way, why don't you leave the church?"

"I don't get it, either," says Jack. "You sound like my sister. She's left-handed, and she's always complaining about how the world is prejudiced against left-handed people. Every time she has to use a pair of scissors designed for a right-handed person, she feels personally offended. She has always struck me as overly sensitive."

The conversation drifts. Anna shrinks down into her chair and feels the hot blood rising into her face.

The pastor of the congregation, who has been sitting off to the side of the room, wonders if he should say something. He wonders what his role as leader of this congregation requires of him, not only in assisting this conversation but also in addressing the issue raised by the forum.

W hat kind of issue is this? Some Christians think that it is simply a "political" issue. It seems to them that people like Anna are trying to change the church in ways that will promote their own interests or the interests of their ideologically motivated group. Some members may perceive Anna's words as a thinly disguised attempt to gain power by dethroning God the Father and remaking him in her own image.[1] Others think that the use of God-language is simply a "personal" issue. They imagine that people like Anna have private, psychological problems that cause them to misunderstand what is said in church. Some members may perceive Anna's words as a cry for help, but one that is best answered by pastoral counseling. Others think that this issue is primarily "biblical." It seems to them that people like Anna fail to acknowledge the authoritative Word of God, which indicates that Christians are to call God Father as Jesus called "Him" Father. Members who think this way perceive in Anna's words a need to read the Bible and to be formed by its witness.

There are indeed political, personal, scriptural, and other dimensions to this issue. Conceiving these dimensions too narrowly, however, and focusing on any one of them too sharply can cause us to miss other features that we ought not to miss.

Like most political issues, this one is not *merely* political. The church is a powerful political institution whose resources, policies, programs, teachings—and words—affect the hearts, minds, and bodies of millions of people. It is incumbent on those who contribute to this institution to examine whether its use of power promotes morally good ends—and to seek change when it does not. Like most personal issues, this one is not *merely* personal, either. A person's thoughts and feelings are part and parcel of her sense of human well-being, and her sense of well-being has an enormous impact on how she relates to others. The experiences of one member necessarily affect the body as a whole. Nor is this issue narrowly biblical. What the Bible says and means about God, and what tradition, experience, and reflection contribute to persons' understanding of God and themselves—all such matters have been in question since the inception of the church, and they will remain in question among persons of faith. The way that Christians choose to wrestle with these questions will determine their characters and the character of their communities.

The way that persons refer to God—within their own minds, in prayer, worship, and conversation—is an issue that has serious political, personal, and biblical dimensions, but it is also, and more fundamentally, a theological and a moral issue. It concerns deeply entrenched and, for many Christians, unreflective habits of relating to God and to others in thought, feeling, and action. An ethic of virtue can bring reflection to bear on these habits and thereby encourage their thoughtful and deliberate formation. An ethic of virtue can help clergy in their own spiritual and moral formation; it can also aid clergy to help parishioners improve their spiritual and moral dispositions in and through the practice of church membership. Before we can appreciate the contribution of virtue ethics, however, we must first appreciate the need for its application; we must apprehend the gravity of the issue and its relationship to matters of faith, character, and community.

Let us begin with the theological dimension of the issue. For Christians, God is the unfathomable ground of being, the source and *telos* of all that is. How can God ever be spoken of in a way that reflects the profundity of God's reality? Indeed, how can God even be thought of by humans? Christians believe that God is the infinite, and thus that God's reality infinitely transcends all images of God that they could ever receive or conceive. How, then, can they think of God without reducing God, in thought, to something that God is not, namely, an object whose reality can be captured in finite human terms?

Needing somehow to think and speak of God, and wanting to do it well, Christians rely on symbols. Religious symbols are terms that point truly, but only obliquely, to what God is. Religious symbols are terms that, in pointing only obliquely, admit that they cannot finally capture that to which they point. God the Father is a prominent Christian symbol. For many, this is a divinely revealed symbol that points truly to a God whose nature is to be like a powerful, wise, and good patriarch. Insofar as God the Father functions properly as a symbol, however, it admits to being a finite mode of approaching God that could never finally comprehend God.

Religious symbols are invaluable in that they allow believers to enter into relationship with a God whose reality always exceeds their grasp; but the use of symbols carries the serious risk of idolatry. A symbol becomes an idol when the one who uses it rests comfortably in the thought and feeling of what God is like — yet one does not, at the same time, experience the unsettling realization that God is also unlike any object that can be possessed by the human mind. God the Father is a symbol that has become, for many Christians, an idol. It has become an image to which they cling for clarity, simplicity, and security, such that this image has effectively replaced the reality of God as the object of their worship. It is difficult for Christians to avoid making this mistake. They want to stand in personal relationship to God, and in order to do so they need to employ personal images of God. Yet if they ignore the way that God's infinite reality breaks into and exposes as finite all such images, Christians end up standing unthinkingly in relation to a mere image.

That the very image of God the Father can become an idol is made clearer when one brings the moral dimension of this issue into view. Many who cling to the imagery of fatherhood invest God with qualities that they associate with ideal earthly fathers— qualities in the presence of which they feel most like safe, secure, beloved children. At the same time, these Christians implicitly invest earthly fathers and other men with power, wisdom, and goodness that they take to be like God's. Many admit, when questioned, that they are most comfortable imaging God as a father (and other male characters) because they revere fatherhood and manhood in general; they like the way that being in the presence of good fathers and other good men makes them feel. In turn, they revere fatherhood and manhood in humans because these appear to them to be uniquely suitable reflections of the divine image. In short, many Christians are attached to the imagery of fatherhood because they are attached to the values of patriarchy, and they intuit (correctly) that the use of exclusively male imagery and language for God upholds the patriarchal order.

Indications that many Christians implicitly idolize maleness in relating to God as male become evident in the reactions that people like Anna get when they question the connection between divinity and maleness—especially if they suggest the use of female, as well as male, imagery partly in an effort to expose the symbolic nature of all gendered imagery. The Bible is replete with female images for God, although this is most apparent in the original languages (see, for example, Dt 32:18; Ps 22:9; Ps 71:6; Ps 131:1–2; Is 49:15; Is 66:13; Mt 23:37; Lk 13:34; Lk 15:8–19; and Jn 3:5–8). When introduced to the image of God as Mother, however, many Christians react with offense, irritation, disgust, anger, embarrassment, or suspicion.

A rational explanation for such reactions is that many people (including many women) value mothers less than fathers, women less than men, or they value the roles or character traits associated in our culture with mothers or women less than those associated with fathers or men; hence, it seems like an insult or in some other way inappropriate to saddle the highest good with lesser female attributes. Moreover, many in our society are invested in familial, social, political, and economic power arrangements that depend upon the unquestioned assumption of male superiority. In such a society, it is not surprising to encounter believers who suspect that imaging God as female could threaten the foundation and structure of their lives.

It is not my intention to prove that attachments to male God-imagery and language support, and are supported by, attachments to tangible features of the patriarchal order. In the present context, I can only raise the possibility. But what a disturbing possibility it is. At issue is the truthfulness of people's relationships to the ground of their own being, the ultimate source and goal of their lives. If there is even a chance that the image of divine fatherhood is associated in believers' imaginations with comfortable arrangements of power, privilege, and responsibility—if there is even a chance that this image and those associated arrangements are vying with God for the status of ultimate concern—then clergy ought to be alarmed. Also at issue is the morality of human relationships. If it is the least bit likely that the use of male God-language has become a subtle means of sacralizing male domination and female subordination, and thus a way of condoning unloving and unjust social relations, then clergy ought to beware.

Clergy must consider how to raise their own and others' consciousness on this matter. If they have already tried to do so and have met with resistance, they must consider how to respond to this resistance. Seeking to change the ways that Christians image and speak of God will likely prove difficult for the church and its leaders. An ethic of virtue suggests that working through these difficulties will require of leaders the cultivation of good character traits that will dispose them to think, feel, and act in ways that are consistently truthful and right, under a wide variety of circumstances, in dealing with diverse, often troubled people, who are embedded in complex, changing relationships. An ethic of virtue also suggests that thoughtful character-work on the part of clergy, leading to more thoughtful God-talk, could inspire similar work on the part of parishioners. Of the many virtues necessary for good church leadership on this issue, we can discuss only a handful.

Let us return to our opening scene and consider some virtues that our pastor must exercise if he is to do well in addressing people like Anna, Dorothy, and Jack, as they begin to examine their ways of imaging and speaking of God. One virtue that our pastor needs is faith. Christians hold that faith originates in an unmerited gift of grace communicated through word and sacrament, but it is nevertheless appropriate to think of faith as a virtue. Faith is a stable disposition to assent to the truth of God—not simply the truth about God, as presented in the Bible or in this or that creed, but the truth that is God. The disposition to assent to the truth of God can also be thought of as the disposition of trusting obedience. Faith is the habit of trusting God to such an extent that this trust influences one's whole way of perceiving the world, one's manner of receiving and responding to persons and their problems, and one's way of choosing consistently to act on behalf of all that is God's.

The first responsibility of our pastor is to develop a sound habit of assenting to the truth of God, and it is in conjunction with this habit that he must cultivate the related habit of speaking truthfully of God. Our pastor must, of course, speak of God in a way that is likely to deepen the faith of parishioners. He must communicate a sense of being called into a personal, saving relationship with God; yet he must, at the same time, communicate a sense of being addressed by a God whose nature is paradoxically beyond all projections. If our pastor is faithful, he will perceive the threat of idolatry wherever it arises, he will be repulsed by it, and he will choose to speak of God in ways that diminish the threat. He will trust that, as he exposes and seeks to alter distortions of faith that surreptitiously support and sanctify immoral relationships, God will not abandon him or his congregation, but will instead reveal Godself in new ways that free and empower them to live closer to the truth.

In order to do well in imaging and speaking of God, our pastor will need other, related virtues. One of these is compassion.

Compassion is a habit of being moved in the perception of those who are in pain. It is a habit of being moved to suffer with them, to want with and for them the alleviation of their pain, and to act in ways that will likely contribute to this alleviation.[2] Compassion is a way of being characteristically receptive and responsive to what others are thinking and feeling, especially about the meaning of their lives, even as one entertains one's own, separate interests and perspective. Under the impact of faith, persons in pain appear to Christians as creatures toward whom God has infinite compassion, for whom God in Christ has seen fit to live as a human being, to suffer and to die. Christian compassion thus emerges as a habit of noticing those who suffer, suffering with them to some extent, and seeking the relief of their/our pain in the shared company of Christ in ways that disclose the healing and sustaining power of Christ.

If he is compassionate, our pastor will regard each participant in our opening scene as a person with a unique and complex personal history.[3] He will perceive Dorothy as someone who is deathly afraid and has been dominated by this fear ever since the murder of her husband. He will see her as one who finds rare relief from terror in an image of God as a Father in Heaven who is somehow in control of the world's events and will see to it that the cocky young man who killed her husband will one day be made to suffer enough for what he did. Exercising the virtue of compassion, our pastor will call all of this and more to mind and heart, feeling a bit of Dorothy's fear rising in his throat in the few seconds that it takes Dorothy to rebuke Anna. He will do whatever he decides to do as someone who is moved by Dorothy, prone to acknowledge and seek the alleviation of her pain, not necessarily in the way that Dorothy thinks best, but not irrespective of her perspective either.

Seeking to perceive Jack with compassion, our pastor might encounter some personal limits. His first impulse, on hearing Jack compare Anna with his left-handed sister, might be to feel disgusted with Jack for being, as he frequently is, so arrogant and thoughtless. Cultivating compassion, however, our pastor will choose to let this impulse subside as quickly as it arises, and he will focus instead on Jack as a precious child of God who is flailing about for something solid in his life to hang onto, but who is tragically unable to secure anything other than his own bad habits. Perceiving Jack in this way, our pastor will begin to co-feel some of the horror that Jack feels as one who seems unable to stop doing and saying things that are hurtful to himself and to the people he loves. Viewed with compassion, Jack will perhaps appear as one who is understandably upset when confronted with the image of God as Mother. For complex reasons, this image makes Jack feel like a wobbly kneed child teetering on the brink of a bottomless pit of need. The fear of feeling the depth of his own need drives him to lash out at those who would make him face the truth about his life. Whatever our pastor chooses to do in relation to Jack, he will do as one who has felt, as partly his own, the horror and the compulsion behind Jack's attitude and speech. He will see that helping Jack with the issue of God-language will require helping him with his God-relationship. As with Dorothy, this will require helping Jack face some of his most painful fears.

In compassion, our pastor will perceive Anna as giving honest expression to her struggle. Knowing some of Anna's story, he will know that she did not grow up with an abusive father who demanded obedience of her; hence, the problem for her is not that worshiping God the Father seems too much like a forced worship of father the God. Then again, Anna has told our pastor of other women who feel this way, many of whom have left the church because no one would take their feelings seriously. Knowing Anna, our pastor will perceive that the problem for her is mainly a moral one. She wants to protect women and girls from unjust injury, and it is becoming evident to her that exclusively male God-language supports a patriarchal order that unjustly injures women and girls. Anna has always thought of her community as one that seeks to promote justice around the world; she is beginning to doubt, however, that the members of her church can face the injustice in their own midst.

Knowing all of this, and listening patiently to what Anna says, our pastor will be drawn, if only for a moment, into her struggle. He will feel with her the need to belong to a Christian community, but also the need to get out from under the weight of this evil that continues to oppress the church. However he chooses to act, he will be guided by the desire to help Anna and others like her to belong, but also to live truthfully and well in their belonging.

If he is compassionate, our pastor will approach the issue of God-language partly by approaching the people who are affected by it, and by being drawn into their stories deeply enough to understand what is at stake for them. It is important to keep in mind, however, that pastors are separate people who have lives of their own. In the exercise of compassion, our pastor will, as a matter of habit, experience his own thoughts and feelings about the issue and about so many other, related issues. He will have his own perspective on God, faith, and the church. He will have his own moral compass and thus his own convictions about what it is to live a good human life as a member of a good Christian community. He will not be tossed to and fro as he identifies with one person and then another; rather, he will be touched by the experiences of several parties while, at the same time, remaining centered and grounded in the depth of his own relationship to God.

In order for our pastor to exhibit virtuous compassion in his response to Anna, Dorothy, Jack, and the others in his care, he will have to exhibit at the same time the virtue of practical wisdom (prudence). Practical wisdom is a habit that enables one to judge well what to do in a given situation. It disposes one to notice that a decision must be made, to discern how important one decision is relative to others that must also be made, to consider with respect to each decision various possibilities for action, to weigh these carefully, to imagine the possible consequences of acting in one way or another, to seek the advice of persons whose experience and judgment one trusts, to reflect profitably on one's own experience, and so on.

Within the context of Christian faith, practical wisdom appears as a disposition to focus, in light of the gospel, on the most significant features of a predicament. It is a disposition to reason faithfully about what to do, drawing on the insights of Jesus and of wise women and men who have sought to follow the way of Jesus, drawing also on insight gleaned through prayer, meditation, spiritual friendship, worship, and service. A Christian of practical wisdom is one who has graciously received and deliberately cultivated a habit of answering well the question, "What is God enabling and requiring me (or us) to be and to do?"[4]

It is practical wisdom, especially, that contributes the "know how" that our pastor will need if he is to conceive and carry out truthful, compassionate action toward several persons at the same time (while also carrying out his other responsibilities). Viewing Dorothy with practical wisdom, he will discern that certain ways of confronting her about her attachment to a strikingly masculine God of control and judgment will likely cause her to withdraw, making it more difficult for him to reach her. He will suspect, however, that until she loosens her grip on this image of God, forgiveness toward her husband's murderer, and thus a rich spiritual recovery, will elude her.

What he chooses to do, in this and every other case, will depend on the circumstances, but he might discern that Dorothy's resistance to Anna, and to the questioning of all-male images of God, is really a resistance to pondering the more compassionate dimension of God's reality, whether in male or female terms. He might discern that Dorothy does not yet feel strong enough to let go of her rage. He might decide to help Dorothy with the issue of God-language by scheduling and inviting Dorothy and others, including some of Dorothy's friends, to some group discussions on the topic of forgiveness. Discussion could culminate in reflections on how various images of God make the participants feel differently about the value of forgiveness in their lives.

Exercising practical wisdom, our pastor will discern the danger of raising questions about the feelings that underlie Jack's arrogance and thoughtlessness, and his resistance to female God-imagery in particular. Jack may feel threatened enough to grab his family and leave the church in a huff. Especially knowing his own temptation to get disgusted with Jack's attitude, our pastor will consider whether it is best to keep his mouth shut. Yet, at the same time, it will be apparent that Jack's resistance to even discussing female God-imagery, especially in the presence of his wife, is linked to his authoritarian stance in his family. Failing to help him discern that his insistence on exclusively male God-language serves to legitimate a godlike rule over his family will mean failing to contribute not only to Jack's well-being but also to the well-being of others who are affected by his behavior. Figuring out how to promote truthfulness will require considerable prayer and reflection. Encouraging Jack to come to him to discuss one or another troubled relationship within his family, using his concern for this relationship to motivate a consideration of the broader power dynamics within the family, and connecting this discussion of power to some reflection on his reigning images of God could prove helpful.

With practical wisdom, our pastor will see the value of honoring Anna's concerns enough to discuss them, at least in conversation with her. Ignoring these concerns may cause *her* to leave the church and to suffer a spiritual trial. He will likely acknowledge that Anna has a point: Christians do tend to idolize male God-imagery when it is not relativized by female imagery, and this idolatry does have serious moral implications that must be addressed by the church. Yet, he will probably try to elicit Anna's patience and compassion by communicating just how difficult it is for the church to change, especially when its leaders and members alike have such complex reasons and motives for resisting this change. Our pastor might promise to refrain as much as possible from explicitly gendered references to God—or to balance the male imagery he uses with more female imagery— during sermons, in teaching, and in prayer, while leaving intact for a time the heavy male imagery encoded in the creeds and the rest of the liturgy. He might indicate to Anna that he perceives this to be an unfortunate but practically necessary compromise for the time being. He will encourage Anna to stay in the church, to cultivate her own relationship with God through the use of an expanding array of images, to share with him and others what she is learning and how she is growing—but also to realize how very slowly the church changes when it must work against the dead weight of centuries of bad habits and self-deception about those habits.

Dealing well with the issue of God-imagery and language requires faith, compassion, and practical wisdom. In the process of discussing these virtues, it has become evident that other virtues are needed as well. Let us conclude by looking only briefly at one more virtue, which is courage. Courage is a habit of responding fittingly to situations of danger. It is a disposition to perceive and think clearly about the kind and degree of danger that is present in a given predicament. It is also a disposition to feel an appropriate amount of fear in response to the danger, as well as an appropriate amount of daring to stand firm in the face of it. Courage is also a disposition to respond with a deliberate course of action or, if appropriate, inaction, which bears up under, evades, or defeats the danger. Within the context of Christian faith, courage is a disposition to respond to danger with the assurance that one is under the providential care of God. Christian courage includes a conviction that, even in death—indeed, especially in death—one will not be abandoned by God.

Our pastor needs courage to confront Dorothy about her impulse to drive Anna out of the community, and her related impulse to drive out difficult questions concerning the nature of God and God's relationship to fallen human beings. He needs courage, for if he offends Dorothy, she is likely to react in a way that makes his life more difficult. She might drop her committee assignment or she might remain in her assignment but bring to it a sullen attitude. She might gossip about what she perceives to be his insensitivity to her plight. Our pastor needs courage also to confront Jack with his impulse to dismiss and belittle others, along with his related impulse to assert the dominance of a God that looks a lot like him. Our pastor needs courage because, if he mis-speaks, Jack could become defensive and even hostile. Courage is needed with Anna, too, for in listening to her, our pastor may feel exposed. He may have to face the fact that his own faith is not what it should be, that his way of expressing his faith up to this point has been inadequate, or that he, too, is getting frustrated with the snail's pace of change on this issue.

Our pastor is afraid of conflict, afraid of hurting people, afraid of not being liked, afraid of losing members, afraid of losing his reason for continuing to pastor this church. With courage, however, he will assess accurately the dangers of confronting the issue of God-language within his community. The fear that he experiences will be appropriate, and it will be accompanied by a fitting amount of daring. He will likely reason wisely that the danger of scaring, alienating, or losing members, or the danger of succumbing to his own frustration, is less than the danger of contributing to the falseness of everyone's God-relationships and the related distortions in their relationships with each other.

Each of us will likely judge differently how this pastor will respond if he approaches the situation before him with these and other virtues. The point is not really to specify how he will respond, for justifying such a specification would require providing more detail than space allows, and even then the matter would be open for debate. The point is more to turn attention to the dispositions of thought, feeling, and action that our pastor— and others like him—must acquire in order to do consistently well in dealing, over a long period of time, with an issue as thorny as this one. The point is also to reveal that the character of a community of faith will be determined, in part, by the character of the one who leads it, and the way in which that leader attends to the character formation of other members. Finally, it must be acknowledged that, from the point of view of virtue ethics, the responsibilities of church leaders appear awesome. It would be a mistake, however, for leaders to feel overwhelmed by this responsibility. Strength for the day will surely come with the gospel's message of forgiveness and with the conviction that the ultimate source of truth is always present and at work in one's midst.[5]

1. It is partly for this reason that I have made the pastor of this case a man. When a female pastor raises the issue of God-language with her congregation, she is much more likely than a male pastor to encounter the suspicion that she is being self-serving. This means that, in some ways, a female pastor's deliberations about what to do regarding this issue will be more complicated than those of a male pastor. I cannot address these complications in such a short piece, but I invite readers to ponder how the analysis presented would likely proceed differently if the pastor of the case was a woman.

2. For a more thorough discussion of the virtue of compassion, see Diana Fritz Cates, *Choosing to Feel: Virtue, Friendship, and Compassion for Friends* (Notre Dame: University of Notre Dame Press, 1997). See also Donald P. McNeill, Douglas A. Morrison, and Henri J. M. Nouwen, *Compassion: A Reflection on the Christian Life* (Garden City: Image Books, 1983).

3. For further reflection on the significance of narrative for Christian ethics see Stanley Hauerwas, with Richard Bondi and David B. Burrell, *Truthfulness and Tragedy: Further Investigations in Christian Ethics* (Notre Dame: University of Notre Dame Press, 1977). See also Stanley Hauerwas and Charles Pinches, *Christians Among the Virtues: Theological Conversations with Ancient and Modern Ethics* (Notre Dame: University of Notre Dame Press, 1997).

4. James M. Gustafson, *Can Ethics Be Christian?* (Chicago: University of Chicago Press, 1975), 156–57.

5. I wish to thank James F. Keenan, S.J., Joseph Kotva, Jr., John P. Reeder, Jr., Mary Pugh, and Joan Henriksen Hellyer for helpful comments on an earlier draft.

Chapter Thirteen

No One Goes Away Hungry from the Table of the Lord
Eucharistic Sharing in Ecumenical Contexts

by Margaret A. Farley

Christian ecumenical gatherings—whether for dialogue, study, social action, or prayer—frequently occasion a desire for and questions about shared Eucharist. This is particularly true in ecumenical theological schools where students from various Christian traditions study, live, and work together for two or more years. In one ecumenical divinity school, there is a weekly community Eucharist, led on a rotating basis by members of different denominations. The questions that arise for each generation of students, particularly (but by no means only) Roman Catholic students, include: Ought we to participate in a Eucharist of another denomination? Should a Roman Catholic Eucharist occasionally be celebrated as the school's weekly community Eucharist? And if so, how will those from other Christian traditions be invited to participate? These questions are experienced not only as theological and canonical questions, but as sometimes deeply anguished ethical and pastoral questions, questions of a shared faith and community life. What can be said in response?

My response to this case, after more than twenty-five years of teaching in an ecumenical theological school, is expressed in the title of this essay: No one should go away hungry from the table of the Lord. Although it is focused on a particular context, it represents the position I want finally to defend concerning the practice of intercommunion among the Christian churches. Three preliminary clarifications regarding my own perspective and assumptions may be useful. First, even though my concerns are for each Christian tradition's approach to these questions, this essay focuses primarily on the Roman Catholic tradition. Any light shed on the problems raised by this tradition will, I think, add some light to analogous problems in other traditions. Moreover, insight into these questions may prove relevant to questions of eucharistic sharing in contexts of intermarriage and of stable second marriages after divorce—both crucial issues especially for the Catholic tradition.

Second, I approach these questions with a very "high doctrine" of Eucharist. I myself believe, for example, in the "real presence" of Jesus Christ in the transformed bread and wine; in the unspeakable encounter with God and with one another by the "taking and receiving" of this bread and this wine; in the eucharistic sharing of Christ's sacrificial offering and the gift of God's life. I even take seriously the genuinely sacramentally inspired forms of reverence for consecrated "reserved" elements. Hence, when I argue that no one should come away hungry from the table of Jesus Christ, it is not because I reduce the meaning of this table to a lowest possible common denominator.

And third, although this case requires an appraisal of principles and rules, it also opens to questions of disposition (character or virtue), both personal and communal. The defense of my own position does not entail a judgment of the wisdom or good will of those who agree or disagree. It aims, however, to show the need for prudence, faithfulness, courage, and liberty of spirit on the way to Christian unity. Both those who yearn for sharing at the table of Jesus Christ, determining all the while that they must wait, and those who yearn for it and discern that they may come forward, can be transformed by eucharistic grace. Neither churches nor individuals, however, can afford to act out of unexamined experiences of power or fear.

In order to explore the question of intercommunion, therefore, and to respond to this case, I will do three things. First, the question needs to be put in some kind of historical context so that both its difficulty and its importance can be seen. I will not attempt to trace its overall history but only to situate its current possibilities and perhaps urgency. Second, I will explore ways of thinking about intercommunion that may make my thesis ("No one goes away hungry from the table of the Lord") theologically plausible. And third, I will reflect on why and how all of this is a matter for ethical concern.

Historical Ecumenical Developments

Major efforts to reunite separated Christian churches go back at least to the Middle Ages, when conciliar attempts were made to heal the breach between Eastern and Western churches. The sixteenth-century break in Western Christianity was followed almost immediately by efforts to overcome the divisions between Protestants and Catholics. None of these efforts ever reached, however, the proportions of the ecumenical movement that has developed in the twentieth century. The establishment in 1948 of the World Council of Churches (WCC) stands out as a major achievement as well as a dynamic new force within this movement—not only because it concentrated efforts at unity among the Protestant churches, but because it included both Protestant and Orthodox participants. And, of course, the importance of the Second Vatican Council in the mid-1960s for the opening of the Roman Catholic Church to ecumenical dialogue and activities can hardly be overestimated. Even in the years following the '60s, when the movement had a low profile and seemed almost to lie dormant, remarkable progress was made in the careful work of bilateral and multilateral theological commissions, in the sharing of ministries of social justice by many of the churches, and in the ongoing transformation of attitudes among the faithful. The Roman Catholic Church came to participate importantly with other churches through the World Council. Though not an official member, Catholic representatives shared in the work of the WCC Faith and Order Commission, in various bilateral commissions facilitated by the WCC, and the Catholic church held full membership in several national Councils of Churches.[1]

Through all of this, however, there remained a "bleeding wound in the ecumenical movement—the divided eucharist."[2] At first a difficult issue for all of the churches, its resolution was easier among many (though not all) of the Protestant and Anglican churches in Western Christianity than it was for either the Roman Catholic or the Orthodox churches. Despite major achievements in theological agreement regarding the Eucharist (most notably in the 1982 WCC Faith and Order Commission's "Lima Report," *Baptism, Eucharist, and Ministry*[3]), the fissures have not been mended. The starkness of this ongoing question has become more and more apparent as concord grows on other issues, as intermarriage of individuals in the diverse churches increases, and as full communion becomes a possibility for many of the Christian churches in the United States.

Recent developments include efforts at "full communion" among five mainline Protestant churches in the United States. Proposals in this regard follow historically upon mergers within the Lutheran Church and the Presbyterian Church, signaling a growing movement toward unity in the Protestant churches. A proposed Concordat between the Evangelical Lutheran Church in America (ELCA) and the Episcopal Church continues to be explored, and the Concordat between the ELCA and three Reformed churches—the Presbyterian Church (U.S.A.), the Reformed Church in America, and the United Church of Christ— is now in place. "Full communion" means that each church confesses a common faith; members of the churches may take communion in each other's church and transfer membership; clergy can be exchanged; and joint efforts in evangelism, witness, and service are possible (including starting congregations, producing materials, and so forth).[4] The Concordats propose theological resolutions of heretofore divisive issues, including issues of the meaning of Eucharist and apostolic succession of clergy.

Beyond their significance for the churches directly involved, they stand as a salutary challenge and painful reminder to the Roman Catholic and Orthodox Churches to address again the serious issues that divide them from other churches.

In the context of an ecumenical divinity school, these movements in the synods and assemblies of the Protestant churches have had enormous effect on the experience of shared Eucharist. New theological formulations have set the minds of many to rest, but new openings to intercommunion have increased the spiritual distress of those who believe they still ought not to approach the table of a church that is not their own, nor invite to their own table those whose membership is in another church. For Roman Catholics, it becomes necessary to review the present possibilities of both adhering to the "letter of the law" and sharing the Eucharist with Christians of other traditions.

I have sometimes argued that there is more flexibility in the Roman Catholic position than is commonly assumed. This is not a wholly successful argument, especially if one is looking for a general magisterial or canonical approval of intercommunion. The 1983 Code of Canon Law certainly moved beyond prior absolute prohibitions of shared Eucharists. Though the general principle articulated in Canon 844 is that Catholic ministers give sacraments only to Catholics, and Catholics may receive sacraments only from Catholic ministers, some exceptions are allowed.[5] The key criteria for exceptions are: Spiritual necessity or spiritual benefit; the avoidance of error or indifferentism; the validity of the sacraments; a shared common faith; and a proper disposition. What circumscribes the exceptions so narrowly, however, are first, the required "emergency" nature of spiritual need (a situation in which one cannot physically or morally approach a minister of one's own church; one is in danger of death or some other "grave and pressing need"[6]), and second, the requirement of a Roman Catholic assessment of the validity of the sacrament. What all of this means in practice is that, for example, according to the letter of the law, Catholics may approach the table of Eastern churches (even, in some circumstances, Eastern churches still separated from Rome) but not the table of Protestant churches in the West; individuals in so-called "mixed marriages" may not, after their wedding ceremony, partake of the same Eucharist through a lifetime of the shared sacrament of marriage; and so forth. In relation to the particular case with which we began, it is generally not possible (apart from further exceptions sometimes made under the rulings of local bishops) for Roman Catholic divinity school students, who take seriously the letter of the law, either to approach the "open table" of a weekly Eucharist offered by Protestant, even Anglican, ministers; or for a Roman Catholic priest to preside at one of these weekly Eucharists and, with the Catholic assembly, invite Protestants to the table.

It is difficult to invoke even the "spirit" of the canons for broader interpretation or relief from what may seem to be a contradiction in one's participation in an ecumenical community of worshiping Christians. What can be done, however, is to appeal to the larger spirit of nonlegal yet significant Roman Catholic texts that articulate an openness to new dimensions of sharing, and on this basis develop a theological and ethical rationale for a more open table. In what follows, I will propose a way of thinking about eucharistic sharing that begins to argue for my thesis: No one, at least not because of ecumenical barriers, should go away hungry from the table of the Lord. This proposal, as I have already indicated, is applicable in particular to situations of ecumenical divinity schools, but it has broader implications at least for mixed marriages, and beyond this to other serious ecumenical activities.

New Theological Possibilities

My theological proposal moves in three steps: (1) the formulation of a theological principle; (2) the development of this principle in terms of the problems it must address; and, (3) a brief view of the underlying theological considerations that are at stake in the principle and the proposal. Principles here are not merely abstract formulations. Rather, they inform and give shape to relationships; insofar as they govern and inspire practice, they are part of the development (either upbuilding or diminishing) of the faith and the life of participant individuals and communities.

First, then, the formulation of a theological principle. Vatican II's Decree on Ecumenism identified two principles that have been the basis for ecumenically shared Eucharist: Eucharistic sharing presupposes and therefore should signify the *unity* of the church; and sharing in the Eucharist should provide a *means* of grace, including grace that *leads to unity*. For many Protestants, the Eucharist as a means to unity is emphasized, and it is sufficient to justify intercommunion. For the Orthodox churches, unity itself is the absolute condition for participation in the Eucharist (that is, Eucharist must be coextensive with membership). For Roman Catholics, as the Decree goes on to say (and as has been reiterated many times since the Council), "The fact that it [eucharistic worship] should signify unity generally rules out common worship. Yet the gaining of a needed grace sometimes recommends it."[7]

The principle I want to propose turns this approach, in a way, upside down. That is, without denying the importance of a condition of achieved full unity and/or Eucharist as a means to this unity,[8] I want to shift the focus from an ultimate unity to the unity, however partial, that already *is* among Christians. From an eschatological point of view, there are degrees of unity. No unity presently achieved (even through shared church membership) is complete; it is not yet full Christian unity. But among the Christian churches, and among Christians, there is nonetheless already a unity. On the basis of *this* unity, Eucharist may be shared. Or better, the Eucharist can be the point of unity, the one deepest form of unity available to Christians. I do not mean by this (as I have already indicated) that our understanding of Eucharist or our enactment of it should represent a "lowest common denominator" among Christians or their churches—quite the opposite, which I hope will become clear as I move to develop my principle in terms of the potential difficulties it must resolve.

The kind of unity usually required by the Catholic church for sharing of Eucharist includes a common faith, common understanding of Eucharist, apostolic succession in the churches offering Eucharist, and valid orders on the part of the eucharistic minister. When exceptions of any sort are made, a shared Eucharist must not, negatively, imply a denial of one's own faith (by seeming to agree with whatever the other believes, even if it is considered by the Roman Catholic Church to be heretical or schismatic) or cause scandal (by giving a deceptive impression that full unity has already been achieved) or occasion indifferentism regarding the need to keep working for a unity that will not be a mere homogenization of differences.

The principle of my proposal would not require unanimity of belief regarding all formulations of Christian faith, nor even regarding the nature of Eucharist. It would not require uniformity of polity, or ecclesiastical structures, among all the Christian churches. It would, rather, accept diversity anchored in the deep unity of a shared commitment to the God of Jesus Christ, to discipleship in relation to Jesus, to a life whose source and end are a participation in the salvific action of Jesus Christ for all the world.

It is generally acknowledged that we face today a very different situation and a different set of questions regarding church unity than at any other time in the past. Our concerns for "recognizing the body" of Jesus Christ are not Paul's; they are also not the fourth-century church's concerns for heresy and schism; they are not the post-Reformation concerns for the scandals of Christian conflict; they are not even the pre–Vatican II concerns for maintaining absolutely unique and separate ecclesial identities. With the experience of nearly forty years of ecumenical interaction, we have learned, as Yves Congar said, that "no church or communion has succeeded in convincing the rest . . ." that it and it alone is the true church with which all should join in a unity that is the reduction of others to itself.[9] Perfect unity remains in the "not yet" of the eschaton. But imperfect unity—the unity whereby heretofore unthinkable agreements have been reached on doctrinal questions, and heretofore unimaginable commonality has come to be in the rituals of worship—this unity is already ours. It is a "pluralist unity," a "reconciled diversity,"[10] a universal church, if you will (not a homogenous whole of which dioceses are quantitative parts), in which diverse traditions can be valued as historically shaped strands without which the richness of the whole of Christianity could not now be.

Such a pluralism, of course, a diversity in unity, would require a recognition of some form of equality among the ecclesial communities of a whole Christianity. We have moved, reluctantly and perhaps confusedly and fearfully, toward this possibility. The Decree on Ecumenism says poignantly, for example:

> Undoubtedly the differences that exist in varying degrees between . . . [members of separated churches] and the Catholic church—whether in doctrine or sometimes in discipline, concerning the structure of the Church—do indeed create many and sometimes serious obstacles to full ecclesial communion. . . . Nevertheless, all those justified by faith through baptism are incorporated into Christ. They therefore have a right to be honored by the title of Christian, and are properly regarded as brothers [and sisters] in the Lord by the sons [and daughters] of the Catholic Church.[11]

And John Paul II, in his 1995 encyclical *Ut unum sint,* wrote:

> . . . in the spirit of the Sermon on the Mount, Christians of one confession no longer consider other Christians as enemies or strangers but see them as brothers and sisters. . . . Today we speak of "other Christians," "others who have received baptism," and "Christians of other communities."[12]

To respect the many Christian churches as equal partners in the life and mission of the whole church does not entail a simplistic belief that "one is as good/true as another." Adherents to each of the diverse traditions will necessarily believe that their own tradition is for them (and in some objective sense as well) a fuller way to follow Jesus Christ, the most life-giving way. Pluralism in an energetic sense does not mean indifferentism. Indeed, when diversity is respected within a deeper unity, diversity is enhanced.[13] Only so does the maintenance of diversity necessitate neither competitive pluralism nor loss of distinctiveness in superficial forms of unity.

Diverse beliefs regarding the nature of Eucharist itself remain, however, a troubling problem for many. Whatever unity there is among Christians, how can they partake of the same table if they understand the reality of what they enact so differently? Even here, however, both the degree of diversity and its significance may be exaggerated. To a remarkable extent, theological agreements have been reached among the many Christian churches. No longer do debates rage about Eucharist as sacrifice or Eucharist as a meal. Almost all Christian traditions today acknowledge the participation of eucharistic ritual in the salvific action of Jesus Christ, the graced presence of God in the sharing of the eucharistic meal, the profound meeting with God and with one another in the "taking and eating," which is essential to the rite of Eucharist.[14] Where differences remain, they are more than semantic but less than failures to recognize the grace of God in Jesus Christ and in the church's action done in memory of his redemptive offering.[15]

If the degree of diversity is less than it is sometimes assumed to be, its significance as a barrier to breaking eucharistic bread together may also be less than is sometimes assumed or feared. One might appeal, for a useful perspective, to the apparent lack of common understanding on the part of the apostles at the Last Supper, and no doubt thereafter if the orthodoxy test put to them were to include specific formulations of what they believed. But other appeals might be made as well today, relativizing the importance of specifically articulated shared understandings. For example, in the Roman Catholic tradition the Eucharist has many meanings—sacrifice, presence, encounter, nourishment, reconciliation, remembrance, enactment, opening to salvation history. In this tradition, it is essential that these meanings be held together. But many of these meanings—if not always all—are essential in other Christian traditions as well. Is it, therefore, not possible to come together within the deep unity of relationship to Jesus Christ, as long as *some* of the multiple meanings of Eucharist are shared?

If the meaning of Eucharist is indeed inexhaustible (though not thereby without any recognizable content), cannot Roman Catholics come to the table of a Protestant church when they are invited, entering into the Eucharist in terms of the understanding of that particular tradition? Must the whole of the meaning important to Catholics be expressed at every tradition's table? And cannot Roman Catholics invite Protestants (as well as members of the Eastern churches) to the Catholic table, assuming at least partially shared understanding of the ritual and the event? Insofar as Catholics believe in the overwhelming, transforming grace of this sacrament, why should they withhold it or, indeed, worry about it, when they are joined by those whom they have recognized as Christian?

Intercommunion as an Ethical Issue

Whether or not Christians can share in the Eucharist across their many traditions is a question for ethics as well as for theology. Four brief considerations will serve to outline an ethical perspective that takes account of the theological proposal I have offered above. First, not even the Roman Catholic Church has ever maintained that intercommunion, while generally ruled out with separated churches in the West, is intrinsically reprehensible, or intrinsically immoral.[16] This suggests that there are ways of understanding it, of at least clarifying exceptions, that can and should be worked out—particularly if an ethical obligation to participate in ecumenical Eucharists can be discerned.

Second, what divides the churches most intensely today, as much within themselves as between or among them, are ethical questions. Unlike prior centuries of controversy in Christianity, we are more likely to be faced with serious conflicts over moral rules and behavior than we are over doctrines of incarnation and redemption, virgin birth, the communion of saints, or even church polity and Eucharist. It is issues such as population policy, divorce and remarriage, and same-sex relations, that are tearing churches apart today.[17] Hence, insofar as church unity is a pressing concern within Christianity, there is grave need to reach to a deeper bedrock of unity, a stronger basis for covenant, from which differences can be negotiated yet respected. A sharing of the eucharistic table offers that bedrock, that covenantal possibility.

Third, deep in the Roman Catholic tradition (and others) are insights about moral growth and development. There is a dynamism in being that inclines to fuller being, in love that yearns for fuller love, and in unity that desires greater unity. The actions, practices, of individuals and communities actualize (or diminish) potentials for fullness of being, love, and unity. Insofar as unity *already exists* among the Christian churches, it has motivated practices such as the search for theological agreement (through the work of bilateral and multilateral commissions); these practices have in turn effected greater unity. Similarly, intercommunion based on an already existing unity (deeper even than particular church membership) offers a graced transformative practice leading to unity (perhaps in diversity) that can still come to be. Intercommunion is not merely a means to a missing unity but an unfolding and actualizing of a present unity that has a future.

For this practice to be possible, all the virtues and graces integral to religious and moral discernment will need to flourish. Until rules are explicitly changed, practice will be determined by the theological understandings and moral convictions of individuals and churches. These cannot be clarified without at least prudence, patience, wisdom, courage, freedom of spirit, and faithfulness to the process wherever it leads. Whatever virtues are required of individuals in concrete situations, these same virtues are required of local faith communities and of churches as a whole. On the way, even imperfect unity and imperfect love can help us to cast out fear.[18]

Finally, what is at stake in these questions goes beyond the shared self-offering and covenanting of individual Christians and churches. Christian traditions acknowledge that Eucharist is not merely an intramural affair; its grace is not only for the Christian community or even the diverse Christian communities. Through the Eucharist, Christians are integrated into a salvific whole. Christians come to the table not for our own sakes alone, but for the salvation and liberation of all the world. To be welcomed to the table is also to be sent forth. The Eucharist is the sacrament by which we are incorporated into the life of God and into the redeeming activity of Jesus Christ. It is in the Eucharist that we are strengthened and gradually transformed into oneness with the whole body of Christ—*Christus amictus mundi*; we are transformed therefore also into bread for the world, the risen body of Christ. Insofar as Christians are divided, separated, in this communion, we are limited in the sharing (social, political, economic, spiritual) that is demanded of us as a way of living in the world.

I end, therefore, where I began: No one should go away hungry from the table of the Lord. Yet there is here a paradox: Insofar as we do come to the table and are fed, we will nonetheless in one sense go away hungry from the table of the Lord—because we live in the already/not yet of unity, of transformation, of fullness of Life. This latter hunger, however—*not the hunger of being turned away from the table*—is a holy hunger: It is both nourished and intensified precisely by participation in the Eucharist. As it grows, we need the Eucharist more. If we recognize the hunger of others because it reflects this hunger of our own, we shall know the moral "ought" of not closing our own table and not forbidding ourselves the food that is offered to us at the tables of the diverse Christian traditions.

1. For a succinct but detailed history of some of these developments, see George Tavard, "Ecumenical Relations," in *Modern Catholicism: Vatican*

II and After, ed. Adrian Hastings (New York: Oxford University Press, 1991), 397–421. Key documents are available in Harding Meyer and Lukas Vischer, eds., *Growth in Agreement: Reports and Agreed Statements of Ecumenical Conversations on a World Level* (New York: Paulist Press, 1984); and more recently, Michael Kinnamon and Brian E. Cope, eds., *The Ecumenical Movement: An Anthology of Key Texts and Voices* (Grand Rapids: William B. Eerdmans, 1997).

2. Kondothra M. George, "Editorial," *The Ecumenical Review* 44 (January 1992): 1.

3. See World Council of Churches Commission on Faith and Order, *Baptism, Eucharist, Ministry,* in Meyer and Vischer, *Growth in Agreement,* 465–503. For an overview of agreements, see Kinnamon and Cope, *The Ecumenical Movement,* 129–210. For historical and contemporary liturgical forms across Christian traditions, see Max Thurian and Geoffrey Wainwright, eds., *Baptism and Eucharist: Ecumenical Convergence in Celebration* (Grand Rapids: William B. Eerdmans, 1983), 99–255. Of course, along with agreements, there are still strong disagreements as well. Not specific to issues of Eucharist, but nonetheless relevant, are current conflicts within the WCC between Orthodox churches and Protestant churches.

4. For identification and discussion of issues involved in the Concordats, see *The Lutheran* 9 (Nov. 1996) and 10 (May 1997). See also *A Formula of Agreement: Between the Evangelical Lutheran Church in America, the Presbyterian Church (U.S.A.), the Reformed Church in America, and the United Church of Christ on Entering into Full Communion on the Basis of "A Common Calling."* See also William A. Norgren and William G. Rusch, eds., *"Toward Full Communion" and "Concordat of Agreement"* (Minneapolis: Augsburg Fortress, 1991); Daniel F. Martensen, ed., *Concordat of Agreement: Supporting Essays* (Minneapolis: Augsburg Fortress, 1995).

5. See *The Code of Canon Law,* trans. The Canon Law Society of Great Britain and Ireland in association with The Canon Law Society of Australia and New Zealand and The Canadian Canon Law Society (London: Collins Liturgical Publications, 1983) Canon 844, 156–57.

6. The descriptions of need are not exactly the same for Roman Catholics, for members of churches in communion, and churches not in communion with the Catholic church. Still, the emergency nature of the need tends to pre-

dominate as a theme in all the descriptions. See Canon 844.1–4; see also *Directory for the Application of Principles and Norms on Ecumenism* (Vatican City: Pontificium Consilium ad Christianorum Unitatem Fovendam, 1993), Sections 129–36.

7. *Decree on Ecumenism,* in *The Documents of Vatican II,* ed. Walter M. Abbott (New York: Guild Press, 1966), 8.

8. That is, I do not want to deny the importance of Eucharist shared specifically by co-members of a given church. I am addressing the question not of who participates in every Eucharist, but of the possibility of ecumenical participation in some Eucharists.

9. Yves Congar, *Diversity and Communion,* trans. John Bowden (Mystic, CT: Twenty-Third Publications, 1985), 162.

10. Ibid., esp. 149–52.

11. *Decree on Ecumenism,* 2.

12. John Paul II, *Ut Unum Sint,* 42, in *Origins* 25 (June 8, 1995): 59.

13. My own observation of both faculty and students in an ecumenical divinity school is a strong case in point. As individuals come to know and genuinely understand traditions other than their own, they come to know and value their own tradition more deeply. As they come to see the richness of the whole of Christianity, they become more deeply committed to their own historical tradition within Christianity, even as they profoundly appreciate the whole.

14. It must be acknowledged that these agreements have been forged primarily between mainline Protestant (Lutheran and various Reformed churches), Roman Catholic, and to some extent Orthodox theologians. The issues are of less intense interest to "free church" traditions and have therefore not occasioned the same efforts at adjudication.

15. For historical perspectives as well as contemporary assessments of ecumenical similarities and differences regarding Eucharist see Congar, *Diversity and Communion;* Horton Davies, *Bread of Life and Cup of Joy: Newer Ecumenical Perspectives on the Eucharist* (Grand Rapids: William B. Eerdmans, 1993); John Kent and Robert Murray, eds., *Intercommunion*

and Church Membership (London: Darton, Longman & Todd, 1973). For historical overviews of theologies of Eucharist, see Gary Macy, *The Banquet's Wisdom: A Short History of the Theologies of the Lord's Supper* (New York: Paulist Press, 1992); Paul H. Jones, *Christ's Eucharistic Presence: A History of Doctrine* (New York: Peter Lang, 1994). For historical interpretation of particular relevance to Roman Catholic beliefs, see David N. Power, *The Sacrifice We Offer: The Tridentine Dogma and its Reinterpretation* (New York: Crossroad, 1987); David M. Power, *The Eucharistic Mystery: Revitalizing the Tradition* (New York: Crossroad, 1992); Edward J. Kilmartin, "The Catholic Tradition of Eucharistic Theology: Towards the Third Millennium," *Theological Studies* 55 (September, 1994) 405–57; David M. Power, "Roman Catholic Theologies of Eucharistic Communion," *Theological Studies* 57 (December, 1996): 587–610.

16. See Richard A. McCormick, *Notes on Moral Theology 1968–84* (Washington, D.C.: University Press of America, 1984), 21. McCormick is here referring to the claim made in this regard by Wilhelm de Vries in his essay, "Communicatio in sacris," *Concilium 4: The Church and Ecumenism* (New York: Paulist Press, 1965), 18–40.

17. This is true within individual churches and among them. A case in point is the intensely growing rift in the WCC between Orthodox and Protestant churches over issues of the ordination of women and of gays and lesbians.

18. Were there space here, it would be important to consider the relevance of what are called "pastoral" solutions in the Roman Catholic tradition. There are strong analogies to be drawn between what is required of individuals for these solutions and what is required of communities and institutions in their considerations not only of exceptions to general rules regarding intercommunion, but ultimately of changes to be made in the rules themselves.

SECTION TWO

The Way Communities Behave

Introduction

As we saw in Willimon's essay, a pastor never is constituted apart from her or his congregation and, likewise, a congregation is never constituted apart from the way it is led. This mutual interplay is only possible by a standard that transcends both congregation and pastor. That standard is the truth of Jesus Christ, the same yesterday, today, and forever. Keeping our eyes on that truth is not a simple matter, however. Only by being conformed to the gospel can we keep our eyes on Christ and this requires grace and, in light of grace, virtue.

For a congregation to grow in virtue is not an easy task. In determining how the community moves forward in virtue and how it lives out its life of faith, it often looks to its leadership, but that leadership is bound by the expectations of the community. The critical understanding of whether those expectations are legitimate is also never an easy assessment. As Roberts showed us, for example, only someone of deep sensitive discernment can appreciate whether—and if so, how—to respond to them. But, then, even the actual authority that the pastor or pastoral team may exercise derives in part from the authority the community gives it: Its leadership is conditioned.

A certain set of vulnerabilities exists, therefore, in the relationship between pastoral leadership and community, a set of vulnerabilities that is often overlooked and ignored. This interplay between pastoral leadership and congregation becomes further complicated by the fact that pastors and congregations often fail to recognize the power each of them enjoys. Ironically, they each seem more aware of the other's power and in this they glimpse, sometimes defensively, their own vulnerabilities. As such, they turn to their own unacknowledged power, a turn that can cause great division.

The irony in this is that the appellation of being Christians, first given and recognized at Antioch, was identified with the care we each had for one another. Unity has been a hallmark of Christianity and yet its fragmented history conveys how short the churches fall of their own standard.

This part is, then, about community and power. It is about how power needs to be recognized and how it plays out, particularly, in Christian congregations and in pastoral teams as they deliberate about and with one another. It attempts to explore, in the first section, unspoken but strong, existing expectations between pastor and congregation in both rural and urban parish life. In the second section, the essays look at other issues that often tear communities apart and ask whether the leadership and community know themselves well enough to make decisions that advance the mission of the gospel. The third section looks at the virtue of justice in the face of power—grappling with the treatment of employees.

Hence, these essays are not about what the churches teach to the world, but rather what its actual practices are with its own kind. Certainly as ethicists, we are interested in what the churches preach to the world in the name of truth, justice, love, and peace, but as virtue ethicists, we keep asking the question, "Who are we as church becoming?" The question will affect not only who we are but, just as important, what we do. As Willimon reminds us: "For the world is right in judging the truth of our convictions on the basis of the virtuous lives that the church and its preaching are able to produce."

Shannon and Patricia Beattie Jung investigate the question of expectations as they exist among pastors and their congregations in a rural setting. Arguing for a covenantal rather than contractual understanding of leadership and community, the Jungs offer two virtues necessary for leadership. The first, which they name andragogy, is the virtue for teaching adults; applied to leaders, it helps them to "nurture among all believers their capacity to use their own gifts in strengthening the witness of the church." The second is the virtue of humility, which recognizes the place of everyone. Together these virtues provide a fundamental ability to lead disciples to evangelize today.

In Paul J. Wadell's essay "Ministerial Malaise and Disillusionment: Recovering Hope in Ministry," we find the realistic difficulties that new pastors abruptly encounter in the early phases of their appointments. Wadell identifies a trinity of wrong attitudes that can create communities that inhibit any chance of having genuine Christian leadership. These wrong attitudes are a messianic, "I-have-to-do-everything-for-my-congregation" self-understanding of the pastor; a consumerist, "we-hired-the-pastor-to-serve-our-needs" prevailing attitude of the congregation, and an anti-authoritarian, mean-spirited, clergy-killing stance of a select, anonymous few. To recover hope in ministry, Wadell reminds us of the standard of Jesus Christ and offers the virtues of courage, gracious realism, respect, and justice for both pastor and congregation to foster good leadership.

Charles Pinches presents the case of a church council which has just decided to appoint a person to chair the evangelism and renewal committee when one member reports that the nominee is living with his homosexual lover. Pinches recognizes that his taking on such a neuralgic case may actually divide the readership of even this volume (indeed, we the editors think he is one-sided in his biblical argumentation!). But Pinches proposes the virtues of patience and hope as key for creating communities that promote a tolerance of one another while recognizing their own sinfulness and their own mission. Only with these two virtues can communities come to modest self-understanding so as to learn from one another what it is to be conformed by the gospel.

Vigen Guroian's essay, "Doctrine and Ecclesial Authority: A Contemporary Controversy in the Armenian Church," provides us a case from the Orthodox community in which the tension is among episcopal and theological leaders. The tension is a classic one for our times: The fear that dogma is being compromised in the name of church unity. The conduct is also classic—one that cries out for deeper humility about the positions we hold and for ordinary respect for others in positions of authority. In these situations, often even the secular virtue of civility is absent.

In a similar vein, the late Cardinal Joseph Bernardin proposed the Common Ground project in a groundbreaking attempt to foster unity among Roman Catholic leaders. No sooner had he announced the project than certain episcopal leaders voiced their concern that dogmatic truths not be compromised in the name of unity. There, as in Guroian's essay, we see that truth and love are the values that all Christian leaders are most concerned with; but, what takes priority when some believe that the truth of doctrine is being compromised?

Bernardin responded to his brothers' concerns by assuring them that fostering loving and respectful unity, so important for evangelical witnessing, does not cast a cold eye on the truth claims of dogma but, instead, provides a qualitatively richer context of dialogue for finding the proper way for promoting those truth claims. In like manner, Guroian's own experience highlights how the journey toward unity, while painfully difficult, will also be the measure of our own integrity. And, as members of the Common Ground project would acknowledge, humility and respect are essential in the promotion of a Christian toleration.

If Guroian's essay is as classic a case as one gets, William Everett gives us as complex a case as we can get: A denomination's regional committee on ministerial appointment is evaluating a pastor who requests approval for seeking appointment to another congregation. The committee learns that the pastor's tenure was at best a problematic one. But they learn that these actions occurred several years earlier and the denomination's statute of limitations has run out.

Everett argues that rules and law, by themselves, are insufficient but that attention to the way virtues operate in our communities is key. In fact, Everett argues that the laws and rules themselves are basically embodiments of the virtue of justice as articulated and promoted by the community. But Everett wants to look at both personal and institutional virtues as well as how virtues function when incorporated into more democratic structures. The essay is a "thick" one, inviting the reader to see new angles on classic virtues and to reexamine whether the structures of our own denominations' governance adequately embody in their rules and practices the virtues necessary for following Christ.

In addressing the measure of justice, Karen Lebacqz and Shirley Macemon return us to Augustine's important insight that some virtues are not real, but only apparent. For Augustine, an apparent virtue was as vicious as a vice. For Lebacqz and Macemon, patience unhooked from justice is vicious. Their case examines how leadership, while ignoring justice requirements of fair pay, often implore their employees to practice the virtue of patience. Lebacqz and Macemon turn the tables, reminding leadership that patience is a virtue for those who willingly suffer in the promotion of justice.

Throughout these essays the movement of women into leadership in the church is often presumed by the cases themselves. In some instances, a woman pastor (Jung, Wadell) is deliberately chosen; in others (Cates), she is deliberately avoided. The failure to treat women as equals in ministry is at stake in the essay by Anne E. Patrick, SNJM. Patrick explores how an ethos of religious obedience in a male-dominated hierarchical context can lead to significant injustices. By juxtaposing the responses of two convents at two very different periods of time, Patrick explores how the virtue of justice (1) liberates us from the structures of secrecy, hidden manipulations, and inequities, and (2) brings into the public forum and into due process the concerns of all.

In the final essay, M. Shawn Copeland provides us with an opportunity to explore how "Collegiality as a Moral and Ethical Practice" functions in the theology department at a Catholic university. By focusing on a case involving the way racism affects our perception of our own colleagues, Copeland provides us a way for seeing that the lack of self-critical reflection affects not only those who are pastors, but those who are theologians as well.

A. Empowering Leaders

Chapter Fourteen

Leadership in Empowering Others
A Case Study from Rural Congregations/Parishes

by Shannon Jung and Patricia Beattie Jung

Sharon Clark, a recent seminary graduate, was assigned to a small rural congregation in Pennsylvania. She traveled to her parish with high hopes and a sense of excitement. She imagined that the congregation could build on its sense of fellowship to become a mission center with strong evangelistic outreach.

Sharon knew better than to share immediately her vision of what the congregation could be. She had been advised to wait a year, to get to know the history and context of the congregation, and to immerse herself in congregational and community life. She did that and found it exciting and demanding work. She usually put in a fifty-five- to sixty-hour week.

One of the things Sharon discovered about the congregation was that it tended to focus on its internal life. The prevailing attitude was that if other people wanted to come to their church that was fine, but no special invitation would be issued. This appeared to be a well-worn tradition which stemmed from lack of an alternative vision rather than from hostility or fear of "outsiders."

The church, though rural, was located only thirty miles from a growing city. People began moving out into the area surrounding the church. Sharon believed that the congregation needed to reach out to these people and, if they were unchurched, invite them to enter into the faith life of the congregation. Indeed she considered it a gospel mandate.

At a council meeting, Pastor Clark proposed a way to address the evangelism need she saw. She asked the council to approve the formation of a visitation team. She would train the team in evangelism fundamentals so they could help her visit newcomers to the community. Her proposal was met with stony silence. After a few uncomfortable minutes, Mr. Bob Rule, the chair of the council, spoke. "Pastor Clark, don't get us wrong. We don't mind having new people come to our church. But we hired you to visit them. We don't think it is right for you to ask us to do your job for you."

Sharon was devastated. Suddenly she felt very alone in her ministry and confused over what she should do.

This case raises questions about the nature of leadership in the church. The case highlights a set of issues that clergy and lay leaders, especially in rural congregations, experience frequently. The analysis of the case we offer here will consider three issues:

1. On a macro level, we will examine the cultural changes that are taking place in our expectations about leadership in voluntary organizations. The church has participated in this change and is moving away from traditional hierarchical leadership styles. That change has necessitated the development of a different style of leadership and the virtues which engender that style.

2. Given this ongoing change, our article will examine the emerging vision of leadership in the church. The roles or self-understandings held by clergy and laity are tied to these changes in organization and accompany the move away from prevailing, relatively authoritarian, contractual structures to more covenantal, empowering models of leadership. This move cannot be accomplished without the development of a more collaborative style and concomitant virtues. Some

attention will be directed toward the theological underpinnings of this latter vision.

3. We will examine the personal virtues as well as the institutional practices and policies that undergird this collaborative model of leadership. We will identify some of those habits of the heart that are needed to guide covenantal, cooperative, voluntary institutions like the church.

In conclusion we will return to the case and suggest a response scenario or approach that might be more effective at engendering the leadership style we judge normative for this particular situation. It should be clear that we will be focusing as much on the self-understanding of the laity as on the leadership style appropriate to clergy.

Cultural Framework for Church Organizational Patterns

The rural setting of this particular case is significant primarily because rural congregations may still disproportionately exhibit a traditional understanding of leadership with its customary division of labor. They may hold more tightly defined expectations of the role of professional clergy.[1]

Top-down leadership is dying with the generation that accepted or acquiesced to it. People are increasingly attracted to groups that emphasize the value of their contributions to them rather than obedience to authority. Thus all nonprofit, voluntary organizations—like the church—are under tremendous pressure to adopt a leadership style that encourages participation by a broad appeal to the intrinsic expressive-emotional fulfillments of such participation. Changes in leadership styles encourage the formation of virtues consonant with those changes. Those virtues accompanying an authoritarian style do not comport well with a consultative one.

Traditional top-down understandings of leadership may still be operational in rural communities and in churches largely composed of those over fifty-five years old. This exists in some rural congregations, especially those in locations experiencing little change or downward economic pressure. But in rural communities and congregations experiencing growth and renewed economic health, expectations have moved beyond a narrowly authoritative style of leadership.[2]

The church, just like other organizations, can no longer assume but must build member loyalty and participation. It has to build community and take its members' values into account. Indeed the survival of voluntary associations depends on committed participation in ways that commercial associations do not.

It is now socially acceptable not to go to church on a regular basis. This is especially true in the countryside where families are working two, three, or four jobs to make ends meet. If they are working the farm, odds are that one or another family adult is also working a second job. The stereotype of idyllic leisurely rural family life is surely an anachronism, if not a historical fiction. For the church this increases the pressure to exercise leadership that is oriented towards meeting people's needs and employing their gifts—providing intrinsic fulfillment and meaning—rather than appealing to Christian duty.

In our case study the council chair clearly articulated a traditional authoritative leadership style based on a division of labor. Traditionally, the pastor was expected to perform "religious" tasks—preach, celebrate the sacraments, lead worship, pray, and visit the sick (perhaps even the unchurched!) while lay leaders were to perform "secular" tasks essential to the church—giving time and money to maintaining the physical plant, developing funds for programmatic and staffing needs, and perhaps looking out for other members' physical needs. By contrast, an empowering or transforming style would engage clergy and laity in building community, nurturing discipleship, maintaining church buildings, fundraising, and doing evangelism together. Pastor Clark had adopted expectations of leadership not insensitive to a traditional style but clearly based more on expressive-emotional or relational appeals. She continues to think of evangelism and outreach as "her" job to some extent, however; she appears to be somewhere in transition between a traditional and an empowering style of leadership. It seems clear from her reference to the laity "helping her visit newcomers" that Pastor Clark is herself in transition between these styles.

In short, in our culture a leadership style that expands the base of participation and involves all participants in decision making will appeal to a wider range of peoples and to multiple generations. Of course there are situations where an authoritative style of leadership may be most appropriate. However, to be effective, leadership needs increasingly to empower others to use their gifts and talents in ministry.

From a theological point of view there is much in the Christian tradition to commend an emphasis on empowering leadership. The doctrines of the "priesthood of all believers" and of "vocation in daily life" tend to support this style. The Scriptures, especially the Pauline correspondence, refers to the community of faith being made up of people having many gifts which, when they are unified and functioning smoothly, build up the body of Christ. The church is portrayed as an organism that calls on the talents and abilities of all disciples.

The style of leadership that will prove most effective today is the one that can itself foster leadership in others. The virtues which elicit participation and encourage others' growth by supporting them are integral to this style; it calls forth gifts and growth in discipleship. It does this by meeting the needs and identifying and respecting the gifts of all. The laity expect to use their gifts and talents for leadership in the church as they do in the workaday world rather than to be told what to do. "Professional" church leaders would do well to adopt a style that is consonant with those expectations. Furthermore, this style of leadership can embody a covenantal vision of the church that witnesses to the biblical vision of discipleship and mission, and encourages broad participation and the discovery of a given parish's mission appropriate to its context. The contractual style can no longer generate a participatory sense of mission and thus cannot effectively give witness to God's Word in our cultural context.

The Self-Understandings of Clergy and Lay People

How the clergy and laity think of themselves will influence what they expect of themselves, each other, and how they will act in order to accommodate the images they have. If the ministry is conceived in traditional transactional top-down terms, then the clergy may think of themselves as being under contract to perform a task. If the ministerial relationship with the parish is contractual, then the cleric is employed to perform services for a specified period of time, perhaps subject to renewal. There is a clear distance implied in the division of labor between clergy and laity, and that calls for a scripted sense of "managing the organization." Emphasis is placed on self-differentiation to the detriment of maintaining connection with others in the church; there is a tendency to think in institutional terms.[3] If, as we would argue, a clergy person is called to lead a congregation in worshiping God and following with everyone else the life of Christian discipleship, mission, and evangelism, then quite different clerical self-understandings must be in place.

Lay people can understand themselves in different ways as well: They can see themselves as clients or as employers who enter into contracts or, more holistically, as believers and disciples. Should they see the church as an institution with a traditional understanding of leadership, then in a corresponding division of labor, they will understand themselves as clients or employers of the organization. They may see themselves as consumers who pay a fee-for-service, albeit spiritual. If they see themselves as consumers or clients, as the chair of the council at the church in Pastor Clark's case apparently did, then they will expect to have the professional do the job that they have hired her to do—as if leading a congregation is analogous to fixing the water pump on a car or setting a broken arm. Similarly, if they see themselves as employers-members of a congregation, they might expect to fill certain roles and contribute certain amounts of time and money and effort in order to maintain the organization. However, those will be conceived as clearly delimited roles.

By contrast, if the laity see themselves as co-disciples, partners and collaborators in church leadership, then they will see the ministry of the congregation as mutual. They may see themselves as partners in a fiduciary relationship, each contributing to growth in discipleship, evangelism, and social ministry of their church. Those clergy and lay people who live out of a *covenantal* leadership style will tend to emphasize the cooperative nature of congregational ministry; as each contributes his or her gifts to the mission of the church, participation in and ownership of this system will increase.[4] This approach to leadership is built on an understanding of the organization as an interacting system composed of many parts or subsystems. There is a pattern whereby the leader becomes a part of the organization or does not. There are clear restraints on the leader who fails to "join his or her organization," that is, to become authentically engaged in the organization as a person.

We have been contrasting two broad styles of leadership— the traditional, authoritative, contractual, managerial style and the emergent, collaborative, covenantal, community-building style. These styles are communicated through the characteristic patterns of action that leaders exhibit, their characters. Congregations and laity exhibit characteristic corporate patterns as well. Congregations and laity are exerting formative influence on the pastor and vice versa.

Clergy and laity will have quite different scripts as their self-understandings change. New roles will develop. At its most pejorative, the self-understanding of laity may be that of being members (clients) who have contracted for services by the professional minister. Over against such a contractual mentality is the covenantal or communal style of leadership, whose primary value is engendering growth in discipleship. Make no mistake; this is a challenging style that replaces the goal of mastering set tasks with the more difficult goal of encouraging spiritual maturation. Laity are no longer to be merely compliant clients but are instead at least co-responsible for and collaborators in the church's ministry.

The overriding question is how to determine what style of ministerial leadership in our world will strengthen rural congregations to live out their lives as the body of Christ. What models of leadership so empower all Christians? How can we engender self-understandings, scripts for ministry, and messages about church leadership that will prove edifying? What habits and practices and policies make that vision concrete?

We are persuaded that these are the right questions. How can Pastor Clark engender such a covenantal, empowering style?

Habits and Virtues for Transformational Leadership

Roland Heifetz offers a social scientific perspective on how to promote such a transforming leadership.[5] He divides problems confronting groups into technical and adaptive ones. When an issue has a clear and definite solution, it is a technical issue or problem—e.g., how to change a flat tire or file for divorce or treat carpal tunnel syndrome. Adaptive problems or issues arise when there is a values gap between the way things are and the way we would like things to be—e.g., how to encourage our children to be more cooperative, how to evaluate a case of patient-assisted suicide, how to resolve a conflict between two legitimate complaints, or how to encourage the growth of discipleship. Viewing leadership in terms of adaptive work, Heifetz's image of leadership entails mobilizing people to tackle such difficult problems.

Leadership, then, is a style, a process of enabling people to interpret and weigh reality. Leadership also enables people to deal with conflict and confusion creatively and with a nondebili-tating level of anxiety so as to decide on satisfactory directions for action. Transforming or empowering leadership is designed to enable others to increase their capacities and realize their gifts. The most admirable leadership is that which is able to foster the emergence of individual capacities within a group effort so as to generate the most valuable possible response. This will involve mobilizing others not to act in a final or definitive way so much as to enable them to face as full a range of provisional options and perspectives as possible.

Clearly leadership that addresses adaptive challenges, such as will be practiced by priests and pastors, is a style that requires schooling in particular virtues. Leadership is more than a set of concepts or principles to be followed technically. This style develops by practicing characteristic ways of relating. It emerges out of a person's character and through particular practices asso-ciated with transforming leadership.

There *are* concrete processes by which leaders can promote others' work towards specific actions, not to say solutions, when those solutions need to be adaptive rather than technical in nature. Here we highlight four elements central to transforming leadership. These elements can be seen as pointing towards par-ticular virtues.

Framing the issues

Leaders can be instrumental in asking hard questions and get-ting others to face difficult, potentially divisive issues. Frequently they can reinterpret those questions and recast peo-ple's expectations so as to develop their ability to respond cre-atively.[6] When there is no single satisfactory answer or the best way forward is unknown, then it is vital for leaders to summon the responses of the entire group by encouraging them to face the realities of the situation. Although the leader may not have "the answer," he or she may highlight elements of several visions as well as illuminative angles and fruitful perspectives for consider-ation by the group.

Respecting others

Rather than managing people, a maneuver that produces considerable reaction in today's culture, the leader can manage the process through which people arrive at a direction for their corporate action. The leader establishes her own integrity as someone who respects the opinions of others and who has certain procedural "ground rules" for the business of decision making. If everyone trusts that his or her opinion will be given careful consideration and that each person will have a say in decision making, much of the "leader's" work is done. Frequently such regard for others is as important—especially in a church or other voluntary association—as the particularities of the decision made. There are skills involved in establishing procedures and helping a group arrive at a solution (which may, of course, include technical information). Theologically the nature of the process that is employed by the group communicates volumes.

Maintaining openness

An important but generally overlooked skill of leadership is to maintain an environment that holds people together in conversation, especially when the going gets tough (that is, divisive).[7] Such a holding environment contains the group in the learning process. It enables people to sense a sufficient level of safety that they can tolerate diverse opinions without having to merge opinions, dismiss the disagreement, or withdraw. The task of the leader here is to regulate the level of stress and to keep the discussion at a level within the carrying capacity of the group. When the tension is contained to such a degree that learning can proceed, church members with different opinions can listen to and learn from one another.

Allowing others to be responsible

The leader needs to be centered enough to allow others to take responsibility for their learning. The leader must be differentiated enough to permit others to face the reality of the situation confronting them; he or she will neither shield others from those circumstances nor abandon them to difficulties. The temptation for clergy is to smother others, depriving them of the benefits of struggling with interpersonal, institutional, and even theological issues. This shielding of strong and independent lay leaders fosters dependency among capable people. This may shore up the clergy person's need to be needed or to see himself or herself as indispensable, but it is quite dysfunctional when there is an adaptive problem requiring corporate response.

In summary, those leaders who are able to maintain appropriate contact and support while facilitating the group's realistic dealing with conflict or difficulty will enable other members of the church to build their capacity to reach satisfactory resolutions. In the process leaders will build their capacity to differentiate from others and not take on the plethora of responsibilities truly belonging to others.

What we are discussing involves moral formation, training in the virtues or character-building, in at least two arenas. First, we concentrate here on the personal habits and skills that accompany empowering leaders, that is, a character or virtue ethics focused on *individual* agents. A second promising area for exploration is that of institutional formation. We are socialized by the company we keep, not only individually but through the customs and mores of the institutions where we are encouraged to practice particular habits and skills. As those who study management theory know well, it is important to tease out the nature and reflect critically on the impact of *corporate culture*.[8]

What personal virtues do leaders need in order to become the transformational leaders who can direct others to meet adaptive challenges? Several come to mind. The first is both the most important and the most difficult to name. It is the quality of being sufficiently self-differentiated that the leader can be intentional about how his or her response will engender growth in the other. Most seminaries aim to teach future pastors a collection of ministerial skills: preaching, worship leadership, counseling, teaching, biblical exegesis—all informed by theological acumen and moral sensitivity. This education fosters the expectation of ministerial performance. Our perspective, in contrast, is that theological education should go beyond training for excellence in ministerial skills to encourage the ability to *nurture among all believers their capacity to use their own gifts in strengthening the witness of the church*. Thus the desired virtue is the capacity to evoke discipleship. Within this are elements of the characteristics needed to teach adults. We might label the virtue *andragogy*, the style of teaching that is appropriate to adult learners. This style begins with the students' gifts and encourages the blossoming of those gifts. It is focused on the other's growth in grace. It has family resemblances to the virtues of prudence and wisdom.

A second classic virtue for Christian leadership is that of humility. Not being so egocentric as to need to have success or recognition always attributed to his or her insight or performance is essential to transformational leadership. Being attuned to increasing the participation and responsibility of other believers entails that one be humble enough to expect to learn from others. Such leadership requires a sincere openness on the part of the leader to have his or her own vision transformed, to be subject to mutual correction and edification.

More positively, humility is about knowing the place of the other person and the value of his or her viewpoint. Humility fosters a prayerful understanding of oneself as limited and dependent on God and others as well as on oneself. It frees the leader to listen with anticipation for what the other has to teach.

This leads to an appreciation of others' viewpoints and an affirmation of a dialogical process which we might label mutuality. What should be top priority in the church is the building up of the kingdom of God. This is a corporate goal of the entire congregation. There is considerable biblical warrant for such mutuality in the images of all members of the body of Christ working together, serving as the vehicles of the Spirit. Another virtue that feeds into mutuality is the virtue of respect for others. If the leader presumes that others may have helpful points of view and that all others potentially may give voice to the Spirit in their midst, then it will be easier to develop those practices which encourage others to speak—to ask questions of and to engage others to raise issues, encouraging others to acknowledge their responsibility. Those practices rest on a fundamental respect for the gifts, insights, and capacities of others and depend on the leader's respect of these.

There are other virtues that both feed into the development of an empowering style and that begin to develop as that style is practiced: Patience is such a virtue. If a collegial leadership became codified into procedures, then such patience might become characteristic of all. Being trustworthy and tolerant are virtues that accompany adaptive leadership. Transforming leadership requires as well a trust that God can speak through the other, can use the other as well as oneself, that no one has a purchase on God's truth.

Practices that Promote a Transformational Style

As a description of practices that promote this style of leadership, we will offer a scenario of how Pastor Clark could address the attitude of the council member who said, "We don't think it's right for you to ask us to do your job for you." The scenario will focus on this particular council and this particular congregation/parish; however, we are persuaded that this attitude is often present in rural parishes and, to some extent, may be more prevalent among members of a specific generation. We are also persuaded that the covenantal style is one that pastors/priests and others in professional ministry need to develop as they lead the church. Clearly this style is itself characterized by a particular style of moral formation—an area that needs such broader investigation as this volume initiates.

Considerable groundwork needed to precede the proposal that Pastor Clark made. The proposal failed to recognize the depth of the corporate assumptions about leadership that were operative in the congregation. The values already formed in the parish have deep roots, and Clark's proposal flies in the face of many of those values. If those values are deeply rooted and form part of the church's culture, then the process for changing them or moving in a different direction will take considerable time. The local congregation needs to undergo a major reformation. Clark will have to lead in a different style, name and identify those differences, interpret them theologically, and nurture the development of this alternate vision of leadership. Before all that, however, Pastor Clark must exhibit a care for the church's members and a deep love and respect for the congregation as it is, rather than how she would want it to be.

We presume for the sake of argument that Pastor Clark has worked diligently, has performed traditional pastoral tasks well, and has cared for the members of the congregation and also the community. Thus the comments of the chair of the council are not an accusation of incompetence or laziness but rather an expression of the expectations standard to a traditional division of labor. Her bewilderment and startled surprise was a response to her transgression of the well-established division of labor in the congregation.

Sometimes it is possible to negotiate leadership expectations during the call process. We certainly commend such conversations but believe it important to recognize that few congregations are self-conscious of their expectations in this regard and, even if they are, those on the call committee rarely can speak for all. It is essential to negotiate clergy and lay leadership expectations very early in one's life in a new parish. It would have been ideal if expectations of mutuality had shaped their ministry at the outset. That is what we called "groundwork" above.

At this point it is vital that Pastor Clark raise the question of expectations again. She might say, "Bob, we need to think about the leadership roles of the pastor and of lay leaders. I understand my call to be that of equipping disciples for mission, and proclaiming the gospel. I know that every member of this church has different gifts and not everyone is called to the ministry of visitation. Nevertheless, I am sure that you would agree that evangelism is one of the things Christ calls all his disciples to do. I hope that we can think about this some more, if not now, then shortly."

It is quite possible that other council members would join a conversation and that there would be divergent points of view. Pastor Clark should welcome those and identify them as divergent. The ensuing discussion might focus on raising issues that are relevant to the church. It would be important for Pastor Clark to welcome all comments, guard against the temptation to dismiss anyone's point of view, and refuse all attempts to make her the only evangelizer in the church. Not everyone in the parish needs to do everything, and if Pastor Clark can negotiate a position where numerous ministries are given permission to flourish,[9] she will have gone far towards empowering the laity. In the process she will have developed some features of an empowering style of leadership.

1. For a penetrating discussion of the impact of church size on leadership dynamics, see Arlin Rothauge, *Sizing Up the Congregation* (New York: The Episcopal Church Center, n.d.). This discussion is summarized in Shannon Jung and Mary Agria, *Rural Congregational Studies: A Guide for Good Shepherds* (Nashville: Abingdon, 1997), 88–89. Also in the latter volume is a discussion of gender issues in church leadership, 106–108.

2. Loren Mead, in *The Once and Future Church* (Washington, D.C.: Alban Institute, 1990) and *Five Challenges to the Once and Future Church* (Alban Institute, 1996), documents the demise of the Christendom model of the church. Even the rural church no longer enjoys the automatic participation of everyone in the community. In addition, many rural communities—especially those with tourist or retirement industries—are experiencing an influx of people during the decade of the 1990s.

3. There is very real value in self-differentiation; *however*, if that precludes the pastor's and others' personal involvement in the life of the parish, then the church is in danger of becoming merely another public institution and ceasing to be a center of discipleship where all are called to do ministry.

4. For an understanding of systems theory, see R. Paul Stevens and Phil Collins, *The Equipping Pastor: A Systems Approach to Congregational Leadership* (Washington, D.C.: Alban Institute, 1993).

5. Roland A. Heifetz, *Leadership Without Easy Answers* (Cambridge: The Belknap Press of Harvard University Press, 1994).

6. Ibid., 84–85.

7. Ibid., 83.

8. For a helpful introduction to the discussion of conflicts between one's personal agenda and the institution's agenda in corporate contexts, see D. Don Welch, *Conflicting Agendas: Personal Morality in Institutional Settings* (Cleveland: Pilgrim Press, 1994).

9. For a discussion of "permission-giving" churches, see Bill Easum, *Sacred Cows Make Gourmet Burgers* (Nashville: Abingdon Press, 1995).

Chapter Fifteen
Ministerial Malaise and Disillusionment
Recovering Hope in Ministry

by Paul J. Wadell

"Have I given my life to something that no longer has hope?"
These were the plaintive words of Anne Marie less than one year
after she graduated from divinity school and only seven months
after she was installed as pastor of a small congregation in the
Midwest.

They were words she never expected to utter. Anne Marie
began her position as pastor full of hope and zeal, ready to
answer a call she had felt in her heart for years. Her one desire
was to lead her congregation to a deeper life in Christ and to help
them grow together in holiness.

But she soon discovered her hope was not theirs. Her efforts
to lead were met with fear, resistance, and even threats. Her con-
gregation did not want a pastor who would preach the gospel, but
a pastor who would "satisfy their needs." And instead of an
atmosphere of hospitality and openness, Anne Marie found her-
self enmeshed in a web of divisiveness, petty jealousies, rumors
and lies, and shameless schemes to sabotage her leadership.
Within weeks she found herself asking, "This is the body of
Christ?"

Disillusionment descended over her and doubt became her
daily companion. It was not long, Anne Marie said, before she
found herself trying "to hang on until my next vacation." Joy had
gone out of her ministry and increasingly she was lonely and

depressed. "I am not sure I can do this for another year, much less the rest of my life. My greatest fear is that if I stay in ministry my gift will wither up and I will die inside."

Unfortunately, Anne Marie's story is not rare. Though denominations do not like to admit it, more and more pastors and clergy find themselves feeling isolated and defeated, strangers, and sometimes even enemies, to the very people they are called to serve. Ministry, they will tell you, increasingly seems not a gracious, hopeful enterprise, but a dispiriting dead end. It is not that there are no good people in the churches, but that many congregations find themselves captive to a belligerent minority whose presence is like a cancer eating away anything healthy and good. Negativism, cynicism, and ungraciousness triumph over charity and magnanimity.

Something is wrong in our churches. This is not to deny that many faith communities are vibrant, healthy witnesses to the gospel; but it is to say that a dangerous sickness has invaded a growing number of congregations, leaving their pastors disheartened. It is not a good sign for the church when a number of clergy describe themselves as depressed and disillusioned.

In this chapter we shall first explore the reasons for clergy depression and disenchantment by focusing on three points: (1) A false identity for a minister; (2) a false identity for the church; and (3) how congregations can be "possessed by unclean spirits." Finally, we shall conclude with suggestions about what virtues and practices can heal congregations, restore zeal and hope in clergy, and allow churches to experience again the freedom, power, and joy of the gospel.

A False Identity for a Minister

Often clergy wrestle with the demons of depression and disillusionment because they and their congregations endorse an understanding of the role of a minister that is inevitably detrimental both to the minister and the congregation. It happens when congregations place unrealistic expectations on their clergy, assuming they will accept a diversity of roles and responsibilities no one person could possibly fulfill.[1] As C. Welton Gaddy wrote in *A Soul Under Siege: Surviving Clergy Depression*, "You are to be pastor, preacher, visitor, staff supervisor, public relations expert, denominational worker, administrator, and teacher as well as model family member, active contributor to the community, and an always available friend."[2]

But ministers can also become their own worst enemy when they try to be "all things to all people" and succumb to the temptation that the best minister is the busiest one. Gaddy calls this a "messianic mind-set"[3] and sees it characterizing clergy who begin to think they are both invincible and indispensable. This is the pastor who believes if something good is going to be accomplished in her church she must be the one to do it. She must attend every meeting, answer every phone call, and honor every invitation because no one can do anything quite as well for her church as she can. What starts as a genuine desire to serve develops into the dangerous conviction that apart from the minister "the important work of the church will not get done."[4] As Gaddy explains, with a "messianic mind-set" clergy confuse "being called to service by God with being commissioned to serve as God."[5]

What also contributes to this illusion of invincibility is an unhealthy obsession with productivity. It is an easy peril to embrace because part of our cultural creed is that the best life is the busiest one. The people to admire are the ones who look most frantic as they walk down the street, cell phones in hand, to their next meeting. The people we are taught to imitate are the ones who work so hard and accomplish so much that they seldom have time for family and friendships, much less for rest and recollection, contemplation and prayer.

The idolatry of defining a good life in terms of busyness, not praise and worship of God, is the very thing the church exists to counter but too often today only mirrors. It happens in ministry when "success becomes more important than service"[6] and "a full calendar" is "indicative of a fulfilling life."[7]

Finally, pastors assume a false identity, and assist in their own demise, when they believe a true spiritual leader is one who never shows weakness and never acknowledges need, but instead is always confident, cheerful, and strong. They may minister to humans with weaknesses and wounds, but they cannot be weak or wounded themselves. They may counsel their parishioners to take time for rest and relaxation, but would never heed such wisdom for themselves. Behind this facade of invulnerability is the unhealthy conviction that a pastor can never let her people see the full truth of who she is, namely, that like them she is a mixture of strengths and weaknesses, confidence and insecurity, certainties and doubts. The danger inherent in assuming this false identity is that a minister who confuses holiness with denying her humanity is bound to crash into the very vulnerability she worked so hard to hide. As Gaddy reminds us, "Attempting day after day to mask hurt, cover fatigue, and convince everyone that all is well when all is not well is the most unbearable stress of all."[8]

A False Identity for the Church

If depression and disillusionment among clergy are fueled by a false and unhealthy understanding of the role of the minister, they are deepened by a false and unfaithful conception of the church. This skewed identity of the church is captured in Anne Marie's comment that in her congregation "every person has their own agenda, their own set of needs. They come to church and expect me to meet their needs. They think if you are not serving their needs you are not a good pastor."

What she describes is a congregation that has become less a community of disciples and more a therapeutic center where otherwise disconnected individuals gather in the hope that their pastor, who functions more as a therapist than as a spiritual leader, will console them.[9] When congregations become therapy centers the minister's role is not to challenge and certainly not to call her people to conversion, but to soothe and amuse them. In such a setting nothing aggravates a congregation more than a minister who actually preaches the gospel, and nothing will doom a pastor more surely than calling her people, in the name of their baptisms, to discipleship. In "church as therapeutic community," the purpose of Christianity is not to call us to holiness through repentance of our sins, but to assure us that all is already well with us. The good pastor is not the truthful one but the nice one.

But as Stanley Hauerwas and William H. Willimon illustrate, such shallowness and sentimentality are not only a corruption of the church, but exactly what makes genuine Christian ministry impossible. If ministry becomes just another helping profession whose purpose is to fulfill needs, not purify them, every individual's desire and every group's agenda are legitimate and demand to be satisfied. The minister who was ordained to help people tell the story of God is permitted only to keep them happy with who they are. In such a scenario ministers disintegrate amidst the conflicting and competing needs of their ever unsatisfied parishioners.[10]

What accounts for such a misguided understanding of the church? Three things suggest themselves. First, as Michael Smith (a pseudonym) noted in "Pastors Under Fire: A Personal Report," congregations have been transformed from churches committed to the gospel to clubs or "sociological fellowships" that are "closed, exclusive and inward-looking."[11] Whereas Christian churches ought to be "inclusive, welcoming, evangelistic, challenging and transformative," "congregations-as-clubs" are deeply threatened by change, newness, and difference[12] and will do everything to resist them. That many congregations today are more like clubs than communities of faith may not be surprising, however, because a social club may be the only model of fellowship most Christians have experienced in our individualistic society.

Second, Christians, like everyone else in society, have been shaped by consumerism and easily think of themselves primarily as consumers and less as baptized followers of Christ. There is quite a difference. A baptized Christian is called to be a faithful disciple, but a consumer's only goal is to be a happy and satisfied customer in a world of expanding choices.[13] In a church shaped by the gospel, the pastor's role is to help people live out their baptisms faithfully and joyfully; in a church shaped by consumerism, the pastor's role is not to preach the gospel but to give her "customers" whatever they prefer.[14]

In "churches of consumerism" pastors are hired, not called, and their role is to indulge the whims and wants of the congregation, not to call them to an adventure greater than themselves. If a pastor fails to do what her paying customers want, the customers will voice their dissatisfaction immediately. In such congregations the language of complaint replaces the language of praise. Anne Marie noted this when she said, "If the service is over an hour, they complain. If my prayers are too long, they complain. Some have even complained that too many people are on our prayer list!"

Third, churches today increasingly think of themselves more as businesses and less as the people of God. Instead of being a community that could challenge and unmask some of the dehumanizing values and practices of corporations and businesses, congregations mimic them. This puts clergy and ministers in a vulnerable position because when churches become businesses rather than communities of discipleship, the pastor becomes an employee, not someone living out a vocation, and the parishioners are the stockholders, not a people eager to imitate Christ. Because they pay her salary, she is to defer to them. Her role as pastor is "to keep the stockholders happy," to "produce and market an attractive product," and to be mindful of the "bottom line." In the "church-as-business," the pastor is not to serve the interests of God but the interests of the "investors." As their employee, she is to manage the business well and make sure the "owners" receive a good return on their investment.[15] Anne Marie confirmed this when she recalled a parishioner who said to her, "You work for me. I put the money in the plate that pays your salary."

Congregations Possessed by "Unclean Spirits"

If mistaken notions of ministry and church assure that the idealism of clergy will collapse in disillusionment, and sometimes even cynicism, this third reality, which G. Lloyd Rediger calls "clergy killers," is like a ticking time bomb set to destroy them. The language is disturbing but accurate because the phenomenon Rediger describes goes far beyond the normal frustrations that characterize every congregation.

"Clergy killers" refers to individuals and groups whose actions result in emotional, psychological, and spiritual abuse of pastors.[16] In behavior that can be subtle and secretive or quite open and confrontational, their aim is to undermine a pastor's leadership not only by fostering divisions within a church but also by attacking a pastor's character through rumors, innuendo, and lies. Rediger says that clergy killers are destructive, determined, deceitful, and sometimes even demonic. They "don't just disagree or criticize, they insist on inflicting pain and damaging their targets. Their tactics include sabotage, subverting worthy causes, inciting others to do their dirty work, and causing victims to self-destruct." They "manipulate, camouflage, misrepresent, and accuse others of their own tactics." Too, Rediger writes, "Clergy killers don't stop. They may pause, go underground, or change tactics, but they will intimidate, network, and break any rules of decency to accomplish their destruction."[17] Clergy killers are vicious, sick people through whom "unclean spirits" enter congregations. If you talk to clergy and ministers today, you learn their number, unfortunately, is growing.

The scenario often unfolds in the following way. A pastor is welcomed into a congregation and given every assurance that the church is healthy, hospitable, and open. There is no sign that any persons within the congregation might be opposed to the pastor's leadership. But then everything starts to change as seeds of discord and discontent are sown. It starts with a small group of people, often the very ones considered to be the "pillars" of the church. Rumors are spread, suspicions proliferate, suggestive questions are raised "with the best of intentions and the good of the church in mind." The pastor senses something is not right, but is unsure what it might be. She no longer feels quite as welcome in parish gatherings. She notices conversations shift when she enters a room. She sees people who once received her warmly now turning away to avoid her.

Working like thieves in the night, clergy killers plot the pastor's demise. Secretly they gather support, hold meetings, and prepare their attack. Unbeknownst to the pastor, she is about to be sacrificed on an altar of slander and lies. By the time she is aware of what has been mounted against her, it is too late; the clergy killers have destroyed her reputation and stolen the authority she needs to lead the congregation. When she asks about the specific accusations and tries to confront her accusers, she is told that confidentiality must be maintained. Finding little support and ostracized by the congregation that once welcomed her, she is forced to resign.[18]

Virtues and Practices to Heal and Restore Hope

No wonder Anne Marie asked, "Have I given my life to something that no longer has hope?" These days many clergy and ministers are asking the same question. But the disillusionment and depression that increasingly have become occupational hazards of persons in ministry are not only destroying pastoral ministers, they are also harming the church. If pastoral ministers are to move beyond the malaise in which many of them feel mired, and if churches are to break free of the "unclean spirits" which possess them, specific virtues and practices must be embraced by both pastors and their people. Many are needed but I want to focus on four: (1) The courage to be the church and the courage to "worship dangerously"; (2) the virtue of gracious realism; (3) the virtue and practice of hospitality; and (4) the virtue of justice.

First, if the discouragement and disillusionment with which many clergy struggle is at least partially due to a false understanding of church, the path to healing and hope requires that congregations repent their unfaithfulness and risk the courage to be the church. This is not the church of the therapeutic community or consumer center, and it is not the church as social club or corporation; rather, it is the church of faithful, committed disciples who help one another "live in the light of the gospel"[19] and witness Christ, but who are also courageous enough to confront one another with the truth for the sake of the body of Christ. If the unity of the church in Christ is to be preserved, Christians must be bold enough to speak the truth to anyone in a congregation, especially the "clergy killers," whose manipulative, divisive behavior poisons and eventually destroys a community.

But how are ministers and parishioners to acquire such courage, as well as any other virtues essential for healthy congregational life? They will be formed in these virtues through their worship and liturgy if they have the courage to "worship dangerously." As Rodney Clapp and Robert Webber argue in *People of the Truth,* Christian worship ought to be dangerous because genuine worship "is not a retreat from reality, but a direct engagement with ultimate reality: God."[20] Unlike "sham worship," which "attempts to manipulate and transform God" in order to make worship safe and conventional, in true worship "we make ourselves vulnerable to the story of Israel and Jesus."[21] Doing so week after week and year after year gradually shapes and transforms the identity and character of the community in the virtues and practices of the gospel. Put differently, in true worship it is not Christ who is conformed to us but we who are continually conformed to Christ. By bending ourselves to Christ, which is fundamentally what it means to live out our baptism, we grow in the virtues that make true Christian community possible. This is why the surest way to overcome the toxic control of the clergy killers is for congregations not to be afraid to praise God and to be empowered by the liberation that comes from such praise. The greatest power Christians have against persons who destroy community is true worship, whether it be a fearless and joyful proclamation of the Word of God or a celebration of the Lord's Supper.

In addition to courage and truthfulness, a second virtue that ought to be cultivated in worship and should characterize both pastors and clergy is the virtue of "gracious realism." Gracious realism is practiced when pastors and their people have realistic expectations of one another. This does not mean only *limited expectations* but also *proper expectations.* It is not proper, for example, for congregations to expect a pastor to fulfill everyone's needs or to be more therapist or social worker than leader in faith. Neither should clergy or congregations have *excessive expectations* of one another. Weakness, frailty, and sin are vibrantly alive in the best of clergy and their congregations. The virtue of gracious realism teaches us to expect this and to respond to it with charity, patience, and forgiveness, but also with justice and accountability. For instance, gracious realism does not mean that those individuals or groups whose consistent impact on congregations is destructive ought to be tolerated.

Gracious realism summons congregations to be generous in offering praise, support, and affirmation of their clergy. It also challenges and, if necessary, confronts clergy to encourage and support their congregations and to have high expectations of them. So much of what unfolds in churches is a matter of attitude. If a congregation approaches a pastor with a begrudging spirit, hostility, or cynicism, or if a pastor sees her people more as enemies and obstacles than fellow friends of God, that church will not know the peace of Christ. But if they approach one another with a generous spirit, "practicing love and grace"[22] and building one another up in Christ, the trust and goodwill necessary for Christian community will abound.

Third, if conflict and misunderstanding between ministers and congregations are to subside, each must become expert at hospitality. This is more than the hospitality of potluck suppers and socials; rather, it is the challenging and transformative hospitality of Christ characterized by openness and respect, and which ought to be a primary consequence of "dangerous worship."

Openness involves listening humbly and attentively to perspectives and positions that not only are contrary to our own but also may be quite threatening and disturbing to us.[23] It means being honest about our own biases, fears, and distortions, and being willing to learn from and be challenged by those who think differently from us. Parishioners and pastors owe this to one another because without openness our differences become obstacles that divide instead of gifts to unite.

Such hospitality and openness is possible only when Christians see themselves as "a community of giftedness," a community that knows that all life is a gift and that they have been given one another as gifts.[24] There ought to be no greater manifestation of hospitality than in Christian churches because if the story of Israel and Jesus teaches us anything, it is that God has entrusted us to one another as gifts. Congregations are given their pastors and ministers as gifts to care for, not destroy, just as clergy are entrusted with their congregations. If both clergy and congregations focused more on cultivating gratitude than garnering power and control, parishes would thrive in the joy and peace of Christ.

But the openness of hospitality must be balanced by respect. Respect is a function of honor, and ministers and congregations should honor one another as sisters and brothers in Christ. If in the liturgy and prayer of the church we develop the moral and spiritual vision enabling us to see everyone, even our enemies, as children of God, we are less likely to denigrate those whose perspectives and plans may challenge or threaten us. If we respect one another first, we can deal with our differences truthfully and hopefully. Respect is the opposite of snap judgments, facile criticisms, or casual backbiting. But respect for pastors, individuals, and congregations also means not tolerating the noxious behavior of persons willing to destroy anyone or anything in order to prevail.

Fourth, restoring the proper relationship between clergy and congregations demands a shared commitment to justice. Justice is the virtue of "right relationship." Thomas Aquinas defined justice as "the constant and steadfast willingness to give to each person what is his or hers by right,"[25] and argued that without justice life together is not possible. That is true in societies, it is true in friendships, it is true in marriages and family life; but it is also true in churches. Without justice the body of Christ fractures.

The evidence is obvious. When, through lies, backbiting, rumors, and maliciousness, Christians act unjustly towards one another, community breaks down and, if such attitudes and behavior dominate a congregation, shared life in Christ is impossible. Although much could be written about the meaning of justice in congregations, at the very least pastors and their people owe one another respect, goodwill, cooperation, kindness, compassion, and patience. But justice also means dealing honestly and responsibly with those members of a congregation, particularly the clergy killers, whose behavior is consistently destructive of the common good; in short, part of justice is fraternal correction. Following the example of Matthew 18, if such people refuse to accept responsibility for their actions and to change, justice demands that they be removed from their positions of power and influence and, if necessary, removed from the community.[26] Otherwise the demonic prevails and sin is given more power than it ever deserves, especially in a community that dares to celebrate Eucharist.

Anne Marie never believed ministry would be easy, but she did believe it would be joyous and full of hope. She knew she would be challenged, but she never expected that something she embraced as a grace might one day destroy her. Her vision of what it means to be a pastor is the right one and ultimately the only truly hopeful one for both Anne Marie and the church. But if that vision is not to disappear in disillusionment, clergy and congregations must avoid the temptations of false identities and risk the courage to be the church, even if sometimes that means wrestling with the demons in their midst. It is a demanding risk but, for Christians, the only choice that does not lead to infidelity and despair.

1. Paddy Ducklow, "Dear Church: We Quit! Marriage and Ministry Depression," *Crux* XXXI: 2 (1995): 31–41, at 34.

2. C. Welton Gaddy, *A Soul Under Siege: Surviving Clergy Depression* (Louisville: Westminster/John Knox, 1991), 40.

3. Ibid., 129.

4. Ibid., 130.

5. Ibid., 41.

6. Ibid., 48.

7. Ibid., 50.

8. Ibid., 69.

9. For an insightful treatment of this point, see Stanley Hauerwas and William H. Willimon, *Resident Aliens* (Nashville: Abingdon, 1989), 112–43.

10. Ibid., 124.

11. Michael Smith, "Pastors Under Fire: A Personal Report," *Christian Century* 111 (1994): 196–99, at 197.

12. Ibid., 197.

13. For a superb analysis of this point, see John F. Kavanaugh, *Still Following Christ in a Consumer Society* (Maryknoll: Orbis, 1992), 3–19 and 105–15.

14. G. Lloyd Rediger, *Clergy Killers: Guidance for Pastors and Congregations Under Attack* (Louisville: Westminster/John Knox, 1997), 20–21.

15. Ibid., 53.

16. Ibid., 2.

17. Ibid., 9.

18. For a sad but detailed account of how clergy killers work, see Smith, "Pastors Under Fire," 196.

19. Hauerwas and Willimon, *Resident Aliens,* 122.

20. Robert E. Webber and Rodney Clapp, *People of the Truth: A Christian Challenge to Contemporary Culture* (Harrisburg: Morehouse, 1988), 68.

21. Ibid., 69.

22. Gaddy, *A Soul Under Siege,* 162.

23. See Thomas W. Ogletree, *Hospitality to the Stranger: Dimensions of Moral Understanding* (Philadelphia: Fortress Press, 1985), 35–46.

24. Webber and Clapp, *People of the Truth,* 58.

25. Thomas Aquinas, *Summa Theologica* (New York: McGraw Hill, 1975), II–II, q. 58, a 1.

26. I am grateful to Joe Kotva for this insight.

B. Arbitrating Conflict

Chapter Sixteen

Debating Homosexuality
Disagreements Held in Patience and Hope

by Charles Pinches

At a church council meeting, nominations are being considered for a chairperson of the Evangelism and Renewal Committee. Discussion of a variety of possible nominees has resulted in one or two names coming to the fore. Ruth, the pastor, asks the group: "Well, does anyone have something more they would like to say about Carl Harris? I think everyone here knows him, although some better than others. It's clear from our discussion so far, though, that all who know him even a little recognize that he has significant gifts that would serve the church well in this important position."

Jack, a faithful older member, raises his hand. "Pastor Ruth," he says, "I hesitate to bring this up, but I feel I must. I know Carl well, as I think everyone here knows. Partly because of our friendship I know something about Carl that some of you don't know, although I know Ruth knows it as well as three or four others here. Here it is: Carl Harris is a homosexual. He and David, who sometimes comes with him to church, live together. They have been homosexual lovers for a long time.

"Now I don't know about the rest of you, but I do not think we should appoint a homosexual to head the Evangelism and Renewal Committee."

Homosexuality is one of the most difficult topics to think about for most Christians, for a variety of reasons. First, of course, is that homosexuality has to do with sex, and (perhaps rightly) we are all quite inarticulate about sex. But there is more than this, for homosexuality is something about which it is difficult not to have an opinion, or at least some sort of feeling or inclination. However, none of us is very sure that the feeling or opinion we might have is based in anything very substantial. For Christians this is particularly important, for we know that the sort of responses that might arise spontaneously, what people sometimes call "natural responses," frequently require transformation in the discipleship of Christ.

Reticence to allow this transformation to occur might account for much of our silence. However, Christians may have faithful reasons to avoid the topic as well. Chief among these is that we all know the issue of homosexuality is currently rending churches. This fact alone should give pastors pause. A well-meaning, young pastor/crusader might bluster into a meeting of the council set to convince its members that faithfulness to the gospel implies that their local church become a safe haven for homosexuals who feel unwelcome elsewhere. But he will most likely leave that meeting with a more divided council, and with a significantly diminished fund of moral and spiritual authority.

That said, it is surely the case that we Christians should be ready at the right times to break our silence and to subject our sundry views about homosexuality to the light of a brother's or sister's criticism. The case I have outlined presents just such an opportunity—the sort pastors should have the wisdom to seize. As Aristotle notes, doing (or saying) the right thing demands attention not just to "what" but "when" and "under what circumstances." Practical wisdom, or prudence, is a virtue that involves subtle perception, one particularly necessary for those who lead. If Ruth is a prudent leader she will perceive that Jack's comment is an occasion to pause for discussion; indeed, prudence demands from Ruth and the council precisely the opposite of the "efficiency" for which prudence is so often mistaken. The meeting must not rush; rather, Ruth and the council members must pause to remind themselves of what it means for them to think about their brother Carl who, as they now know, is a homosexual.

As they do this, they must begin with the premise that Carl Harris cannot be for them simply a "homosexual." No, he is Carl. This stands, I believe, as a sort of benchmark of faithfulness in any discussion the contemporary church might have about homosexuality. For the church council to be considering if Carl is the right parishioner to head the Evangelism and Renewal Committee, they must have previously welcomed Carl into their church community. This means that, for the faithful church, discussions concerning homosexuality cannot begin abstractly, for many particular homosexuals are brothers and sisters in the church. In stronger language, the gospel requires that the Christian church not exclude homosexuals as "homosexuals."

I do not mean to preclude a frank discussion about a prospective member's sex life by those churches who carry a tradition of carefully examining those who would join them. The church should not reflect the world in maintaining it is nobody else's business, including the church's, as to what someone decides to do with her or his sex organs. (Indeed, reference to "sex organs" as if these were one more item of personal possession already partakes in a dualism about body and soul that all Christians must eschew.) So a prospective member in these churches should not take offense if he is examined on sexual questions before he is admitted. However—and this is the point—no church is truly the church if it hangs out a sign that homosexuals are not welcome. Of course as we all know, and as the apostle James reminds us in his discussion of how rich and poor are differently received at the churches to whom he is writing, there are more ways of hanging out signs than merely tacking them to the door. The way James begins his discussion is apropos: "Do you with your acts of favoritism really believe in our glorious Lord Jesus Christ?" (James 2:1)

We can now note that the discussion in the council meeting has begun in the context of a certain faithfulness. Carl Harris, a homosexual, has been welcomed and has become an admired friend of Jack and others. Mind you, he was not welcomed as a "homosexual," for some on the council were unaware that he is one. Yet that, in fact, is as it should be. For just as the church should not hang out a sign (in any number of ways) that homosexuals are not welcome, it should refrain from hanging out a sign that says "homosexuals please come." It should not because such a sign grants a prior validity to the distinctions of the world. Unlike the army, the church is not looking for any sort of person in particular.

Perhaps this is where Ruth, the pastor, should begin: by reminding the council that in its discussion of Carl it is not setting "policy about homosexuals" but rather is deliberating about whether and how Carl's homosexuality should be a factor in this appointment. The council must see Carl, friend, brother, child of God, who is a homosexual, not the "homosexual Carl." Together with Pastor Ruth, the council must teach this to the whole church, including, importantly, Carl himself. For as a homosexual in our current culture, Carl is likely under constant pressure, not just from hostile homophobic sources but from the "gay community" itself, to see himself as a homosexual before he sees himself as God's child.

Of course the church's welcoming Carl, and Ruth's recognition of this as an act of Christian faithfulness, does not yet specifically address the matter the council must now consider. What will it say? Should Carl Harris get the call for Evangelism and Renewal?

To diminish the disappointment later, let me say now that I cannot answer this question. It is up to the council. (It is good to remember that when we imagine a case that poses a genuine dilemma for some [imagined] real people, and then resolve it in writing, we are doing something quite different from what those real people [the ones we are imagining] do when they resolve it.) And, of course, what the council members decide will depend a great deal on which church they stand within and, consequently, which authorities they are bound by. It is wonderful that in this book we can pool wisdom from diverse traditions about ethics for clergy. But it is also true that the courses of action we pursue within different Christian traditions will and should vary according to those traditions' differing loyalties. For instance, Roman Catholicism stresses the need for the unitive and procreative elements in all acts of sexual union, whereas this is less emphasized in most Protestant denominations.

I do not mean to leave Pastor Ruth and her council here without further comment.[1] We can consider what sorts of things the council should consider, even if we cannot weigh them exactly as they would or should. However, pausing in the midst of our discussion of homosexuality to admit that we do not know exactly God's will on the matter is an important exercise, not just intellectually but pastorally. Pastor Ruth might be prudent once again to point out to the council that the church is called to carry on even in times of considerable uncertainty about which way it should turn on a particular matter.

This suggests that there is more to the council's debate about Carl or the church's debate about homosexuality than reaching a resolution. Indeed, it is in conducting these debates that the discussants will need an important set of virtues. I am not thinking of niceness or even cordiality. As the debates of the patristic church reveal, disagreement in the church need not avoid anger and there is room, even, for tactical maneuvering. Rather, we must debate with patience and hope. To begin, these virtues rule out two responses that are common in air made thick by disagreement. The first of these, impatience, begins in the dismissal of the other and his (tiresome) views. So if, for example, Jack's opening comments are met by protestations from council member Russ regarding Carl's right to privacy, a response Jack could have predicted would come from Russ, he (Jack) is nonetheless bound to patiently listen to Russ's points. Impatience, particularly of another's point in a debate, often carries a tinge of disdain, as can tolerance, the "virtue" so extolled in our current culture but nonetheless, when it stands alone, mainly directs us to pursue our own separate ends. Impatient disdain is the more likely vice in the church's debate about homosexuality, for the disputants perceive something precious is at stake and they want to win. Impatience egged toward disdain can quickly change to cynicism, a vice that especially opposes hope. And cynicism, modeled so well in the society around us, will clear the disputant's path to a politics of power by which he may crush the other into silence. Churches are divided in this cynical resort to power—either when dissenting voices actually are silenced by power or when they prematurely perceive that they have been.

By contrast, the virtues of patience and hope direct us not only to listen to the other but also to recognize the past for which he or she speaks. Patience, as I have suggested, evidently rules out quick and summary resolutions at the same time that it engages the other in argument, listening carefully. Particularly in the council's discussion of Carl, patience cannot turn to passive waiting; something must be decided, so patience must prayerfully proceed. Yet it must proceed in hope; and hope, which looks to things to come, must for that reason look to things that have been. Hope, the first of the three theological virtues, is of course related to charity, which Aquinas calls the form of all the virtues. Yet, in preparation for charity, Christian hope reminds the church of the tensed or timeful nature of its discussions of human conduct such as homosexuality.

Homosexuality has a deep history, both personal and institutional. Sex in each person's life is itself a history, often of deep personal struggle, particularly for homosexuals. Institutionally, there is history as well. On the one side, known to homosexuals, is a history of rejection and fear; on the other side is a history of the formation of an ethic of marriage that directs and disciplines heterosexual desire even as it affirms that desire.

Genuine hope does not ignore these various histories which are, as noted, histories of struggle. They cannot be swallowed into one. Hope shows us the way to go on amidst incompleteness, with stories that as yet have no conclusion. We hope for the completeness but, as hoping, also knowing it is God's and not our part to bring it about. Heterosexual Christians will be tempted to complete the story on their own terms; yet homosexuals by their very existence, let alone their stories, challenge the simple story of sexuality some heterosexuals might prefer. Hope in this sense may require that the answers we advance as heterosexuals or homosexuals have a tentative air about them, even as we make practical decisions in such matters like Carl's appointment to the committee chairmanship. Such tentativeness need not be a sign of weakness or indecision, but rather of a hope that all our present struggles will not be in vain, including both the struggles of our disagreements and of our particular lives wherein we prayerfully seek for the godly transformation of our desires.

Here we must once again return to the council members. They cannot avoid a decision. However tentatively, they must discuss how to count Carl's homosexuality, and count it in one way or another. Carl's personal history will and should be of concern to them, but they will need to consider the history of the church's own deliberations about homosexuality as well. And this can begin nowhere else but in Scripture. We should be honest, as is biblical scholar Richard Hays, when considering the Bible's explicit references to homosexuality: "Though only a few biblical texts speak of homoerotic activity, all that do mention it express unqualified disapproval."[2] So if someone wishes to argue biblically for homosexual practice, something else besides these texts needs to be put forward. It might be possible to hold that, for instance, the particular references can be overcome by some more general consideration that is absolutely key to the biblical witness. Paul, after all, was unequivocally negative about women praying with their heads uncovered (1 Cor 11: 5–6) but, as most Christians hold, Paul's views on this point are to be located historically and culturally, and are not binding.

This is part of Biblical Hermeneutics 101 where we were all introduced to the problems with a certain sort of biblical literalism. For responsible Christians, however, the problems with biblical literalism cannot lead us to ignore at will this or that biblical condemnation. The passages must be faithfully investigated and reasons given for why Christians today can set them aside. Hays does this investigation, and here is what he finds: In the Romans 1:18–32 passage, particularly important because Paul offers there a theological formulation of the phenomenon of homosexuality, we find that sexual desire—male of male or female of female—is a "dishonorable passion" that follows from the human race's having "exchanged the truth about God for a lie." As Hays observes, it makes all the difference that here homosexual passions are not the cause of human alienation from God; rather, they are the *result*. Paul means, then, to characterize our disordered state after the Fall; for him, homosexual passions are emblematic of any number of passions that can be understood as disordered. God's wrath, which in the passage is provoked by prior disobedience, "takes the ironic form of allowing [human beings] the freedom to have their own way, abandoning them to their own devices."[3] The homosexual passions and practices Paul cites serve as a ready and rhetorically powerful example of this disorder; they are not, then, sins that stand by themselves. Indeed, Paul's argument in the first three chapters of Romans is to lead us to the conclusion that we are all without excuse.

Using Romans, Jack can suggest that Carl's homosexual desires are evidence of disorder in human desire that is the result of sin. But if he is faithful to the structure of Romans, he will add that this is a pervasive disorder that he (Jack) may himself display in, for example, his desire for a certain comfort and security gained by means of a substantial IRA accumulation, or in his not infrequent errant heterosexual desires, even, perhaps, for his wife. That is to say, Jack cannot pick one disorder over another and read the Bible. For according to the Bible, disordered desire is pervasive in the fallen state we share. Moreover, the state is inherited. As Richard Hays makes clear, Paul steers far clear of the pernicious idea that Carl Harris's homosexual desire is the cause of his disordered state before God, the part of him from which God most turns his face. Paul would hold that Carl's homosexual desires are "disordered passions," but this places those passions in a vast category of disordered desires to which distinctions of type or degree simply do not apply.

How might Jack use this biblical understanding to argue that Carl Harris should be excluded from the appointment? Surely he can hold that Carl Harris's homosexual practice is relevant because the church council should be looking for people who strive to be conformed to Christ who, though in all ways tempted like us, remained without sin. But if the council appointed Jack to his position, even though he likes to stow away a hefty chunk each month to ensure that he and his wife, Mabel, will be able to keep up their golfing habit well into retirement, why shouldn't it appoint Carl to head the committee if he displays otherwise in his life the love of Christ? One might reply, of course, that Carl has set up his life so that he will yield to the desire, for he lives with David. But, as Jack and Mabel's golf habit illustrates, evidently this can be true of lives in a whole variety of ways. We should call one another out of these patterns, of course, and perhaps the council should speak with Carl about his homosexual practices at the time of his appointment—even if it (inconsistently) didn't use Jack's appointment to the council in a similar way. If it does so, of course, it must be ready to recognize complexity, as well as goodness. Suppose, for instance, Carl and David's relationship is one in which they successfully strive to be faithful one to the other, to grow in love. As such it may serve to discipline their inordinate desires, perhaps more than Jack's and Mabel's hetero-sexual relations. Or perhaps the council will discover that just at the time Jack and Mabel head to the links on Saturday morning, Carl and David buy, bake, and serve breakfast in the homeless shelter down on Fourth Street.

To sum up, if we begin by thinking (as the Bible does) of homosexuality as disordered desire that is the result of sin, the practicing homosexual cannot be distinguished from anyone else insofar as we all have and act upon disordered desires. The struc-ture of Paul's argument in Romans is not just a powerful bit of rhetoric; rather, it is central to the Christian faith. It is designed to remind us that we are all sinners, that each of us participates in the disordered state that might be illustrated in any number of ways. For Carl Harris, one of these is homosexual desire—something Christians cannot ignore. But it is a mistake of epic proportions, an anti-Christian mistake, to think that homosexuals are, by virtue of their homosexuality, to be distinguished on this score from any of the rest of us, or that they are any less able to show forth God's glory and to offer service to God's church.

To this point, our discussion has centered upon desire, not unfittingly because it is impossible to speak about sex without speaking about desire. Christians need to be honest about what desires human beings have; yet for them, the mere existence of a desire is not enough to justify it. Sexual desire of any sort is not self-justifying in the church. No doubt some, like Elaine Pagels, are right to see certain earlier preoccupations, of the likes of Augustine, with sexual desire as what we might now call "hang-ups." But the basic notion that pervaded this earlier time, that we each must subject ourselves and our desires to the discipline of Christ, has become clouded in our own time, and may need rejuvenation. This is why it is not out of line to suggest that the council should question Carl about how he supposes his sexual desires are being changed and transformed to bring him closer into conformity with Christ. As I have suggested, it may be that Carl could give a better account of this than could Jack about his heterosexual desires. However, there is this difference: According to the view we have from Saint Paul, Carl's and David's sexual desires are incapable of a complete transformation so long as they continue to have sex. If one accepts Paul's starting place (it could be disputed, no doubt, but I have not disputed it here), this creates a problem for Carl. This is not to say anything in particular about Carl and David's relationship—which may exceed in goodness many heterosexual relationships like Jack and Mabel's. Rather, it is to make a general claim about all homosexual relationships, namely, that qua homosexual relationships they resist a final ordering to God.[4]

I mean to emphasize the generality of this claim, which is, you will recall, precisely the opposite of the opening emphasis in this article. It seems to me, in fact, that the church's success in navigating the troubled waters of current debates about homosexuality will depend on its capacity to carefully and self-consciously move between these two levels or types of claims. Can the church welcome Carl and David, hold up their specific lives (which, in many respects, are exemplary) for admiration, perhaps even appoint Carl as chairperson of Evangelism and Renewal, at the same time that it patiently holds (in general) that active homosexual relations are not God's ultimate intention for the sexual lives of his people?

To put the point that way is to imply that God has some general intention for the transformation of our sexual desires. And this is what the Christian church has maintained, either in singleness or in marriage. Singleness and marriage are, in effect, general calls issued to all Christians, general invitations to transformation as sexual and relational children of God.[5] In practice, their promise will be grossly underrepresented in particular cases. The church, which marries, will nevertheless contain within it any number of bad marriages. As particular relationships, many of these will reflect God's glory far less clearly than the relationship between Carl and David. However, the church will be committed to sustaining them as marriages, as well as sustaining singleness, in a way that it will not be committed to sustaining homosexual relationships as homosexual relationships.

But why? What's so special about marriage or singleness that a homosexual relationship cannot also partake in? This is a key question for our time. For, indeed, the recent call by those who would have the church "marry" homosexuals is a challenge to the church to articulate why the marriage of male and female is so important. Plainly a sentimental, romantic, or purely biological account of marriage in the church will not cut it, although evidently these are the sort of accounts most prevalent in our time. In its more lucid moments, the church has turned to lifelong sexual fidelity and/or the procreative aspect of heterosexual sex in upholding marriage. Both of these will need to find a place in the account, although the first by itself could include homosexual relationships. The second is particularly available to Catholics, although it may have repercussions about the use of birth control that, some have argued, are not sustainable in our world.

By calling for a theological reflection on marriage, I do not mean to minimize the force of past teaching in the church about it, particularly in the Catholic and Orthodox churches where marriage remains a sacrament. Yet it seems true, not only in the Protestant churches but in these churches as well, that despite the fact that one of the main things churches do is marry, they have become inarticulate about why God would have some of us marry. One way to get the church to say more clearly why some Christians should marry is for the practice to decline among the general population. There are some slight signs that this may be occurring. Another more direct way is for homosexuals to ask the church whether they can be married, too. The church should welcome their questions.

The bearing this more general concern about marriage has on our case is not small, although it remains general, and our case is particular. Jack might argue that participation by church members in one of two states, marriage or singleness, serves as an important pointer to those outside the church concerning who these people are who call themselves "Christian." So, he could suggest, Carl's witness will be compromised. Yet, depending upon the specific type of witness this church has in the world (for example, is there a large gay population in the region?), and upon the character and faithfulness of other willing candidates, perhaps that council should appoint Carl to head the Evangelism and Renewal Committee. It is difficult to know without knowing more about Carl—more, that is, than that he is a homosexual.

---

1.   The question of what we should say or believe about homosexual practice is before the church, and we must make our way, by argument, to some

considered judgments. I attempt to do this later in the paper. However, as I mean to accent, our judgments about this difficult and potentially divisive issue must be approached with great care. The virtues, I believe, can help us do this. I am hopeful that those who differ with my position, which I later outline, will not be kept by their difference from considering how the virtues might help us disagree well.

2. Richard Hays, *The Moral Vision of the New Testament: Community, Cross, New Creation* (New York: HarperCollins, 1996), 389. The "explicit" passages Hays cites are Leviticus 18:22, 20:13; I Corinthians 6:9–11; I Timothy 1:10; Acts 15:28–29; and Romans 1:18–32.

3. Ibid., 385.

4. I advance this in the tentative way I have suggested hope directs. Christians hope for the full establishment of God's kingdom. Through Christ and the church they believe they know something of its general shape — otherwise in what do they hope? However, the specific shape the resolution that God will bring about in the kingdom is not yet seen. In this way it is not contradictory to hope for a resolution to the struggles and joys of a particular case of homosexual love while holding at the same time that qua homosexual relation it resists God's full intention for human life.

5. For a suggestive account of the relation between these two ways of life in the church, see Stanley Hauerwas, *A Community of Character* (Notre Dame: University of Notre Dame Press, 1981), 186–93.

Chapter Seventeen

Doctrine and Ecclesiastical Authority
A Contemporary Controversy in the
Armenian Church

by Vigen Guroian

On December 13, 1996, at the close of a three-day meeting at the Vatican, Karekin I, Catholicos of All Armenians of the Holy See of Etchmiadzin, and John Paul II, Bishop of Rome and Pope of the Catholic Church, jointly issued a declaration of common faith and purpose. In most respects, the Common Declaration was not an unusual document—the sort routinely promulgated by heads of churches when they meet together. The Catholicos and the Pope expressed their hope that the Armenian Orthodox Church and the Roman Catholic Church might draw increasingly toward full communion and unity. They affirmed modern efforts to resolve historic differences among all of the churches; they proclaimed a common Trinitarian faith; and they applauded cooperation "in all the fields of diaconia" and peacemaking.[1]

In these elements, the Common Declaration was not, as I say, unusual. However, the Catholicos and the Pope also entered into a brief discussion of "the great advance that their churches have registered in their common search for unity in Christ." This was followed by a statement about christological belief, in which the two leaders sought to move beyond their respective church's historic disagreement about the two natures christological formula of the fourth great Ecumenical Council of Chalcedon, held in 451. Whereas, the Roman Catholic Church has embraced the Council's two natures doctrine, the Armenian Church adheres to a qualified Monophysitism that affirms the fullness of Christ's divinity and his humanity without speaking of two natures. The Armenian Church traces its teaching back to the universally accepted fourth-century church father St. Cyril of Alexandria.

In the Common Declaration, the Catholicos and the Pope did not use the two natures terminology. They stated:

> *[We] welcome the great advance . . . [in our] common search for unity in Christ, the Word of God made flesh. Perfect God as to his divinity, perfect man as to his humanity, his divinity is united to his humanity in the Person of the Only-begotten Son of God, in a union which is real, perfect, without confusion, without alteration, without division, without any form of separation.*

There was ample modern precedent for this kind of an agreement. In past decades the heads of the non-Chalcedonian Coptic and Syrian Orthodox churches joined with the papacy in making similar statements. The Armenian Catholicos, however, was harshly criticized from within his own church for doing the same. His critics maintained that the language of the Common Declaration bore the meaning of the two natures formula of Chalcedon and nakedly contradicted the "One Nature" teaching of the Armenian Church.

The Anatomy of an Ecclesiastical Controversy

*F*or six months an acrimonious debate ensued within Armenia and throughout the Diaspora. This episode not only invites an inquiry into the nature and uses of ecclesiastical authority but also raises canon law questions about church discipline. Nevertheless, these are not the matters that I will be examining. Instead, I am going to narrate the course of the controversy with the aim of setting in relief the ethical issues respecting the character and conduct of the participants. That story reveals a breakdown of standards of civil discourse, even at the highest levels of the hierarchy, and raises questions about the moral formation of the clergy in general. It is not my aim, however, to pass judgment on the speech and public demeanor of some of the Catholicos's antagonists, although the story certainly exposes shortcomings. Rather I seek to take instruction from this failure of civility in order to reflect briefly on resources and strategies that might remedy the shortcomings that came to light in this episode.

Over a distinguished career of more than thirty-five years as a priest and bishop, Karekin I, occupant of the most honored patriarchal see in the Armenian Church, rose to world prominence as an Orthodox leader committed to ecumenism and rapprochement among the churches. Karekin Sarkissian had played a role second to no other Armenian clergyman or theologian in vital consultations on Christology. Indeed, he had penned a significant study on the Council of Chalcedon and how it was received historically by the Armenian Church.[2] In addition, as a young priest he had been a principal Armenian observer at Vatican II. Thus, Karekin I's visit to Rome and signature to the Common Declaration was entirely consistent with his theological knowledge and ecumenical commitments.

Nevertheless, the Catholicos's action ignited an explosive mixture of arguments about high doctrine and challenges to ecclesiastical authority. The controversy resembled debates in the fourth and fifth centuries far more than familiar late-twentieth-century church agonistics over issues of social justice and the like. Indeed, the principal actors of the early Christian centuries were resurrected in spirit and their beliefs were lent voice once more. Furthermore, a doctrinally illiterate laity was faced with a form of theological discourse that sounded arcane to their ears. The vast majority of laity were hearing for the first time, excepting the prayers and anathemas of the liturgy (to which modern ears are distinctly deaf) the names of the principal theological contestants of Christian antiquity and the positions they took: Athanasius and Cyril of Alexandria, Theodore of Mopsuesta and Nestorius of Antioch.

At the start of 1997 an essay appeared in Armenia and later in the Diaspora by Fr. Mesrob Aramian, director of the Gandzasar Theological Center in Yerevan. Aramian boldly condemned the language of the joint statement and bitterly criticized the Catholicos. In March, Aramian's case was brought before the Supreme Spiritual Council at Holy Etchmiadzin, over which Karekin I presided. Soon afterwards, two members of the Council, Archbishop Nerses Bazabalian, long active in the ecumenical affairs of the church, and Archbishop Karekin Nersessian, Primate of Yerevan, called upon Aramian's diocesan bishop Barkev Mardirosian, Primate of the Diocese of Nagorno-Karabagh, to discipline the priest. On April 11, Bishop Mardirosian and two other bishops, Archbishop Diran Gureghian, Primate of Russia, and Bishop Hagop Kilinjian, Primate of Uruguay, visited the Catholicos to lodge their objections. They issued a statement to the Armenian press expressing the view that His Holiness had misrepresented the Armenian christological doctrine and exceeded his authority in signing such a joint statement without consulting with the College of Bishops.[3]

In an open letter to the Catholicos, published first in Yerevan and later in Canada, Bishop Mardirosian rejected the demand that he discipline Fr. Aramian. Instead, he bitterly criticized the Catholicos. The bishop accused Karekin I of "have[ing] drawn a sword on our faith." He continued: "You as Catholicos are responsible and obliged to serve as the model for rules and orders . . . but you were the first [to break the rules] without consulting the Supreme Spiritual Council—you have signed a doctrinal paper." In answer to the charge that Fr. Aramian was a fanatic, Mardirosian responded that Fr. Aramian is a "fanatic" only in the sense that he has "tried to defend the doctrine of the church" against an illicit revision of that doctrine accomplished by the Catholicos in Rome. As for the request to discipline Fr. Aramian, the bishop declared, "Why discipline him? So I can be a man-pleaser, or to be the defender of my church . . . My discipline of Fr. Aramian . . . is: 'May you be blessed for your faith' . . . I do not share what you have signed in Rome. . . . You may consider that I did not go with your entourage to Rome"[4] (Mardirosian was in the delegation that visited Rome with the Catholicos). This open letter from a primate of the Armenian Church to the Supreme Head of that church is, in my estimation, extraordinary. The sheer spleen in the bishop's comments is itself breathtaking, worthy of Martin Luther's most vitriolic polemics against the Pope.

Aramian himself raised some serious arguments and demonstrated a studied interpretation of the sources. Based on his analysis of these sources, he maintained that the declaration seriously contradicted the teaching of the Armenian Church and conformed in the essentials to the "the basic statement of Chalcedonian Christology." But Aramian may have crossed the line from legitimate disputation to spurious and malicious speech when he insinuated that Karekin I was motivated chiefly by self-gain and political expediency. Indeed, Aramian accused the Catholicos of preparing the Armenian Church to abandon its historic relationship to the other Oriental churches and join the Chalcedonian camp. He characterized the Catholicos's visit as a "strange ecumenism" and raised this specter: "One wonders whether a Georgian conversion to Chalcedonianism is not being prepared for us."[5] Was this talk not tantamount to accusing the head of one's church of treachery against that very body?

A Brief Review of Armenian Christological Teaching

I have intimated already the principal historical reason why the Armenian Church is not in communion with either the Roman Catholic Church or the greater body of Eastern Orthodox (e. g., Greek or Russian) churches: It is that the Armenian Church dissents from the fifth-century christological formula of Chalcedon.[6] At that time the Church of Armenia worried that the "two natures" formula jeopardized the ancient scriptural confession of "one Lord, one faith, one baptism" (Ephesians 4:5). There were fears and suspicion that the formula logically divided the One

Lord Jesus Christ into two beings, as bishop Nestorius and his followers had done. The Nestorians had spoken of two beings joined in the physical individual known and seen as Jesus of Nazareth—the human individual gestated in the womb of his mother, Mary, and the Second Person of the Holy Trinity who came to dwell within that individual during his earthly life. Members of the Chalcedonian camp who were prone to distinguishing Jesus' actions into those ascribable to his manhood, such as when he hungered and ate, and those belonging to his godhood, such as the performance of miracles, were suspect of committing a Nestorian error. In the eyes of the Armenians, Pope Leo's Tome addressed to the Council had erred in this heretically diophysitic direction. And so they concluded that the definition of Chalcedon did not emphasize sufficiently the essential unity of Christ's Person in his being and in his acts. Christ is one, the Armenians insisted, and he acts as one single being in his one divine-human Nature at all times and on every occasion.

The Armenians adhered strictly to the language of the first Great Ecumenical Council of Nicaea (A. D. 325). That Council in its Creed had employed the term nature with a quite specific connotation of concrete existence. Thus, God is one being and nature. And the Son is of the same being and nature of the Father. This is how the Council interpreted the words of Christ in the Gospel of John 14: 9–10: "Whoever has seen me has seen the Father . . . I am in the Father and the Father is in me." The theologians of Nicaea used "nature" with a sense analogous to what is meant by a solid in modern physics. Solids, like diamonds or ice cubes, are discrete substances and cannot be mixed together, as can liquids or gases. So when the Chalcedonian party spoke of two natures in Christ, Armenians balked. How could Christ be two "solids," two natures? If the supporters of Chalcedon were using nature differently in order to connote something analogous to a liquid or a gas—nature as a kind of abstract and amorphous essence—new problems arose. A gas or a liquid can be mixed with or emulsified into another gas or liquid. But if nature were used in this sense, then what was there to prevent people from saying that Christ had three or four natures? Air is made up of not just oxygen and nitrogen but also hydrogen and carbon dioxide, and so forth.

The Armenian Church held to what it understood as the original language and intent of the Council of Nicaea. And in the sixth century it formally rejected the Council of Chalcedon with its two natures teaching. Through the centuries, the Armenian Church continued to speak of Christ as One Person and Nature of the Divine Word who became Incarnate, a complete human being. The eternal Divine Word and only begotten Son of the Father acted (or assumed) full manhood by being born of a woman and participating in all of our human ways, excepting sin, and even dying humanly on the cross, and still he was God.

On December 13, 1996, Karekin I, Catholicos of All Armenians, and Pope John Paul II rejoined the ancient debate and sought a way beyond the old disagreements. However, the critics pointed to the Common Declaration's phrasing, "in a union which is real, perfect, without confusion, without alteration, without division, without any separation" and argued that this implied the two natures doctrine. In a rigid ahistorical manner these words might be interpreted that way. But Armenian churchmen and theologians from the Middle Ages forward to the modern ecumenical era had found the means to embrace this sort of terminology. Karekin I, a contemporary student of this history of interpretation, knew he was acting in complete faithfulness with distinguished predecessors.

The most important of these predecessors was St. Nerses the Graceful (1102–73), the great twelfth-century Catholicos who sought a rapprochement with the Byzantines. St. Nerses judged: "If 'One Nature' is said for the indissoluble and indivisible union and not for the confusion, and 'Two Natures' is said as being unconfused, immutable and indivisible, both are within the bounds of orthodoxy."[7] Likewise, he wrote, "to say [that] there are Two Natures, thereby meaning the union of the Two, is by no means contrary to the truth, provided one Christ be not divided into Two."[8]

Karekin I did not press the interpretation nearly as far as his twelfth-century predecessor. He did act consciously, however, within the context of a long history of Armenian engagement with the Byzantine and Roman churches on this issue and in light of modern ecumenical successes in sorting out meanings and clearing up linguistic confusions. His opponents looked at things differently. I, too, was attacked in the press for taking up the Catholicos's cause in an article I wrote in the spring of 1997 published in the May 24, 1997 issue of the *Armenian Reporter International*.[9] Reverend Dr. Vrej Nerses Nersessian, a librarian and curator of the British Library, charged: "V. Guroian has again reiterated his longstanding Protestant prejudices regarding the Orthodox Church by his accusations that in my article, there is a kind of 'patristic fundamentalism and rigid historical scholasticism.'"[10] Being called a "Protestant" in such contexts is the same as being accused of having abandoned the Armenian orthodoxy.

Nersessian was even less generous toward Karekin I. In a February article entitled "Beware of Faulty Writing," Nersessian essentially accused the Catholicos of being duped by the papacy. The papacy has not withdrawn its claims of supremacy and infallibility in doctrine, argued Nersessian, and so it is not to be trusted. "Where is the change in milieu and context which His Holiness has discerned but our Holy Fathers have missed?" Nersessian questioned. He continued: "In the narrow candle-end approach the Catholicos and his entourage of archbishops, like entrepreneurs, are lugging the Holy See in their suitcases across the world and diminishing its standing in a monstrously arrogant or foolishly blinkered way." [11]

Archbishop Mesrob K. Krikorian of Vienna, a longstanding participant in ecumenical discussions, soon responded to Nersessian. Krikorian argued that Nersessian misrepresented the context and spirit of the Catholicos and Pope's meeting and the Common Declaration. "The Common Declaration might be inspired by the spirit of Vatican II and of later ecumenical documents," Krikorian explained, "but it contains nothing in favor of the jurisdictional primacy and infallibility of the Pope and against

the sovereignty and dignity of the Armenian Apostolic Church."
Krikorian also sharply admonished Nersessian for his disrespect-
ful public speech against the occupants of the See of Holy
Etchmiadzin and the Holy See of St. Peter. "Of course, it is
everybody's right to freely and publicly express their opinions,
even faulty and senseless ideas, but nobody has the right to
offend dignitaries: critical words should not surpass the limits of
fairness and politeness."[12]

Nersessian responded to Krikorian in yet another article.
"What the Archbishop calls 'arrogance,' I call 'humility' towards
the patristic and monastic tradition of the Armenian Church
fathers. Anyone who abandons the traditions of his church,
forged and defended for over 1700 years, is a scoundrel and a
traitor."[13] The explicit object of Nersessian's anger was
Archbishop Krikorian. But any reader the least bit sensitive to
meaning and nuance would have had to wonder whether he was
not directing these same charges against Karekin I.

The Ethical Dimension of the Debate
Or Where Civility Failed

An especially disturbing dimension of this entire episode was
the lack of self-discipline and ethical constraint displayed by
some of the clergy who entered the fray. Name-calling and
recrimination surfaced regularly in the Armenian media. The
observer might rightly wonder what sort of examples were being
set for laity by high-ranking clergy as they slugged it out in
Armenian papers and journals. In May of 1997, Aram I,
Catholicos of the Great House of Cilicia in Antelias, Lebanon,
the second most venerated patriarchal see in Armenian
Christendom, rose to a defense of Karekin I and called to account
this unseemly conduct. Interviewed in the *Armenian Weekly*
newspaper, Aram I told the editor:

> I . . . [am] deeply disturbed regarding this unpleasant
> and incomprehensible phenomenon. I feel sorrow for

those high-ranking servants and priests of the Armenian Church who are criticizing the Catholicos of All Armenians. . . [H]ealthy, constructive public debate about the Armenian Church's credo, rites and mission, in general, is normal and sometimes necessary. But within the Armenian Church we have a centuries-old understanding about order and respect for hierarchy. Woe to us! If we sidestep or overturn those traditions in the name of freedom of speech. If clergymen or laymen have anything to say or bring to the attention of their ecclesiastical superior about any subject they should do so in person or within the bounds of meetings, not through public declaration.[14]

Aram I was endeavoring to identify and prescribe the legitimate boundaries of discourse and criticism within the church. The fact that he felt the need to do so already betokened a lamentable breakdown of common respect and civility among high-ranking clergy. I am not suggesting that in the history of the Christian church there have not been occasions when similar or worse lapses of civility and respect for authority and office have occurred. But these do not excuse new occurrences.

The baseness of the debate over the Common Declaration belongs to a much larger and deeper crisis of moral formation and training of clergy in the Armenian Church. The ramifications of this crisis are several, ranging from poor morale within the parish priesthood to unseemly competition among bishops and the lack of ordinary etiquette and manners in the church's conduct of affairs. The sources of the crisis are complicated and cannot be thoroughly reviewed here. Nor do I think that this crisis is unique to the Armenian Church. It is found in other churches and, alas, in the culture at large.

A long time ago, St. John Chrystostom instructed his parishioners in another age of moral confusion that not by "ten thousand precepts of philosophy" would Christians win the minds and hearts of men and women but principally by the quality of their lives. "For it is not what is said that draws their attention, but their inquiry is what we do. . . . Let us win them therefore by our life."[15] Manners and morals in the church are not merely matters of decorum and externals of behavior. Their breakdown affects the evangelical witness and mission of the church. That is the lesson Chrystostom was trying to teach. Where fundamental beliefs and matters of belonging are at issue, passions are bound to run high. Those whom the church invests with the solemn responsibility to transmit and sometimes defend Christian beliefs and identity should receive a training that cultivates virtues of humility, temperance, and forbearance.

The success or failure of such training in virtues admittedly is hard to measure; and moral perfection is a lifetime's endeavor, not something that can be stamped instantaneously upon a student or seminarian. But this type of training is desperately lacking at present in the preparation of Armenian clergy. Seminaries need to recapture and reappropriate some of the wisdom of moral discipline and spiritual *askesis* (or asceticism) within ancient monastic tradition. After all, monasticism historically has been a movement of moral and spiritual renewal within the church.

The same St. Nerses the Graceful who was an example of ecumenical dialogue and *rapprochement* in the twelfth century also saw the need in his day to write a *General Epistle* to the whole church that gave counsel on conduct befitting the church. When Nerses became Catholicos in 1166 there was turmoil and corruption in the Armenian Church. As Thomas J. Samuelian notes in his preface to a recent English translation of the *General Epistle*: "It was a church of self-important bishops, wealthy princes, greedy priests, and faithless people. Robes, pomp, and ceremony"[16] prevailed over humility, simplicity of living, and selfless service.

Virtues vital to witness and salvation were at issue then as they were in the acrimonious debate over the Common Declaration. Every church has its own special resources within the tradition. Nerses the Graceful's *Epistle* belongs especially to the Armenian Church. It ought to be studied and reflected upon by every seminarian in my church. Saint Nerses names meekness and humility, holiness, benevolence, justice, self-restraint, and temperance as especially vital to the office of primate. He identifies the vices of vainglory and arrogance as the episcopate's special temptations. "Being meek, humble, honest and with humility calls to mind one who resembles Moses and David, who were long ago shepherds of the people of Israel. . . [I]t is unfitting for a bishop to be arrogant and haughty like a tyrant toward the obedient."[17]

Saint Nerses also points out that a special test of character for the church is when clergy argue. He explains that the conduct of clergy in such instances must remain consistent with the virtues he has listed and discussed. "First, we are not to give way to evil thoughts in our mind, but to oppose them with temperance and to drive them out of the heart so their enactment will not follow. . . . [Do] not speak such words as the worldly do, which are unsuitable to a holy station . . . [Do] not become angry against those who trespass against you, but . . . be humble. . . Be neither quarrelsome nor contentious. Since you are a disciple of Christ, indeed His vicar, accept the example of His meekness as He commands those who were His disciples. . . [T]he Lord Himself gives this blessing to the meek and the peacemaker."[18] He warns in particular against "oppos[ing] the words of enemies in useless battles and harmful arguments, or while arguing yell[ing] things to . . . enemies and detractors like the worldly."[19] And he adds: "[B]e slow to move to argument and . . . quick to move to reconciliation and peace."[20]

I must pause at this counsel. Even though there is nothing especially remarkable or surprising in it, it contains a wisdom, however, that demands special attention. I have described what I believe was a lapse of civility during the controversy over the Common Declaration. And I do not retreat from that judgment. Nevertheless, it must also be emphasized that vital concerns over doctrine and identity were involved. As disappointed as one might legitimately have been over the speech and behavior of the participants, especially those who opposed Karekin I, the passions that rose to the surface were often fueled by genuine concerns about dogmatic truth and faithfulness to the historic identity of the Armenian Church.

If my analysis risks unintentionally suggesting that it is all right for moralism to trump the truth claims of dogma, I want to correct that misapprehension immediately. Saint Nerses rightly admonishes and instructs members of the clergy with respect to their special calling to practice the evangelical virtues of love and reconciliation and to avoid rancor and mutual vilification. Yet there is such a thing as a noble combat in defense of spiritual truths and dogma. And this, too, can be an expression of love of God and the church. In such instances, a trying tension may arise between the need to defend salvific truth and the need to practice evangelical love in the world and reconciliation within the body of Christ. The principal point here is that the truth in the dogma of the church would have been better served in the course of the debate had greater civility, loving respect, and imaginative dialogue prevailed.

As it stands, the controversy over the Common Declaration was an embarrassment to the Armenian Church. In my judgment, the spiritual authority of the Armenian episcopate was badly compromised. Real harm was done. After six months of bitter accusation and counteraccusation, the contending parties finally grew tired of carrying on any longer. Wisely, Karekin I himself did not enter the verbal fray. Nor did he retreat, however, from his commitment to the Common Declaration. Yet neither were the opponents' challenges to his authority satisfactorily answered. During the debate and after the debate, the contending parties exhibited no public willingness to be reconciled, while the laity were left to wonder precisely where the truth and authority of the church resides.

Saint Nerses confronted similar matters in his own life and wisely saw the need to prepare clergy and laity to deal with them in a manner faithful to dogmatic truth, mutual love, and evangelical witness. The fact that he was moved to issue the *General Epistle* speaks volumes as to the less than satisfactory conditions he found when he rose to the highest ecclesiastical office of the

Armenian Church. For years afterwards it was a regular practice throughout Armenian Christendom for portions of the *General Epistle* to be read in the parishes on Sundays. One should not discount the impact that such a discipline of reading and consideration of ethical standards within daily church life can have. It does not exist in the Armenian Church today, nor does it play a central role in seminary training. But it ought to.

The story I have told is a case from modern church life that shows how crucial it is for the historic Christian churches to conduct ecclesial formation which includes rigorous leadership training in morals and manners. This problem, however, is by no means limited to the churches. Our society as a whole is failing in the moral education and formation of its business and political leaders. A parallel to this church episode is the debate over the impeachment of President William Jefferson Clinton in the United States House of Representatives that ensued in December of 1998. The debate turned to rancor and dripped thick with demagogic arguments and appeals to fear, not limited to one side or the other. Civic discourse broke down, which indicates something significant about the character of our political leaders. As I write, the nation waits to see whether the Senate, the so-called deliberative house, will be able to rise to a higher level of civility and public discourse than was seen and heard in the House of Representatives.

1. "Common Declaration Signed by Pope John Paul II and Catholicos Karekin I," *L'Osservatore Romano,* Weekly Edition, 51/52 (December 1996): 2.

2. Karekin Sarkissian, *The Council of Chalcedon and the Armenian Church* (New York: The Armenian Church Prelacy, 1965).

3. "Clergy Delegation Asks Karekin I to be Mindful of Preserving Armenian Church's Christological Position," *Armenian Reporter International* (April 19, 1997): 1.

4. "I Won't Hide the Candle Under the Table" (trans.), *Horizon* (May 5, 1997): 13. This is an Armenian language weekly published in Canada. The article originally appeared in the April 23, 1997 issue of the Yerevan paper, *Molorag (Planet)*.

5. Mesrob Aramian, "The Joint Vatican Declaration Contradicts the Christological Tradition of the Armenian Church," *Armenian Reporter International*, Forum Supplement (April 12,1997): 2.

6. This section draws on my analysis contained in an article I wrote regarding the controversy over the Common Declaration. It first appeared in the New York-based *Armenian Reporter International* (May 24, 1997): 27–28; and later, in July was published as "Fully God and Fully Man" in the *National Catholic Register* (July 6, 1997): 5.

7. Quoted by Mesrob Ashjian, *Armenian Church Patristic and Other Essays* (New York: The Armenian Prelacy, 1994), 179.

8. Quoted by John Henry Neale, "Part II: General Introduction," in *A History of the Holy Eastern Church* (New York: AMS Press, 1976. Reprint of the 1850 edition), 1088.

9. See note 6 for reference.

10. Dr. Vrej Nerses Nersessian, "Response to Vigen Guroian: Deliberations Are Not Enough," *Armenian Reporter International* (June 14, 1997): 3.

11. Dr. Vrej Nerses Nersessian, "Beware of Faulty Writing," *Armenian Reporter International* (February 22, 1997): 3, 24, at 24.

12. Mesrob K. Krikorian, "Senseless Pride Is Not a Virtue," *Armenian Reporter International,* Forum Supplement (April 12, 1997): 1–2, at 1.

13. Dr. Vrej Nerses Nersessian, "Reply to 'Senseless Pride Is Not a Virtue,'" *Armenian Reporter International* (May 3, 1997): 3.

14. "An Interview with His Holiness Aram I, Catholicos of Cilicia," *Armenian Weekly* (May 31, 1997): 3.

15. John Chrystostom, *The Homilies of St. John Chrystostom,* in vol. 4 of the *Library of Fathers of the Holy Catholic Church* (Oxford: John Henry Parker, 1889), 32–33.

16. St. Nerses Snoralhali, *General Epistle,* trans. Arakel Aljalian (New Rochelle: St. Nerses Armenian Seminary, 1996), viii.

17. Ibid., 46–47.

18. Ibid., 49, 50.

19. Ibid., 38.

20. Ibid., 60.

Chapter Eighteen
Serving the Church and Facing the Law
Virtues for Committee Members
Evaluating a Pastor

by William Johnson Everett

You are a member of a denomination's regional Committee on Ministerial Certification and Appointment, which oversees the movement of candidates toward ordination as well as their general progress through their career. It is in charge of the certification of clergy and oversees their placement in local churches and church organizations. Its members include clergy as well as lay people. In problematic matters, your Committee can turn to the regional legal counsel to the denomination, who relies both on relevant civil law as well as on the church's internal law, which has developed over many years.

In the course of its work, the Committee is asked to deal with a conflict between a congregation and its pastor. The claims are complex and manifold, and evidently have some history to them. Following ordinary procedures of mediation according to church law, the Committee helps resolve the conflict by enabling the congregation and pastor to reach an agreeable separation that honors the needs of all parties.

Subsequently, the pastor requests approval for seeking appointment to another congregation. In the course of its routine inquiry, disturbing news begins to filter back to Committee members informally from members of the previous congregation. Underlying the more public claims of the congregation made earlier against the pastor there seem to have been various sexual indiscretions and behavior by him that had led over the years to an elaborate pattern of secrecy and manipulation. The members in question could not raise any of this at the time because of their personal embarrassment and their fear of retaliation from their former pastor. In the earlier proceedings their personal objectives for separation from the pastor could be met through the formal procedures of the church. Now, however, they feel an obligation to find a way to prevent this pastor from visiting the same behavior on others.

At first the Committee, although it has received these reports only as informal information, feels it can move ahead to a formal investigation according to church law. The sources of the information seem credible enough that the matter should be taken up, though discreetly, as a personnel matter under the cloak of ordinary procedures for re-appointment. The committee senses an obligation to the members as well as to the pastor, and think it is important for the sake of the denomination's credibility to find the truth.

At this point the Committee hits a snag. All of the alleged actions occurred several years earlier. According to church law, a statute of limitations disallows actions regarding such claims. To take formal action would violate this rule.

The Committee members are convinced that the parishioners were not far off the mark in their allegations, even if they had initially accepted some of the pastor's advances. Other circumstances of the pastor's life and separation from the congregation seem to confirm these claims. Moreover, the Committee members feel they ought to honor the parishioners' deeply felt desire for anonymity in the face of possible retaliation or humiliation. At the same time, they want to protect other congregations from possible misbehavior. Indeed, in some sense they feel a civil obligation to avoid lawsuits if they do not take action, regardless of the church's statute of limitations. Finally, they believe that they have duties toward the pastor to abide strictly by church law, which exists to protect not only congregations but also pastors. Here, too, their actions might lead to a civil suit if they violate well-established rights of citizens in areas of employment, repu-tation, and livelihood. Theologically and ecclesiologically, they also sense the need to uphold cherished parts of their heritage, which may well be at stake in proceeding precipitously or clan-destinely toward the pastor.

The Committee begins to work through a series of consider-ations that bear on how it ought to weigh claims about the con-duct of the pastor over against the claims of proper procedure. The procedural limit seems to pose an absolute barrier to formal investigation, even if in this case it stands in the way of ascer-taining a matter of substantive justice. Its claim is clear, public, written, and observed in fact. Its claim carries with it the force of justice. The body of church law that contains these procedures is a formal declaration of its commitment to all members of the church, including those suspected of wrongful behavior.

Moreover, failure to comply with its own legal requirements could subject the Committee or denomination to a civil suit, since American courts have increasingly been willing to hear civil cases for breach of contract and violations of by-laws, even in ecclesiastical cases. Over the years the distinction between civil justice and ecclesial justice has become blurred in the popular mind as well as in the courts. The room for discretion in church decisions has been narrowing. The Committee does not want to expose itself on this flank, an exposure that would in fact exacer-bate the situation even more through the publicity it would arouse.

Even short of a civil suit, moreover, the Committee is bound by church law to make a public report of any formal investiga-tions. Centuries of suspicion about secret decisions and tribunals have led the church to make public disclosure for all its decisions and official actions a top priority. In some sense, everything the Committee does falls under the requirements of publicity. Its dis-cretionary room is constricted. Its capacity for secret negotia-tions is quite limited.

However, once having decided that it can not launch a formal investigation, the Committee still feels bound by its own judgment about the specifics of the case and its concern for the good of the church. It can not simply pass the pastor on to another congregation. The weight of the evidence, even though resting on the character and credibility of the parishioners, is too great to be set aside. However, if the Committee does act in some way outside the formal rules, it also has to keep in mind the parishioners' needs for anonymity, the needs, claims, and rights of the pastor, as well as its own fiduciary obligations to the wider denominational structures.

How then, should the Committee proceed? How would you act in such a situation? What kinds of values, perspectives, assumptions, and loyalties would inform your decision?

Specifically, this case presents us with two main problems. First, to whom or to what institutions are the Committee members responsible? How do they balance these various responsibilities with each other? Second, what virtues should or can they rely on in moving through their decision? What are the qualities of character and disposition that will best enable them to do the right thing? With these two concerns in mind we turn first to the question of how these virtues relate to rule-oriented conduct, which in this case has brought the members to some difficult dilemmas. I shall then frame the Committee's questions of responsibility and virtue in terms of accountability within the various publics shaping their lives.

Much of our ethical life is governed by rules. These rules are the webs of expectation that make institutional life possible. Without them we return to the arbitrary decisions of parents and monarchs or, more chillingly, of dictators. Religious movements, especially because of their appeal to personal charisma or to parental nurture, have often developed rules, laws, canons, and judicial procedure in the face of moral turpitude by their leaders. These rules arise because appeals to the leaders' virtue has usually fallen short of securing the accountability required by a wider public. The norms of justice, it seems, require more than virtuous leaders. They require public, rule-governed behavior.

No matter how ecstatic their beginnings, religious movements of innovation, renewal, or reform inevitably develop the routines of law to preserve norms of justice within the religious group. At the same time, these rules have also sought to preserve the peculiar principles that generated the religious movement. Catholics seek to preserve the integrity of sacramental life, Methodists the life of conference and itinerancy, Presbyterians the pure preaching of the Word, Lutherans the free operation of grace, and Pentecostalists the free movement of the Spirit.

But are laws enough? And are they enough for the church? What ethical thought should guide us at the limits of the law? In each denominational tradition, as in every polity, the rules of the church inevitably find their limits as well. Although virtue may not be enough for organizations, it is necessary for their actual daily survival, especially where their laws and rules fall short. Virtues speak to the qualities necessary in leaders, laws to the structures of accountability within which they must act. In this brief essay I want to explore the kinds of virtues necessary for leadership where the law's workings are ineffective or violate key goods of ecclesial life. These are the kinds of issues raised in the hypothetical case before us.

The case confronting this denominational committee reveals the limits of an ethics of rules and law in several ways. First, we see a conflict among rules, such as "respect confidentiality" and "respect full disclosure." We also see conflicts between ethical rules, like "seek the truth," and legal rules like "observe statutes of limitations."

Second, we see at the institutional level possible conflicts between legal systems designed for the church and those designed for civil society. What are the claims of church autonomy and what are the claims of civil law?

Third, we confront ambiguities about the application of rules within institutions. How far does a committee's mandate extend? When is it exceeding its authority? How narrowly should the rule on limitations be applied?

Fourth, we find the distinction between law as the "protection of rights" and law as a "means for seeking the common good." Much of our civil law arose to protect the rights of citizens against governments as well as other persons and groups. Thus, the statute of limitations exists to protect rights to a fair trial. However, much law also exists to seek certain goods, whether of health, survival, beautification, environmental integrity, or economic well-being. We are constantly judging these laws in light of the goods they purportedly seek. The Committee in this case is seeking the "good of the wider church" in the midst of laws that protect "ecclesial citizens" as well as seek that ecclesial good.

Finally, these limits of the law and of rule-guided behavior bring us to the boundary question of obligation. Why are we obligated to certain rules or laws? How do we rank the publics to which we are obligated? How do our obligations to God, to Christ, to the church, or to persons shape our ethical decision making at the limits of the law? All of these limit questions raise issues addressed by ethical concepts of virtue.

One way of framing the question of how to proceed in this case is in terms of the virtues of the persons involved in the question as well as the virtues of the institution in which they are acting. Let us begin with the simple definition of a virtue as a strength of character that creates the capacity for moral existence. This strength in persons can be seen in terms of the character of their will, disposition, imagination, and purpose. All of these psychological attributes are formed over time into habits. Similarly, institutions can be seen as exhibiting virtues. These are institutional strengths that make moral existence possible for their members and for other institutions as well. Institutions may seek to cultivate virtues of justice, fairness, or openness. Both of these kinds of virtue are at work in this case.

Institutionally, this ecclesial body has the habit of treating its members as citizens with a wide panoply of rights. Thus, the institution is restrained in disciplining and guiding its members because it assumes, let us say, that they have an independent theological existence rooted in their baptism. This is quite different, for instance, from an institution that treats its members like children of stern but loving parents. There, the habits of nurture, direct chastisement, guidance, tutelage, and protection are much more evident in the policies and practices of the institution. Both institutional habits have been important in the historic life of Christianity and also appear in this case, though it is clear that the citizen habits of this institution dominate significantly the parental habits. Not only do the parishioners have citizen-like rights but so does the pastor, who is not merely an employee to be discharged at will but a kind of citizen in an elected office in the church.

This mixture of citizenship and parentalist virtues in the institution confronts the Committee with personal as well as group challenges. Clearly, the Committee, as a group with its own character, has to chart its way into the gray area beyond the law's limits. Essentially, it must navigate according to the lodestar of ecclesial good. But the night is dark and cloudy. Each individual in the group must also draw on certain virtues to participate in this voyage. How might we speak about these virtues?

In order to get at these virtues we need to frame their institutional setting more precisely and draw to some degree on a theory about institutional life. We can envision institutions as a complex web of mutual expectations and obligations. These expectations crystallize around particular structures, like committees, boards, councils, senates, conferences, and the like, as well as around roles, such as president, secretary, treasurer, pastor, deacon, and trustee. The function of law in this network is to facilitate trust among the members so they can work together for the common good of the institution. Without this primordial trust and its daily ratification through law-abiding behavior in the institution, the institution itself breaks down and it fails to fulfill its purposes.

Theologically, we can see this centrality of trust in our concepts of faith, of God as covenant-maker, and of ourselves as covenant-creatures. We can see it in our concepts of grace as the capacity to entrust ourselves to God in response to God's entrustment of the divine mystery to us. Although this theological ground can be nuanced in various ways, it is a central way we can get at the connection between our life in faith and our life in institutions. In either case, we live in a web of trust that seeks durability in law.

At the same time, our life in trust lives with constant mistrust. Our life experience and our knowledge of history present us with trust that is broken, with trust placed in false places and people, with trust that disables us. One expression of this mistrust in our institutional life can be seen in how we decide which groups or officials we can trust with what knowledge. How public can we be about a matter? Some statements can appear with little fear in the widest, most expansive publics. Scientific claims are like this. Other claims, as in a criminal trial, require the more limited public of a courtroom, lest an inflamed mob or a callous media horde carry out its snap judgments. Still others, like a shameful violation of other people's trust, need the shelter of private confession, which can only be a "public" in a representative way. *In extremis* we finally stand alone in "God's public" through prayer and contemplation.

How we negotiate the tensions and differences among these publics requires great discretion. The Committee faces the tension between publicity and secrecy in its work. Its wider institution strongly evidences the virtues of publicity, such as open disclosure, full debate, and collective judgment. These institutional values generally operate to enhance trust by giving each person some control over how he or she is treated in the institution, even if very indirectly. However, there are times, as in this case, when too much publicity threatens the fragile network of trust, either between pastor and parishioners or among the Committee members themselves. The Committee's search for the good of the institution, balanced with the good of the members in their various roles, demands a strictly limited publicity for its activity.

This kind of situation highlights the importance of the classic virtue of prudence. I would like to specify it in this situation as discretionary judgment. The virtues of discretionary judgment require a capacity to hold opposing values in tension as well as to select the appropriate level of publicity in which to seek the overall good of the institution. This imaginative work of discretion also requires the fundamental classical virtue of courage. Courage itself, aside from the sheer disciplining of our natural fears, can be seen as a choice of which public we wish to be remembered by. It is not merely a matter of avoiding potential shame and disapproval, but of which public we want our deeds remembered in. To whom, finally, are we accountable?

Each of these publics, no matter how small, requires this exercise of courage. Each public requires in us the capacity to give intelligible voice to our convictions in the face of possible disconfirmation by the claims of others. Legal publics exist to manage the scope and severity of this disconfirmation, even as they shape how we express our claim. Ecclesial publics, because they expect even deeper self-disclosure, must provide a greater array of small and large publics in which people can gain the virtues necessary for faithful existence. It was the violation of expectations within some of these limited publics that generated the Committee's quandary in the first place. Now it must draw on the virtues of its members as well as of itself as a group to negotiate the passage out of these violations into a possible regeneration of trust in the wider institution.

How, then, might we speak of the appropriate virtues for this discretionary work among the little and large publics of the church and civil society? We can imagine the members of the Committee proceeding in this way: They might first try to establish some common assumptions in the group about the nature of the challenge they face. I have cast the problem as one of public trust. Both the alleged wrongdoings and the process by which the Committee deals with these claims involve the violation and reconstruction of public trust in the institution and between it and the environing society. This is the ecclesial good that should guide its discretionary judgments. The ethical question poses itself in terms of what personal and group virtues are necessary to the achievement of this higher level of public trust.

In a situation at the boundaries of clearly defined law, the members of the group need to heighten their capacity to trust one another. This begins with an agreement about the situation they face and the primary good they seek to advance. In order to heighten their internal trust they need the virtues of honesty, clarity of expression, sincerity, ability to listen, and the ability to persuade and be persuaded. The latter two strengths are ways of understanding the virtue of humility within a network of communicative trust. Sometimes, to achieve this trust, groups will ask everyone to recite their life story and reveal any possible conflicts of interest relevant to the case at hand. Sometimes this self-revelation is helpful but other times it avoids the question of whether the members have the capacities to help the group move ahead with its ethical task and aim. In any event, this formation of what the German philosopher Juergen Habermas calls "communicative competence" and of simple trustworthiness cannot occur without these communicative virtues.

Notice here how this task draws on classic virtues like humility or honesty but recasts them as the task of building trust through communication rather than through obedience to external orders. The disciplines by which virtues crystallize as habits are not modeled in this case on the image of making our passions instruments of our reason and will. That, it seems to me, is the received, somewhat unconscious way we perceive them. Rather, these virtues arise in the discipline of communicative interaction. They arise in the process of self-disclosure, listening (with more than our ears), and struggling together for a common world of understanding. This decisive shift in our understanding of these virtues occurs because the wider framework of understanding rests on a conception of public life rooted in ultimate convictions about God and God's ways with the creation. The ecclesial institution is seen here as a testing ground and rehearsal space of our capacity for this public life as well as of our capacity to deal with our sin and needs for secrecy.

Beyond its internal work of trust-building, the Committee needs to keep remembering that it is in some sense a representative assembly. Its members and the group as a whole are the means by which the larger institution has assembled to deal with its common life. The imaginative work of representation is crucial to the moral life, for it establishes in our characters the publics to which we are loyal and accountable. It shapes the kinds of concerns that are uppermost in our minds when we speak, listen, argue, and negotiate in our immediate assemblies and meetings. In this situation the members imagine themselves as representing the church's wider assembly, the relevant congregations, and the civil public. Beyond that they also need to imagine themselves as representing the universal church, past, present, and future. Finally, each of them remembers himself or herself as representing the Christ into whom they have been baptized. That is, each of them is to represent the spirit of Christ in that meeting. Each of them is a representative of Christ's presiding power in that assembly. In this sense, each member understands himself or herself, to extend this conceptual scheme, as participating in the very public where God's Spirit presides. This is the kind of imaginative representation that shapes our understanding of conscience, which is, to reframe Pope Paul II's phrase in *Veritatis Splendor,* an imaginative reconstruction of our internal conversations with and before God.

This is a tall order indeed. This virtue of representation rests on our imaginative capacities, our capacities for empathic understanding, and our capacity to be transparent to our represented publics without yielding our own unique creative capacities. Both the Committee as a whole and the persons within it need to manifest this virtue of representation. The capacity for representation is not unlike that of acting, in which we take on a role and try to re-present the persona of the character in a play. It requires the work of rehearsal and the acquisition of an imaginative repertoire that is often lost in a world focusing simply on our own expression of our unique selves.

In seeking to represent the conversation and argument of these wider publics in its own deliberations, the Committee goes not merely beyond the law but beneath it, back to its own grounds and purposes. The law is seen as existing to preserve the basic web of trust that makes social and institutional life possible. By seeking to re-present the basic publics of the church's life, the Committee, though operating discretely and in that sense in some secrecy, can also anticipate and guide whatever degree of public argument might arise out of its decisions and actions. Its secrecy is not a secrecy of hiding from the law but of working beyond its limits. It is a return to the embryonic assembly, with its principles of public trust, that originated the church's law in the first place. The two forms of secrecy may look the same to the outside publics, but the latter can stand the light of publicity and the former cannot. It is a crucial difference and one that we can often collapse when we forget that it is our task to represent these wider publics rather than our own narrow interests.

The case with which we began poses some classic dilemmas of institutional life, whether in the church, in secular corporations, or in civil life. In framing these dilemmas as dilemmas of publicity and secrecy, of discretion and simple adherence to law, and of procedure and institutional goods, we claim some new angles of vision on classic virtues of humility, courage, prudence, and honesty. The virtues of public trust and of representation, though not spelled out at this point in detail, point us to the way we need to rethink our understanding of virtue in terms of capacity for trustworthy communication and imaginative participation in the ultimately open public to which God calls us. While we cannot determine a successful outcome to the Committee's deliberations, we can hope that reflections like these might helpfully inform their search for the good of the church within the complexities of human aspiration and human failure.

C. The Measure of Justice

Chapter Nineteen

Vicious Virtue? Patience, Justice, and Salaries in the Church

by Karen Lebacqz and Shirley Macemon

Dear Staff-Parish Relations Committee:

Greetings in the name of Christ! I write to you with both prayer and pain in my heart. Two years ago, you praised my 13 years of service to First Church and asked what you could do to "make my life better here." I asked for a raise so that my wife and I could buy a house. With two growing boys, our two-bedroom apartment isn't big enough. (Remember, my salary is nearly that of some other ministers on staff at First Church, but I receive no housing allowance or other benefits. That means the total compensation of ordained associates is one and a half times what I receive.) You assured me that I would receive a significant increase in salary, not contingent upon full ordination. You led me to believe that a significant raise would be forthcoming more than a year ago.

Two years have gone by, and I have not received the promised raise. Last year I sought clarification from you, and again I understood that a raise was imminent. After waiting patiently, I now call upon the Committee to honor its implied promise. While I have no desire to leave First Church, the disparity between my salary and those of others rankles. In addition to the disappointment I feel, I must attend realistically to the needs of my family. I love First Church and have tried to serve it diligently over these years. Now I wonder if I should look more seriously at other possibilities. What are your intentions in this matter?

Sincerely yours,
Ron Cookson, Director of Youth Ministry

Dear Ron,

We have received your letter regarding compensation. We want to assure you that your work here at First Church is highly valued. Your skill with the youth has brought joy to our church on many levels. We do not want to lose you!

At the same time, we must ask for patience. We realize there is a discrepancy between your total compensation package and that of the ordained ministers on staff. Unfortunately, we have received little help from the national offices as to how to adjudicate such situations. Thus, we must work carefully, lest we set an unfortunate precedent. Moreover, as you know, our senior minister is on paid sick leave, we have just added another minister, and several staff have recently been increased from part-time to full-time. First Church faces a possible deficit of some $75,000 for salary and personnel expenses this year. It is not a good time for additional financial requests!

With regret, therefore, we must ask you to bear with us. We know this is difficult to hear, and must seem a cross to bear. Please remember that socioeconomic status is not a sign of divine approval. Christian ministers are called, as Paul said, to "follow the way of love" which is neither proud nor self-seeking, keeps no record of wrongs, but hopes and perseveres. We urge you to keep in mind the purposes of First Church that brought you to us originally, that bind us in Christian love, and that make all of our work more bearable.

Yours in Christ,
The Staff-Parish Relations Committee

Whether it is lack of funds or disputes over how to use assets, money creates problems in the church. In this case, money issues raise difficult questions for virtue ethics. We will argue that this case pushes us to see the need for a system of virtue ethics rather than a dependence on individual virtues alone, and that lifting up individual virtues without such a system can be a dangerous undertaking in which virtues become vices.

The case here is rather typical: A worker believes that he is worth more than his current salary. From his perspective, he has been treated unfairly—a promise was broken. The Committee responsible for salaries is facing budget strains while struggling to determine appropriate bonuses and pay raises. The Committee urges "patience."

Who among us has not been urged to be "patient" at some point? Who has not heard the plea that finances are tight and our needs must be put on hold? When is it appropriate to be patient and when not? Is there a point at which patience becomes not a virtue but a vice?

In our case, the Committee depends on Paul's Letter to the Corinthians: "Love is patient, love is kind. It does not envy, it does not boast, it is not proud . . . it is not self-seeking . . . it keeps no record of wrongs." Love "always hopes, always perseveres" (see 1 Cor 13:4–7). Though Paul does not use the word "virtue" but speaks rather of "fruits of the spirit," Joseph Kotva suggests that these fruits of the spirit can be seen as Christian virtues; some are shared with other virtue systems, and some are distinctive to Christianity.[1] For Paul, Christians are "called to patience and kindness, but warned of jealousy, arrogance, rudeness, irritability, or resentment. We are called to self-control concerning boastfulness or insisting on one's own way. We are encouraged . . . to endure everything."[2]

Using such a list of qualities, we can imagine a member of the Staff-Parish Relations Committee saying to Ron, "You should not be jealous of the other ministers. It is arrogant for you to push for a higher salary. Don't resent what others have, but be patient and glad to serve in Christ's name." Indeed, the Committee in our case study comes very close to hinting at precisely such a position. Any jealousy or resentment that Ron feels over the disparity in salaries would be seen as a vice to be purged, while patience emerges as the primary virtue.

In our view, such a position is a misuse of virtues. Precisely because Christians have available a listing of "fruits of the spirit," Christians may be especially prone to such misuses of virtues. We think with deep regret and shame of how African Americans were told to be "patient" and "wait" for justice to be done.[3] We think with pain and misgiving of the many women who have been counseled to be "patient" with abusive spouses. Patience in particular is a virtue prone to misuse, and so our focus in this essay will be on patience and its proper place in a *system* of virtues. We will argue that patience gets its proper place only in relationship to justice, and that justice in wages makes some difficult demands on churches.

The Place of Patience

The word "patience" comes from the Latin *patiens*, from *pati*—"to suffer." It is no wonder, then, that we hear a request to be "patient" as a request to "suffer in silence" or to wait without complaint. By asking Ron to exercise patience, the Committee no doubt intends that Ron should wait until they can handle things their own way and in their own time, and that he should wait without complaint, even if doing so means that he suffers. This is the common meaning of patience today.

In his classic study of the cardinal virtues, however, Josef Pieper offers a different understanding that will illumine the situation at First Church. Patience, says Pieper, is not "an indiscriminate, self-immolating, crabbed, joyless, and spineless submission to whatever evil is met with."[4] Patience, therefore, does not mean simply to "endure everything." Rather, patience is a way of enduring—a certain quality of spirit that refuses to be *disheartened* even when one knows that one is sustaining injury.

It is keeping one's spirit strong while enduring injustice. Patience is not simply sitting and waiting.

Patience is a way of enduring. What is endurance, then? In virtue tradition, endurance is a mode of resistance to evil. It is a component of *fortitude*, which is a steadfast realization of the good "in the face of injury or death, and undeterred by any spirit of compromise."[5] Fortitude—the strength to work for the good no matter the cost—encompasses both attack and endurance. When evil can be eradicated, it is to be attacked; when it cannot be eradicated, it is to be endured. Patience is the quality of spirit that allows one to endure—to sustain the struggle against evil in spite of the odds. Patience, then, is not simply waiting, but is the strengthening of the spirit precisely to sustain the struggle for good or for justice.

One can indeed urge Ron to be patient, then, but doing so does not mean urging Ron to sit and wait. It means urging Ron not to give up the desire to see justice prevail. Patience is needed because justice does not always come easily, and it is sometimes easier to give up the struggle than to persist. To be "patient" in the classical sense of this virtue is to have the spirit to persist and to sustain the struggle in the face of odds. To be patient is to be like the Canaanite woman in Matthew 15:21–28 who respectfully stated her case until Jesus responded by healing her daughter.

Patience is rightfully powerful within a system of virtues where *justice* is primary. *Fortitude* is the stance that supports the struggle for justice. *Patience* is key to fortitude. Justice must be enacted in this situation. Ron must speak out against injustice, "endure," and continue calling for justice. His "patience" does not lead him to wait forever to see justice done, to keep clarity about the rightness of the cause. He must not lose his spirit for speaking out and calling for justice even when it is not forthcoming. It is in this sense that Ron is called to exhibit patience. Patience as a means to enact justice, then, is quite different from what the Committee may intend if their request is equivalent to a request to "wait."

Justice and Salaries

Even when we agree that patience is appropriate as it leads to justice, and that justice is the primary virtue here, the Committee's dilemma remains. What does justice require in this case? What would constitute a "fair" salary for Ron? How is this to be determined? Once determined, how can a just compensation be effected if the church's compensation budget has already been expended?

A full discussion of these questions requires details that are beyond the scope of this essay. We can offer some preliminary thoughts, however. First, we note that the Committee may not be well served if it goes to the literature looking for guidance on salary practices.[6] In *The Multiple Staff Ministry*, for example, Marvin Judy notes the symbolic importance of money but quickly suggests that church staff need to be helped to gain satisfaction elsewhere: "A strong sense of identification with the goals of church staff often goes far to cause one to overlook what he considers to be an injustice in pay, and leaves the individual a more efficient employee and basically a better person."[7] Judy as much as suggests that virtue (being a "better person") consists of accepting rather than protesting salary injustices, and that churches should try to turn staff attention away from justice demands. This is exactly what the Committee does in its response to Ron when it suggests that he remember the goals of the church. To suggest that virtue consists in accepting injustice rather than in protesting it is a genuine perversion of Christian virtue tradition, in which patience serves to sustain the struggle for justice and for the realization of good.

Second, like many churches, First Church has vested a great deal of authority in the senior minister. Salary levels are technically the purview of the Staff-Parish Relations Committee, but in practice have been determined by the senior minister, who gives bonuses or raises to those who plead their cause most persuasively to him. Such practices are common but seldom lead to a just salary structure. Not surprisingly, the senior minister's attempts to provide "salary justice" on a case-by-case basis exacerbated the budget crisis and led to vast inequities in compensation. This situation exists not only in churches but potentially in any organization where salary increases are not tied to quantitative or qualitative metrics. The door is then open for raises based on likes and dislikes. Women and members of underrepresented groups suffer particularly under such practices because those responsible for determining salaries may not as easily appreciate their situation.

Third, a contract is not a guarantee of fair compensation. We are happy to report that no one at First Church suggested to Ron that he had signed a contract and simply needed to live with the results of that decision. However, the case can be made that the practices and polity of denominations and congregations increasingly adopt a business model and "contractual" view.[8] It is common in business practices to assume that a "fair" salary is whatever is agreed to at the time of hiring, specified in an implicit or explicit contract.

Contracts lie in the arena of commutative justice. In his classic study, *Economic Justice*, John Ryan describes a "rule of free contract" in which "[commutative] justice is realized whenever the contract is free from force or fraud. In such circumstances, both parties gain something and presumably are satisfied; otherwise, they would not enter the contract."[9] Such a rule underlies a common understanding of justice in American society. Robert Nozick gives voice to this understanding in his acclaimed study, *Anarchy, State, and Utopia*.[10] For Nozick, justice consists entirely of commutative or contractual exchange—so long as there has been no force or fraud, whatever is agreed to is by definition fair or just. Moreover, inequalities present no breaches of justice in this view so long as each exchange or agreement has not been forced or fraudulent.

Ron has been employed by First Church for fifteen years. Ron agreed to an original salary, considered fair at the time, and has received cost-of-living increases as well as some adjustments to reflect changes in his responsibilities. These increases have not, in fact, kept up with changes in the "market," so that others hired long after him and with considerably less experience are now making more money than he is. (Both authors of this essay have had precisely this experience.) Is it "fair" for others' salaries to be higher than Ron's simply because he agreed to an initial salary and the market has since changed? The "rule of free contract" and the libertarian theory of Robert Nozick would say "Yes." In such a view, what has happened to Ron may be unfortunate but it is not *unfair.*

However, John Ryan would disagree. Ryan holds that the rule of free contract is unjust. He notes (as have later critics of Nozick[11]) that many labor contracts are not "free" in any genuine sense: "The laborer does not agree to this wage because he prefers it to any other, but merely because he prefers it to unemployment, hunger, and starvation."[12] Often the employer is in a stronger bargaining position than is the prospective employee— for instance, if there are numerous applicants for the job, the salary can be set rather low. In such a case, if Ron wanted the job, he would be compelled to take the salary offered. If he needed to remain in a certain geographic region for family or health reasons, he would be even less free to bargain over salary.

Pieper argues that a contract, even *if* it is agreed to by both parties, can still be unfair. First, in Pieper's understanding of the four cardinal virtues, commutative justice deals with giving the other what is "due"[13] not simply what is contracted. This is in contrast to distributive justice, or "fair" disbursement of the common good, which we will discuss below. Central to determining what is "due" is a notion of "*restituo.*" *Restituo* (derived from the same root as our term "restitution") means restoring to the other that which is already his; hence, it implies that we must recognize that it is his.[14] In this case, Ron is asking the Committee to *recognize* that a higher salary is his due and right, in light of his training, experience, and skill, and also in light of their implicit promises to him. A crucial component of this argument—a component that virtue theory adds—is the recognition that the goods are "due" not because of a signed contract but because of the fundamental demand of justice that we recognize the worth and value of the other.

However, we would also argue that the issue of fair salary cannot be settled simply at the level of commutative justice, so we turn to distributive justice. *Distributive* justice addresses the fair disbursement of the common good. Goods are distributed by the person or persons who hold the role of steward of the goods. Previously, the senior minister had this power and exercised it as he saw fit. On the occasion of his leave, the committee members become stewards of the goods in a real sense and must reconcile promises made with funds available. Distributive justice calls for the goods to be distributed "proportionately." This means considering the "person" and his dignity. As Pieper puts it, "taking part in the realization of that good in accordance with the measure of *dignitas,* capacity, and ability that is distinctively his, this is the share that 'is due to' the individual and which cannot be withheld . . . [without violating] justice. . . ."[15]

Concretely, this means that the Committee must take into account two additional aspects of the situation. First, is the salary proffered a "living wage" that allows the worker to support himself and his family (e.g., to get into the housing market)?[16] If not, then the person is not recognized and justice has not been done. It is clear that Ron's current salary does not allow him to provide for his family in appropriate ways, such as being able to buy a modest home near the church. Second, the "dignity" of the person includes any special aptitude for the work or demonstrated "worthiness" or "meritorious service distinguished by public recognition."[17] It is clear from the record that Ron has performed "meritorious service distinguished by public recognition," as the music program of the First Church Youth Group has a national reputation. Under the demands of distributive justice, the Committee needs to provide to Ron enough to recognize his stature in his field, enough to support him and his family, and enough to offer him what is "due" to him as a contributing member of the community.

Although the Committee carries primary responsibility for seeing that distributive justice is done, it is not the only agent of justice here. At First Church, as in most local congregations, the quantifiable "common good" is the income from donations, facility use, and investments. Unlike industry, there is no profit goal; the common good is used to support the mission of the church. Salaries are part of this distribution, as they support the mission of the church. If salaries increase while the funds available do not, then there is less to support other forms of mission. We suggest, therefore, that virtue theory would also call the remainder of staff to account for how their salaries affect the common good. "In this instance [of distributive justice] the individual is not an independent, separate party to a contract . . . as in *justitia commutativa*. He is faced with a partner of higher rank, of which he himself is a part."[18] The "partner" here is the congregation. As members of that congregation, the staff are responsible to see that funds are used for the mission of the church in a fair manner. If persons of similar "worthiness" or "meritorious service distinguished by public recognition" receive vastly different remuneration, is one lucky while the other is the unfortunate recipient of an unjust wage, or are they both recipients of unjust wages? As justice is a cardinal virtue for all Christians, other staff must also exhibit this virtue and work to ensure that the compensation pool is fairly distributed and that they do not receive an unfair share.

Conclusion

Even though virtue theory illumines some of the issues at stake, wage distribution remains notoriously difficult. The questions we put here to others might also be put to us![19] We have no perfect resolution to Ron's case. Rather, we have a caution—that Christians beware of using a virtue such as patience outside of a careful context in which that virtue is embedded in a system of virtues. We also offer a perspective: Resolution of these matters calls for an understanding that *patience* is a component of *fortitude* that ultimately supports the struggle for *justice*. The proper stance of patience, therefore, is not spineless submission but a spirit of endurance that continues the struggle for justice. Typical salary practices, such as assigning responsibility for salaries to a senior pastor, often lead to inequitable and unjust compensation. The literature on compensation for church workers often runs counter to a virtue ethic approach. Just salaries are neither simply a matter of contract nor even of commutative justice alone, but of distributive justice in which disbursements are made with a view to the common good, which requires respecting the dignity of each person. Hence, responsibility for justice in compensation rests not only with the Committee that grants and approves compensation packages, but with all members of the church, including other staff who may be receiving unjust compensation. It is not only Ron who should struggle ceaselessly for justice to be done, but the Committee itself, even if doing so means that it must confront the congregation and other staff members with patterns of unjust practices that have built up in the church.

1. Joseph Kotva, Jr., *The Christian Case for Virtue Ethics* (Washington, D.C.: Georgetown University Press, 1996), 120.

2. Ibid., 121.

3. In his powerful "Letter from a Birmingham Jail," Martin Luther King, Jr., gives voice to the frustration of those who are told to "wait" for justice to be done: "For years now I have heard the word 'Wait!' It rings in the ear of every Negro with a piercing familiarity. This 'Wait' has almost always meant 'Never.'. . .We must come to see . . . that 'justice too long delayed is justice denied.'" In James M. Washington, ed., *A Testament of Hope: The Essential Writings and Speeches of Martin Luther King, Jr.* (San Francisco: Harper San Francisco, 1986).

4. Josef Pieper, *The Four Cardinal Virtues* (Notre Dame: University of Notre Dame Press, 1966 [first published 1954]), 129.

5. Ibid., 131.

6. The otherwise excellent volume by Julie L. Bloss entitled *The Church Guide to Employment Law* (Matthews, NC: Christian Ministry Resources, 1993), for example, does not discuss fairness in wages at all, but only whether churches are covered by minimum-wage standards, and whether they must comply with Title VII of the Civil Rights Act that prohibits discrimination, and EEOC guidelines that prohibit sexual harassment.

7. Marvin Judy, *The Multiple Staff Ministry* (Nashville: Abingdon Press, 1969), 62.

8. "Because the church as a whole has succumbed to the business model of operation . . . the pastor has become [simply] an employee. . . . " G. Lloyd Rediger, *Clergy Killers: Guidance for Pastors and Congregations Under Attack* (Louisville: Westminster/John Knox Press, 1997), 53.

9. John A. Ryan, *Economic Justice: Selections from Distributive Justice and a Living Wage,* ed., Harlan R. Beckley (Louisville: Westminster/John Knox Press, 1996 [first published 1906 and 1916]), 102.

10. Robert Nozick, *Anarchy, State and Utopia* (New York: Basic Books, 1974), chapter 7.

11. See, for example, Bruce A. Ackerman, *Social Justice in the Liberal State* (New Haven: Yale University Press, 1980), 188, 233, and passim.

12. Ryan, *Economic Justice,* 103.

13. Pieper, *The Four Cardinal Virtues,* 76.

14. Ibid., 78–79.

15. Ibid., 99.

16. Ryan, *Economic Justice,* 115. Ryan states that a worker "has a right to at least a *decent* livelihood . . . that may be summarily described as: Food, clothing and housing sufficient in quantity and quality to maintain the worker in normal health, in elementary comfort and in an environment suitable to the protection of morality and religion . . ."

17. Pieper, *The Four Cardinal Virtues,* 100.

18. Ibid., 82.

19. As Pogo said: "We have met the enemy and they is us!" Walt Kelly, "POGO" comic strip, Earth Day 1971.

Chapter Twenty

"His Dogs More Than Us"
Virtue in Situations of Conflict Between Women Religious and Their Ecclesiastical Employers

by Anne E. Patrick, SNJM

What does a virtue ethic require of Catholic women religious who find themselves in intractable conflicts with their ecclesiastical employers? This chapter will explore the question in light of the paradigm shift in the understanding of moral goodness now underway among many Christians, which involves a change from a patriarchal understanding of virtue to an egalitarian-feminist one.[1]

In what follows, I shall illustrate the difference this paradigm shift is making by analyzing two cases of conflict between women religious and the churchmen who employed them, one from the Diocese of Brooklyn in the 1930s and another from Key West, Florida in 1989–90. The first instance shows women of strong character who made difficult choices that were essentially guided by the patriarchal understanding of what "good sisters" should do. The second case shows women of equal dedication to the church's mission, whose egalitarian-feminist understanding of their moral ideals and obligations led to a dramatically different series of responses.

It is important to note three things at the outset of this comparative case study. First, although these cases focus on the women religious and their differing ways of practicing virtue when treated unjustly, clearly sisters share in the sinfulness of humanity. There are indeed instances of their own unjust behavior that warrant ethical scrutiny, although such is not my focus here. Second, the categories of patriarchal and egalitarian-feminist paradigms of virtue are abstracted from the complexities of life. I employ this typology for its heuristic value without intending to oversimplify the human experiences involved or to deny that middle positions exist between the two extremes. Finally, I have weighed the question of whether justice would be better served by fictionalizing these accounts because they are told from the churchwomen's point of view and the churchmen involved in the conflicts might tell them quite differently. The decision to present the actual details as found in the convent archives and through interviews with sisters was reached for two reasons. First, the value of honesty between ministers and laity is central to the ethical analysis, and seems well served by providing historical facts; "silence" about truths that are scandalous tends to perpetuate injustice, whereas there is more hope of addressing systemic problems when the facts are brought to light. Moreover, the details of the recent case were well-known to the public at the time they occurred, because the dispute received considerable attention in the Florida press and national mention on the Cable News Network.

The chapter's title, "His Dogs More Than Us," was chosen to honor the experience of all Catholic sisters who have endured something like the injustice known by an eighty-nine-year-old nun interviewed in July 1998. Without bitterness, she summed up her years in an abusive employment situation by saying quite simply, "Father cared more about his dogs than about us."[2]

"His Dogs More Than Us"
—A Case from the Brooklyn Diocese, 1939

The nun who objected to the pastor's preferential concern for his dogs was one of five Sisters of the Holy Names of Jesus and Mary withdrawn by her provincial superior from the Catholic parish in St. James, Long Island, when the school year ended in 1939: the *superior and principal of the school, three young teachers, and a sister who cooked for the convent and did sacristy work in the church. The last received no pay; the four nuns involved in the school each received a stipend of $33 per month. The dogs were three—a Spitz and two shepherds—and Sister Joan Teresa, also interviewed in 1998, recalls them as "kind of nasty." One had ripped the veil of Sister Margaret of Jesus, and most of the women religious were afraid of the pastor's well-kept animals. They also lived in some fear of Father Clarence E. Murphy's power over their own lives, for he controlled the heat and hot water and forbade them to talk with parishioners or to accept rides from them, although the sisters had no car.*

Several sisters alive today recall their assignment to St. James as a "hardship post" because of the overly controlling pastor, although they loved the people and found their teaching work rewarding. A young sister's friendly conversation with a parishioner would be noticed by Father Murphy, and a complaint made to the superior. There was no furnace until the sisters put on a school play to raise money for one, but even after heat became a possibility, the pastor kept the thermostat turned down and locked. The pupils wore coats in the classrooms, and each winter one or another of the sisters would be hospitalized for an illness such as pneumonia. On those occasions when Sister Casimira, the superior, felt impelled to beg Father Murphy for more heat, she would ask the other sisters for special prayers. Her situation was similar to that of the fictional superior in J.F. Powers's short story from the 1940s, "The Lord's Day." In that story, the need was for a stove "that worked," and the pastor's response was not to replace the stove but rather to chop down the last trees remaining in the parish school yard, on the feeble premise that the trees were preventing the stove from drawing air properly.³ The nuns in the real case fared no better. In their convent home, the sisters could have hot water for bathing only on Wednesdays and Saturdays. They remember with gratitude the times when members of their religious community came by train from Coney Island, where they staffed a thriving school and enjoyed a very positive relationship with the generous pastor of Our Lady of Solace Church, Father Francis Froelich. On these rare visits, the superior from Coney Island would bring cookies and candy to St. James, for she knew that the sisters there were getting by on a very slim food budget, supplemented by donations from parishioners' vegetable gardens.

Finally, after years of unsuccessful efforts to improve things, and in the wake of Sister Casimira's hospitalization for pneumonia, Mother Mary of Lourdes, the provincial superior, concluded she could no longer leave her sisters in this intolerable situation and informed the bishop of Brooklyn, Most Rev. Thomas E. Molloy, of her decision. He countered by saying that if the sisters left St. James they would also have to leave their other mission in his diocese, the much loved school on Coney Island. Nearly sixty years later, Sister Joan Teresa recalled her provincial superior's response: "Very well, your excellency, we will withdraw from the diocese."

Whether Molloy actually hoped the provincial would reconsider keeping sisters at St. James in order to hold on to the excellent situation at Coney Island is not known, but what is clear is that Mother Mary of Lourdes had reached a point where she judged it wrong to ask sisters to endure St. James any longer. Although the practice of religious obedience was very strict at that time, community members knew that the provincial had difficulty appointing new sisters to the mission. And what the sisters remember above all is that when their provincial told them they were leaving the parishes, she enjoined them not to discuss this with anyone. The chronicles (official records) of the two convents are studies in the sort of restraint exercised by women who were striving for the ideals of virtue held up to them under the patriarchal paradigm. An entry for May 28, 1939, comments on the final May procession at Sts. Philip and James parish in St. James, Long Island: "Our pastor speaks at great length about the devotion to Our Blessed Mother and the imitation of her virtues," and one for June 25 remarks on the school graduation ceremony: After Father Murphy had presented prizes for scholastic achievement, "Benediction of the Blessed Sacrament brings to a close the simple yet impressive graduation, the last to be held under the direction of the Sisters of the Holy Names."

There is no word critical of the priest or bishop in the chronicles and, indeed, the superior who had been hospitalized with pneumonia, Sister Casimira, was never known to have complained about Father Murphy's unreasonable control and stinginess. *"I don't want to have to account to God for being irreverent to priests,"* Sister Joan Teresa remembers her saying. The final entry for St. James, dated July 1, 1939, notes simply that the superior and the cook departed for Maryland, and *"This marks the final departure of the Sisters of the Holy Names, who have labored so zealously during the past seventeen years for the glory of the Holy Names of Jesus and Mary."* The statistics at the closing of the mission at St. James showed there had been five sisters and ninety-six pupils. The Coney Island mission sacrificed at the bishop's insistence had been a much stronger operation; there were five hundred pupils in Our Lady of Solace School when the thirteen Sisters of the Holy Names withdrew. One can infer that leaving this parish was much more difficult for the sisters, and that they enjoyed a much better relationship with their pastor, on the basis of things that are included in the chronicles for that mission, which contrast starkly with things left unsaid in the chronicles for the problem parish. According to Sister Charles Raymond, a teacher at Coney Island, their local superior had broken the news of the provincial's decision to remove them sooner than she was supposed to reveal it, after nuns who were shipping boxes of books to another school had been asked by postal clerks if they were moving. The official word came only one week before graduation, as the chronicles for June 18, 1939, state: *"Mother Mary of Lourdes, Provincial Superior, pays us a visit and officially announces the news of our withdrawal from the diocese of Brooklyn because of lack of teachers. We accept the decision of Authority and beg graces from the Holy Ghost for those upon whom fall such painful duties."*

Although the sisters' chronicles for St. James give no indication of the pastor's opinions and, indeed, imply that he uttered no *words of gratitude about their seventeen years of labor in the parish, the entries for June 25, 1939, at Coney Island carry an altogether different tone. This pastor did not tell the full story to his parishioners, but he did his best, within the model of virtue reigning at the time, to show his appreciation for the nuns and to invite the people to accept the loss of their services without resentment. The final pages of convent records include these entries:*

> *OFFICIAL ANNOUNCEMENT—This morning at the various Masses, Rev. Francis Froelich, Pastor, explains to the parishioners the reason for the Sisters' withdrawal. His words of appreciation for the work accomplished by the Sisters of the Holy Names, and the assurance of his sincere regret at our departure, tend to make his people understand and help to remove any ill feeling which might exist among them because of the present circumstances.*

> *GRADUATION—Thirty-eight of our eighth grade boys and girls receive graduation honors this afternoon. Rev. Francis Froelich, Pastor, reminds them of their duties as Catholics and as American citizens, and again emphasizes the loyalty they should prove to their school and to their Sisters. Father seized this last opportunity to express once more his gratitude to the Sisters.*

The wording of these chronicle entries is governed by a concern not to question the judgments of religious authorities, whether those of bishop or provincial superior. But it is clear that their author is worried that the laity may be hurt by the sudden departure of the sisters from their children's school because of "lack of teachers" elsewhere. The last entry for Coney Island, dated July 3, observes that "Since June 28 the sisters have gradually left, to take up their work [summer study] at the various universities and today the remaining three bid a final farewell to the work which has been ours for twenty-one years. God wills it thus and we humbly submit to his designs in our regard."

"Save the Nuns"
—A Case from the
Archdiocese of Miami, 1989–90

Silence and humble submission were notably absent in the more recent case of conflict between women religious and their ecclesiastical employers, which showed women operating under dramatically different ideals of what it means to be a "good sister" than were exhibited in the pre–Vatican II era. Instead of emphasizing obedience, denial of conflict, and institutional loyalty, the paradigm of virtue inspiring their responses to difficulties laid stress on justice, honesty, and personal responsibility. No longer was God's will assumed to be contained within the directives of ecclesiastical authority; rather, the presumption was that women and men in ministry ought to dialogue together in an effort to discern what God might want for the people. And if dialogue proves impossible, then the people who will lose the women's ministries have a right to know what has been going on. Sisters are no longer willing to "cover" for the clergy or to absorb the blame for decisions beyond their control.

In August of 1989, at the invitation of the pastor of St. Mary Star of the Sea Church, the same religious community that had reluctantly withdrawn from the Brooklyn diocese fifty years earlier sent four women to reestablish their mission in Key West, Florida. The returning Sisters of the Holy Names were warmly welcomed by islanders and church officials, including the pastor, Father Eugene M. Quinlan, and the archbishop of Miami, Most Rev. Edward A. McCarthy. This community of women religious had previously ministered in Key West, primarily in schools, from 1868 until 1983, and had played an important role in the island's history. Their voluntary departure because of a significant decline in their numbers after the Second Vatican Council had left a void in Key West, and in 1988 Father Quinlan, who came as pastor in 1986, contacted the community.

Initially the pastor's purpose was to make arrangements for relocating the graves of sisters buried on land they originally owned, but which had been turned over to the archdiocese in the 1960s when the religious community could not otherwise meet debt payments for building projects that had been necessary for its work on the island. This contact in 1988 soon led to discussions of the sisters returning to minister in Key West, and on January 20, 1989, Father Quinlan wrote to Sister Kathleen Griffin, the provincial director, describing four possible positions and expressing "my fondest desire that the Sisters will return to St. Mary's."[4]

After prayer and planning among several sisters with their provincial leaders, four were chosen to re-found the mission. Sister Dolores Wehle, who had previously worked for eighteen years in Key West (nine years teaching in the parish school, and nine serving as its principal), would come as Director of Religious Education, and Sister Eileen Kelleher as Associate Director of Religious Education; Sister Mary Patricia Vandercar would do historical research on the parish and convent, and Sister Audrey Rowe, who had taught in Key West during the 1950s, would focus on visiting the island's many AIDS patients and others suffering from illness. In August 1989 there was a joyful celebration when these women religious came to Key West, reestablishing a long-valued connection between the sisters and the islanders.

Within a few months, however, the seemingly fine second foundation had fallen apart. At a parish staff meeting on December 5, 1989, a long-simmering misunderstanding between the pastor and the sisters over whether the two women with expertise in religious education should be expected to teach classes in the parish school erupted into an emotional exchange that led to the pastor's declaring that the sisters' contracts would not be renewed for the following year. In a December 7 letter to

Sister Kathleen Griffin, Father Quinlan expressed his under-standing of the problems and stated his decision, indicating that salaries would be paid through August 15 but the four sisters would have to leave their leased residence by July 1, 1990. Griffin responded on December 22 that "the nature and content of your letter came as a great surprise," and said she needed to pray and reflect on the matter and would visit Key West again in February. On January 8, 1990, Quinlan wrote to Griffin that his decision was final, though he regretted that "the aspirations I visualized over the founding Sisters returning to Key West have not been met."

According to Sister Rose Gallagher, Apostolic Director for the women's community, on January 15, 1990, there was a meet-ing of Griffin and herself with the Vicar for Religious in Miami, Sister Denise Marie Callaghan, for the sake of exploring "approaches to solutions," but these proved fruitless. Essentially the archdiocese viewed it as a local matter and did not question a pastor's decision. Gallagher sums up the community officers' failure to gain a hearing beyond the vicar's office thus: "Neither the Vicar for Religious nor the provincial were able to obtain any appointments with the archbishop or archdiocesan officials, or even acknowledgment that correspondence or phone calls were received between mid-January and May."[5]

On February 28, 1990, Sister Eileen Kelleher wrote to Father Quinlan and to Archbishop McCarthy to tender her resignation as "Minister of Adult Education" and to explain her reasons for leaving before the contract expired. To Quinlan she pointed out that he had objected to several initiatives she had proposed after listening to parish members, which ranged from planning a parish retreat day to forming a group for separated and divorced Catholics. She lamented the lack of a functioning parish council or liturgy committee, and expressed dismay at the discovery that she was being paid from parish school funds, when she under-stood her position to be concerned with adult religious forma-tion. To the archbishop she mentioned that she had uprooted herself from a thriving parish ministry in Schenectady, New York in order to address "the greater need" in Key West, but that her efforts on behalf of adult education and sacramental preparation had been blocked at every turn by the pastor. She concluded by voicing a prayer that "someone will be attentive" to the people's great needs. Quinlan tersely acknowledged her resignation and asked her to turn in all parish materials by its effective date, March 8; the archbishop did not respond.

Meanwhile the provincial superior agreed to meet with a group of parishioners who had requested this in order to "gain some understanding of why the sisters were leaving so that they, too, could seek solutions," as Gallagher recalled. Shortly thereafter, Griffin and the other three members of the sisters' provincial council prepared a letter that was addressed to the archbishop and the members of St. Mary Star of the Sea Parish.[6] This letter of March 29, 1990, was also shared with all the New York Province Sisters of the Holy Names. This public letter is a step that would have been unthinkable in the days of Mother Mary of Lourdes's conflict with the bishop of Brooklyn. The fact that it was sent illustrates not only the great changes in sisters' ideals of virtue since the 1930s but also the enhanced position of the laity in the post–Vatican II church. The letter opens by explaining the reason it was prepared:

> *Since we believe that only Father Eugene Quinlan's story will be shared at the Archdiocesan and perhaps local level, we wish to lay out for you the sequence of events surrounding the return and dismissal of our sisters in Key West as we Sisters of the Holy Names experienced them.*

> *Our community's great joy, enthusiasm and sense of celebration at the return of four sisters to Key West in August 1989 have changed, in a few short months, to deep sorrow at the news that we are being asked to give up our mission among you and leave after less than a year.*

There follow several pages of narrative, based on provincial administration records of events from 1989, which describe the way plans had been made to return to Key West after the community's reduced numbers had led to their voluntary withdrawal in 1983. The letter includes a powerful statement of the historical connection between the sisters and Key West:

> *The people of Key West hold a unique place in the hearts and in the history of the Sisters of the Holy Names. One hundred twenty-two years ago, in 1868, before bridges, railroad or air travel, we came to Key West, bought and cleared our land and began our ministry of education in the faith. During periods when there were no priests on the island we were present with you to gather people for worship, to baptize, to teach. During severe epidemics we were present to nurse the sick, comfort the dying and conduct burial services. During the Spanish–American War we converted the school into a hospital and nursed the wounded. During calm and hurricanes, in periods of great economic growth and severe depression, we were present with you, in good times and bad. The return of four sisters to Key West was prompted by our desire to resume a long ministerial history of response to your needs.*

The letter concludes with the sisters' clear statement of the message they most wanted to leave with the people, something that their predecessors at Coney Island were not able to express:

> *It is not our choice to leave. While Father Quinlan may choose to exercise his authority to dismiss these four sisters who freely and lovingly chose to return to Key West, his choice can never erode or dismiss the affection and the bonds we sisters have with you.*

Scrutiny of the women's narrative reveals that the seeds of the misunderstanding over classroom responsibilities were sown in the early stages of the negotiations for the return of the sisters, for the provincial officers had not known that "the salaries of at least two of the sisters are paid by the school even though they do not work for the school." The women had presumed that job descriptions would be refined cooperatively after some on-site experience and dialogue and, apparently, Quinlan had not told them he was funding the religious education positions from the school budget. Meanwhile school administrators were counting on having nuns in their classrooms, but Sister Dolores Wehle (who had been principal of that school for nine years) understood her role to be one of working with teachers, not pupils, and Sister Eileen Kelleher expected to be doing adult faith formation.

On March 21 the provincial superior had come to Key West, where she spoke with the pastor and deacon, the sisters, and the laity in separate meetings. The March 29 letter states that "Father reiterated the finality of his decision that the sisters must leave," while parishioners were still "seeking a compromise, believing that Father Quinlan has left an 'open door,' in their view." It further observes that "the parishioners and Sister Kathleen [Griffin] noted that the sisters' names and positions are still not on the parish bulletin although they were assigned last June and arrived in Key West in August."

After their meeting with Griffin, a group of concerned parishioners undertook a public campaign to "save the nuns." Their response exhibited both their post-conciliar optimism about having a "say" in matters concerning their parish life and also their trust that church officials would respond to the pressure tactics often employed by interest groups in the United States. Thus on April 22 they published a full-page ad in the Key West Citizen, *featuring a picture of the foundress of the community, Blessed Marie Rose Durocher, above the banner headline "Save the Nuns." The ad also included historical material from the sisters' open letter of March 29, and declared in bold type, "It is not their choice to leave." Readers were encouraged to write to the arch-*

bishop and other churchmen and to display the ad in their windows. Two more display ads appeared in subsequent weeks, one carrying the entire text of the March 29 letter from the provincial council. Other activities organized by the laity included distributing hundreds of "Save the Nuns" buttons and having nightly gatherings to recite the rosary at the Lourdes grotto near the church. This campaign resulted in frequent coverage in the Miami and Key West papers, and even mention on the television Cable News Network. According to Sister Rose Gallagher, the campaign finally led to the archbishop's contacting the sisters:

> A biplane flew over the island after all the masses one weekend in April trailing the message, "Father, please keep the nuns." It was this event that prompted the first contact from the archdiocese. The archbishop phoned the provincial to tell her to remove the sisters as soon as possible. The provincial met with her council, talked with the sisters in Key West and then finalized their departure in May, three months ahead of time.[7]

Some sixteen months after the sisters' departure the Miami Herald reported in a September 5, 1991, article that Father Quinlan would be leaving Key West to become pastor in Marathon, Florida. The story noted that "Quinlan, 57, spent thousands of hours working on behalf of the sick and helped secure a property for . . . a group that supports people with AIDS. But it was his decision to force the nuns out of Key West that brought him the most publicity."[8]

Quinlan's successor has since been supplied by the archdiocese of Miami; some sisters have visited Key West on occasion but the community has no plans to resume ministry there. And, the archdiocese holds title on land where sisters labored for over a century, which has appreciated considerably in value since the women gave it up in the 1960s to avoid bankruptcy over a loan incurred for the sake of continuing their ministry in Key West. In

1996 the parish published a sesquicentennial booklet in which the Sisters of the Holy Names figure prominently for 115 years, from their arrival in 1868 until their voluntary withdrawal in 1983. In the entry for 1989, no mention is made of the return and rejection of four living sisters, although Father Quinlan's reburial of eighteen deceased sisters "next to the grotto which they had built in the early twenties" is noted. The pastor's subsequent transfers and eventual "medical retirement" are also mentioned under 1989, although he left the parish only in 1991. The year 1990, with its divisions over the unsuccessful "save the nuns" campaign is omitted from the historical record.[9]

Implications of These Cases for Virtue Ethics

Although an idealized picture of the early church declares, "The community of believers were of one heart and one mind," (see Acts 4:32), there is evidence that disputes and conflict have been part of Christian life from the very beginning. The examples of conflict between women religious and their ecclesiastical employers described above are hardly unique in the church's history and, indeed, sisters are by no means the only Catholics to have felt powerless when they were in dispute with church authorities. But the cases under consideration here are interesting from the standpoint of virtue ethics because they illustrate a clear development in the ideals of virtue held by women who occupy an important role in Catholic ecclesiology. This development is arguably an instance of a larger paradigm shift where virtue is concerned, which has been in progress among Christians ever since the experiences of World War II and the trials at Nuremburg put in question the great emphasis on submission and obedience that had held sway in the past. When it began, the paradigm shift placed responsibility instead of obedience at the center of Christian ethics, and among Catholics there followed an emphasis on "co-responsibility in the church," which took hold at the time of the Second Vatican Council, largely through the influence of the Belgian cardinal, Leon-Joseph Suenens.[10] Subsequently the paradigm shift has been greatly influenced by insights from feminist theory, to the point where it can now be called a change from a patriarchal to an egalitarian-feminist understanding of virtue.[11]

The patriarchal paradigm of virtue is based on a now-discredited view of women's alleged ontological inferiority to men, which although rejected at the conscious level by most persons today, nevertheless continues to exert residual influence. This paradigm tends to see virtue in light of the domination-subordination motif that has long characterized relations between men and women, colonial powers and the colonized, and rulers and the ruled. Virtue is primarily a matter of reason exerting control over the passions and the unruly body, as well as over impulses to insubordination within social systems. As a result, subordinates are expected to cultivate the virtues of obedience, docility, and loyalty. Moreover, ideals for character tend to be segregated along gender lines, with men trained to think in terms of justice and rights, and women expected to excel in humility, charity, and chastity.

The egalitarian-feminist paradigm, by contrast, is built on the principle of the equal ontological status of women and men, and it emphasizes *respect* for human dignity and material creation rather than control. Instead of obedience, the central virtue for this paradigm is justice, and it tends to promote gender-integrated ideals for character. Discipline continues to be valued, but is viewed less rigidly than under the patriarchal model. Rather than expecting men to take care of the public sphere and women to keep the fires of charity burning at home, this paradigm sees love and justice as mutually reinforcing norms that should govern both sexes equally. Although the present imbalance of power within the Roman Catholic Church where gender roles are concerned is defended by Vatican authorities on theological grounds, believers influenced by the new paradigm regard these arguments as limited human positions rather than divinely endorsed realities. The two types of virtue paradigms are, of course, abstractions and, in real life, few characters fully embody either one; there is a wide range of "middle" positions along the spectrum from patriarchal to egalitarian-feminist understandings of virtue.

The present time of transition may be likened to the tumultuous ending of a sexist ice age. As a result of the dramatic changes this entails, persons committed to church service are destined to deal with a good deal of conflict, misunderstanding, and disappointment. This is the case across the board, regardless of gender and whether one's stance is basically patriarchal or egalitarian-feminist. Here the focus has been on the practical difficulties experienced by women religious, who have traditionally been subordinated within Catholic structures, and whose stories have not been widely known in the church precisely because of the sexist ideology and notions of goodness long held by Catholics. Undoubtedly the dramatic decline in membership among communities of women religious in recent decades is partly due to the clash between the ideals of love and justice articulated in church documents and the experience of male domination that perdures in Catholic institutions. Today in the United States there are fewer than half the number of sisters than there were in 1966, and women with healthy self-concepts are increasingly skeptical of involvement in an ecclesiastical system where their talents are destined to be circumscribed by a sexist power differential.[12]

Certainly many sisters are happily employed in parish or diocesan settings today, but their fate depends on which priest or bishop currently has authority over them, and things could change drastically with a new appointment. As the cases from Brooklyn and Key West show, when conflicts arise between women religious and their ecclesiastical employers, the power of office enjoyed by clergy of all ranks too often trumps considerations that would otherwise be relevant. There are some exceptions that offer grounds for hope, but in too many instances it happens that women who try to "fight this system" are destined to lose, at least in the short run.

In these conflict situations it tends to be the case that sisters who understand virtue under a patriarchal paradigm will respond by following what may be called a "military obedience and institutional loyalty" model, as did Mother Mary of Lourdes when faced with the ultimatum of the bishop of Brooklyn in 1939. She saw her duty as threefold: protecting the well-being of the sisters by removing them from St. James, accepting the resultant ouster from Coney Island, and keeping the record of events as hidden as possible to protect the image of clerical authorities. In this context she insisted that the sisters should not know they were leaving Coney Island until the last minute, and she forbade them to discuss the true reason for their departure, especially with the parishioners. By contrast, those inspired by an egalitarian-feminist paradigm will be guided by a "personal responsibility and social justice" model, as was the case in Key West fifty years later, when the provincial administrators felt it appropriate to inform the sisters and the laity that the provincial director, Sister Kathleen Griffin, had been unable to obtain a hearing from the archbishop and that the sisters had not chosen to leave.

Given the tensions of a transitional period, there are three virtues that especially commend themselves to women religious who contemplate ministering as church employees: prudence, honesty, and justice. Prudence, which helps in the practical attainment of goals, requires that sisters enter into ministry situations not only with the idealism of their commitment to the gospel but also with a good measure of institutional realism. It is not enough to negotiate contracts that provide for just compensation, as the Key West case makes clear. It is also necessary to probe into matters such as where funding for new positions is coming from, how decisions affecting the operation are made, and how the church official in charge tends to handle conflict. One can think of many pastors and a good number of bishops who would have handled the issues that arose in Key West in a much more mutually satisfying way. Just as a diocesan or parish administrator should conduct a background check of references for a prospective church employee, so should a sister undertake some scrutiny of the track record of those for whom she will work. Prudence cannot obviate all possible problems, but it will prevent some.

Honesty is a virtue that has often been sacrificed under the patriarchal model of virtue for reasons of institutional loyalty, fear of giving scandal, and desire for preserving a measure of status and security. And yet there is still truth in the maxim that honesty is the "best policy." Although there was hurt on all sides over the Key West debacle, the pain from having to leave Coney Island abruptly and without a real explanation seems to have lasted much longer, at least for the sisters involved. Certainly the willingness of Sister Kathleen Griffin and her provincial council to state the record of events as the sisters experienced things was appreciated much more by her community than would have been a decision to withdraw without disclosing the reasons, as happened under Mother Mary of Lourdes.

It has taken the tragedy of the clergy sexual abuse scandals, which began to be addressed with appropriate measures only after publicity and lawsuits in the 1980s, to teach those in power that denial of problems does not make them go away. Bringing more honesty into all church employment matters remains a continuing task for Christians, who have often been schooled to prefer silence and indirection to confrontation and, as a result, may need to cultivate skills of appropriate and effective self-assertion.

Justice is the third virtue commended here, and its meaning needs some clarification in view of the fact that the patriarchal and egalitarian-feminist paradigms interpret it differently. As Margaret A. Farley has observed, under the "old order," which presumed the inferiority of females and understood God's will to require the subordination of women to men, understandings of love and justice did not include the possibility of criticizing sexism. Modern recognition of women's full human dignity, however, is bringing into being a "new order" that requires new interpretations of these traditional principles. With respect to justice, she argues that adequate understandings of both individual and common good require a shift from strict hierarchical models of social organization to more egalitarian ones. She notes that ". . . the good of the family, church, etc. is better served by a model of leadership which includes collaboration between [male and female] equals" than by one which places a single male leader at the head of the community.[13] In the end, new understandings of justice and love are found to be mutually reinforcing norms for an egalitarian-feminist ethic:

> [I]nterpersonal communion characterized by equality, mutuality, and reciprocity may serve not only as a norm against which every pattern of relationship may be measured but as a goal to which every pattern of relationship is ordered. Minimal justice, then, may have equality as its norm and full mutuality as its goal. Justice will be maximal as it approaches the ultimate goal of communion of each person with all persons and God.[14]

Certainly more work needs to be done in translating such insights about the principles of love and justice into new understandings of the related virtues, but some things are clear already. Justice must be understood not as a matter of merely fulfilling contractual obligations but as one of striving for right relations in all situations. Moreover, especially because women have been socialized to assume roles of nurturing and self-sacrifice on behalf of others, it is crucial that they include their own well-being among the goods that are rightfully defended against injustice, even that found in the church. The affirmation of gender equality should affect not only transcultural virtues such as justice but also, more specifically, ecclesial ones such as religious obedience. Religious cultures must be held to account for the way they promote or inhibit the practice of virtues needed for the ministry to flourish—especially prudence, honesty, justice, and fidelity.

Those ministerial situations in which clergy and women religious do function in just and mutually supportive ways, as seems to have been the case in the flourishing parish on Coney Island in 1939, are harbingers of a future in which an even fuller degree of justice and love will be evident in church administration and ministry. Women and men inspired by the egalitarian-feminist paradigm of virtue today are helping to bring this hope closer to realization.

1. For a discussion of the paradigm shift in Catholic understandings of virtue, see Anne E. Patrick, *Liberating Conscience: Feminist Explorations in Catholic Moral Theology* (New York: Continuum, 1996), especially chapter 3, "Changing Paradigms of Virtue: The Good Life Reconsidered."

2. The author here thanks several Sisters of the Holy Names who provided information about their experiences in the Brooklyn diocese of the 1930s during interviews conducted in Albany, NY, July 2–4, 1998. These women have resumed their baptismal names since the Second Vatican Council, but were known by special religious names for decades prior to that: Sisters Marjorie Brainerd (Joan Teresa), Clara Brunelle (Charles Raymond), Edna May Gagnon (Robert Marie), and Anna Martha Murphy (Joan Patricia).

3. J.F. Powers, "The Lord's Day," *Prince of Darkness and Other Stories* (New York: Image Books, 1958), 11–18.

4. Eugene M. Quinlan to Kathleen Griffin, January 20, 1989, Sisters of the Holy Names of Jesus and Mary Archives, Albany, NY. Subsequent references to correspondence and unpublished documents are all based on materials in these SNJM New York Province Archives. Besides drawing on archival documents and newspaper accounts, the author has benefited from clarifying conversations with several of the women involved in the case, particularly Sisters Kathleen Griffin, Dolores Wehle, and Eileen Kelleher.

5. Rose Gallagher, "Outline of Key West Events, Dec. 1989–May 1990," SNJM Archives, Albany, NY.

6. Sisters of the Holy Names Provincial Administration to Most Reverend Edward A. McCarthy, D.D., Archbishop of Miami, and Members of St. Mary Star of the Sea Parish, March 29, 1990, SNJM Archives, Albany, NY. Besides Provincial Director Griffin, councilors signing the letter were Sisters Rose Gallagher, Rose Christina Momm, and Patricia Brennan. The entire letter was reproduced in a full-page advertisement sponsored by the "Save the Nuns" campaign, which appeared in the *Key West Citizen* on Sunday, May 6, 1990, 12–B.

7. Rose Gallagher, "Outline of Key West Events, Dec. 1989–May 1990," SNJM Archives, Albany, NY.

8. Ozzie Osborne, "Pastor's 5-year Tenure in Key West to End," *Miami Herald*, "The Keys" (September 5, 1991): B–1.

9. "A History of St. Mary Star of the Sea Catholic Church," Key West, 1996.

10. Titles reflecting these developments include, Albert R. Jonsen, *Responsibility in Modern Religious Ethics* (Washington, D.C.: Corpus Books, 1968); Dorothee Solle, *Beyond Mere Obedience*, trans. Laurence W. Denef (New York: Pilgrim Press, 1982); and, Leon-Joseph Suenens, *Coresponsibility in the Church* (New York: Herder & Herder, 1968).

11. See Patrick, *Liberating Conscience,* 77–79.

12. The different values assigned to priestly vocations and those of religious brothers ("lay" by choice or circumstance) and sisters (canonically ineligible for ordination) are shown in the fact that worries about the loss of clergy were articulated much sooner and louder than notice was taken of what was happening to the nonordained religious in the years after Vatican II. The departures of women were considerably more numerous than those of priests, however, and the loss of brothers was also dramatic. It took fifteen years for the drop in the number of priests in this country to approach one thousand, from 59,193 in 1966 to 58,398 in 1981, which represented a decline of just over one percent (795). Meanwhile, within the same period, religious brothers had declined by more than four thousand (by 1981 there were 4,489 fewer brothers, a drop of more than 36% from the 1966 figure of 12,255) and nuns had declined by nearly sixty thousand to 122,653 in 1981 (58,768 departures and deaths within fifteen years caused a 32% drop from the 1966 peak of 181,421 sisters). As the century draws to a close, there are fewer than 90,000 women religious in the United States, a decline of more than 50% from the peak figure. All statistics are from P.J. Kennedy & Sons, *Official Catholic Directory*. For contextual background, see Lora Ann Quinonez and Mary Daniel Turner, *The Transformation of American Catholic Sisters* (Philadelphia: Temple University Press, 1992); and, Patricia Wittberg, *The Rise and Fall of Catholic Religious Orders: A Social Movement Perspective* (Albany: State University of New York Press, 1994). As the stories from Brooklyn and Key West corroborate, historian Jay P. Dolan had reason to characterize sisters as "the Catholic serfs" in his study, *The American Catholic Experience* (Garden City: Image Books, 1985), 289.

13. Margaret A. Farley, "New Patterns of Relationship: Beginnings of a Moral Revolution," *Theological Studies* 36 (1975): 645.

14. Ibid., 646

Chapter Twenty-one
Collegiality as a
Moral and Ethical Practice

by M. Shawn Copeland

Sarah received her doctoral degree in biblical studies from the Catholic faculty of a German university.[1] Her area of concentration was the New Testament, with specialization in Pauline literature; her research focuses on womanist interpretation of certain of the epistles. Sarah has published one book that was well received, ten articles, and has another book under review for publication.

Sarah is beginning her sixth year of teaching in a U. S. Catholic seminary, operated by a religious order of men. Roughly 350 seminarians, sisters, laywomen and men compose the student body of the seminary, but only a handful of the students comes from underrepresented ethnocultural groups. The faculty numbers forty-five and are drawn mainly from the supporting order, but includes a few members who are Protestant. There are five women on the faculty, four of whom, including Sarah, are Roman Catholic. Three of the women are religious sisters; two are laywomen. Sarah, a laywoman, is the only nonwhite member of the faculty.

Sarah should be preparing her dossier for tenure and promotion, but she has begun to reconsider. Each of the past five years has been increasingly difficult. Too often at faculty meetings, Sarah's suggestions are acknowledged politely, then ignored; too frequently the thoroughness of her reports is questioned. On one occasion, a project that she put forward was rejected, only to be welcomed at a subsequent meeting when repeated by a male colleague. When that project was reviewed for external foundation funding, Sarah was asked to prepare additional supporting documentation, but was never told of the on-site visit of the foundation representatives.

Two years ago, when Sarah was scheduled to teach first-year Greek, the Chair of the Biblical Area questioned her credentials. Sarah was asked to attend the Chair's Greek classes to ensure her competence. When Sarah refused and pointed out the unusual nature of the request, the Chair ended the conversation abruptly. She then appointed a new faculty member, a white male, to teach the course, but she did not ask him to attend her Greek classes to ensure his competence.

Sarah is puzzled by ambivalent course evaluations from students. On the one hand, they comment favorably on her teaching style and find her professional yet sympathetic in her dealings with them. She respects, values, and supports their call to ministry. On the other hand, the students say that her courses are too demanding and that they cannot relate to an interpretation of Scripture from a womanist standpoint. In a conversation with some students who have appreciated their classroom experience with her, inadvertently someone lets it slip that some faculty advise students not to enroll in Sarah's courses.

Sarah wonders why so few of her colleagues have sought her out for scholarly conversation or dinners or social events. The indifference of the other women on the faculty has caused her real pain. Only John, a member of the school's supporting order, helped her adjust when she arrived and has continued to engage her in more personal and human terms—discussing her work and his own, celebrating her achievements with her.

I

Sarah is a black person, the only nonwhite person, in an environment in which authority and leadership are held by whites, and racism positions her so as to make her visible in distinctive ways. Sarah is a *black woman* and in this environment, racism culls her out from the other women and blinds them to possibilities of collegiality with her. At the same time, Sarah is a black woman in an *over-male-identified* environment.[2] Practices of tokenization, erasure, systematized white racial privilege, and "male overreward"[3] render this environment vulnerable to the (dis)values, beliefs, and assumptions of white racist supremacy, thus setting the conditions for the possibility of the biased practice of collegiality.[4] This is not only a marginalizing and oppressive ecology, but a sinful one.

Like other black academics, Sarah is not confronted daily with racist physical threats to her person; but she does encounter blatant and subtle dispiriting manifestations of racism. In the academic environment described in the case, Sarah is erased doubly—as a professional and as a human person. She is reduced to an entry, and a double entry, at that, on the crude ledger of affirmative action. Her contributions to faculty meetings are received with polite tolerance or condescension, only to be ignored. Yet, in order to contribute to the common good of the school, to be known and understood by her colleagues, to function as a professional, Sarah cannot remain silent. She must risk speech, and "to speak is to occupy place in a social economy."[5] But, as Hortense Spillers goes on to suggest, for racialized subjects like Sarah:

> history has dictated that this linguistic right to use is never easily granted with human and social legacy but must be earned, over and over again, on the level of a personal and collective struggle that requires in some way a confrontation with the principle of language as prohibition, as the withheld.[6]

This clarification helps us to understand the ways in which white institutions force, yet forbid, Sarah, and people of color, to discover her own voice. If her words and ideas are neither acknowledged nor engaged, then it is as if she has never said anything at all. And, if what Sarah has to say is received as the words or ideas of *the black* faculty member, her disciplinary expertise, education, and instructional experience are made invisible in the seminary's social economy. What *is* visible is what is undesirable—her blackness; and it is met with suspicion. Sarah's erasure by her white colleagues at faculty meetings is subtle, but her exclusion from the foundation meeting is obvious and blatant.

As a black woman with a doctoral degree and highly special-ized linguistic and exegetical skills, Sarah's very embodiment constitutes a dissonance from the "normative" appearance of those responsible for higher education. Sarah presents her black self as the expert she is, but when she does so she displaces what, heretofore, has been normative for academic expertise, namely whiteness and maleness. Cultural critic Michele Wallace points out that when black women take on the roles of intellectuals and writers they (and all women) function symbolically as white men. But, Wallace declares, "black women are [considered] the least convincing in this role, the least trustworthy."[7]

In the discussion with the Chair or in other instances in which she finds her qualifications coming under excessive scrutiny, Sarah may insist, mildly, at first that she too has had a Catholic education, that she too loves the Tradition, that she too is con-cerned about its preservation and transmission. With such responses, Sarah is attempting to help her colleagues detect the racism implicit in their inordinate concern about a black woman's qualifications. Or, Sarah may ward off their questions quietly. When she does this, she is protecting herself from internalizing the image of herself as other, as inferior, as incompetent. In white institutions, this is a difficult battle for blacks and other people of color. Being constantly challenged—about the content and meth-ods of one's pedagogy; about student reactions; about academic credentials (because it is assumed that the job was acquired through affirmative action and, therefore, that proper qualifica-tions were set aside)—takes a toll.[8] Unless Sarah has supportive family, friends, and/or colleagues outside the institution who can reflect back to her the meaningfulness of her academic achievements and competence, her self-confidence will be eroded. The constant battle against suspicion, negativity, and indifference will wear down her spirit and, not surprisingly, will begin to affect her performance.

Sarah's situation is not singular. It is no surprise that black women scholars are perceived as marginal to the production of theological, philosophical, and public knowledge. Research indicates that for women of color, the award of an advanced degree does not translate immediately into professional parity or respect. And, it is time to discard the myth that black women easily find academic employment. Full-time, nonwhite women comprise only a tiny percentage of the total of seminary and college or university faculty—by some analyses, less than three percent.[9] From the beginning, the black woman's path to academic employment is strewn with formidable obstacles. Essayist bell hooks writes:

> During my years of graduate work in English, I was often faced with the hostility of white students who felt that because I was black and female I would have no trouble finding a job. . . Ironically, no one ever acknowledged that we were never taught by any of these black women who were taking all the jobs. No one wanted to see that perhaps racism and sexism militate against the hiring of black women even though we are seen as a group that will be given priority, preferential status. Such assumptions, which are usually rooted in the logic of affirmative action hiring, do not include recognition of the ways most universities do not strive to attain diversity of faculty and that often diversity means hiring one non-white person, one black person.[10]

Hiring that one nonwhite person, that one black person can be read all too easily as tokenism. Kellis Parker makes the point that:

> [t]he hiring of one [black] is as bad as the hiring of
> none because neither position changes the symbol of
> black exclusion. . . . Tokens are incapable of chang-
> ing the ethos of all-white institutions. It is this ethos
> that white people have nurtured and developed for
> centuries that dominates the process of thought at uni-
> versities.[11]

Tokenization, then, places Sarah on display, even as it calls her professional activities into question: "What is she doing? Is she doing what she is 'supposed' to be doing? Why is she here? Is she [really] qualified to be here?"[12] What has she published? Are these publications about black issues?

At the same time, ironically, tokenization commodifies Sarah. For example, she may be asked to take on assignments that give her visibility in the local community or her photo may be used in advertising or her research given attention in seminary publications. Sarah's colleagues, privately, may admit to mild envy; but in the competitive and rarefied atmosphere of the academy, this envy too easily gives way to belittling hostility or *resentment.* Her colleagues fail to grasp that such attention to the only black faculty member serves the public image of the seminary and covers up her objectification. This visibility merely offers the illusion of a black woman holding autonomy or power in a white institution. Recall that Sarah holds the faculty rank of assistant professor, nontenured junior status. In academic hierarchy, this position allows her no decisive power over her own fate (tenure). Such forms of public attention may give Sarah "place," but they do not give her authentic "importance."[13]

Sarah is never *simply* herself, never a particular person; she always is a symbol of her race. This means that Sarah bears the burden of her race and race bears the burden of her performance. As a symbol, Sarah is allowed little scope to develop sufficiently her academic creativity. Sarah focuses much of her research on African American religiocultural perspective. Because the content of that perspective generally is disvalued in the monoculturality of the academy, she can expect little encouragement, authentic critique, or reward. But when Sarah brings up her research on early Christian asceticism, her colleagues are surprised at her interest.

Because she is a symbol, Sarah is denied as well the freedom to make mistakes as a finite human being. Suppose Sarah hesitates in answering a student's question in lecture or misses an editor's deadline; suppose she neglects to return an email message or a telephone call. Because Sarah is never simply herself and is always a symbol, her white colleagues have societal license to interpret her and her behavior through the lens of negative stereotypes about blacks. Sarah (the black woman) is hired because of affirmative action and, therefore, she is unqualified. Sarah (the black woman) is inefficient, not up to the mark.

These stereotypes are equally effective in the obverse: The black woman (Sarah) must be too overburdened to take a seat on the influential committee. The black woman (Sarah) should be consulted about diversity in the seminary, but her advice would not be as useful on rethinking the introductory course in New Testament, although this is her area of expertise. The black woman (Sarah) is expected to research and write about black topics and, if she fails to do so, her white colleagues will question her racial identity—the black woman is *not* black enough. But what the black woman (Sarah) does research and write from a womanist perspective will be designated by those same white colleagues as nonrequired and nonessential to the curriculum.

If Sarah should hint, even tentatively, that such behavior and reactions border on racism, her colleagues will object. Almost certainly someone will say, "I do not see color." Or someone else will insist, "I am color-blind. Race makes no difference to me." Spoken nearly *always* by whites to nonwhites, these statements belabor the obvious and expose just how important the obvious is.[14]

By erasing the most distinguishing characteristic of Sarah's physical or bodily presence, her colleagues intend to compliment her. Their approval of her comportment, dress, diction, etiquette, and appropriation of European-American culture aims to tell

Sarah that she is not like other blacks.[15] To erase or dissolve a visible difference that evokes such visceral response is no gesture of appreciation or regard; it is one of contempt and disdain. These comments offend, even if offered in good faith. They insinuate that the other is *best* made over in the image and likeness of the dominant group. Such uncritical idealism erases not only color but also the alienating conditions under which Sarah has had to seek inclusion.[16]

The complement to erasure is assimilation. When Sarah's colleagues say that they "don't see color," they mean that Sarah has assimilated. Even as a strategy for managing entry into the white mainstream, the logic of assimilation dictates that whites (or those in power) define the standards according to which "other" entrants are judged. Consider the over-male-identified academic environment. We would expect all the women to bond together for companionship and support; however, in their own attempt at assimilation, the other (white) women participate in marginalizing Sarah. As bell hooks observes, "at its very core . . . [assimilation] is dehumanizing. Embedded in the logic of assimilation is the white-supremacist assumption that blackness must be eradicated so that a new self . . . [a colorless or desexed self] can come into being."[17] Still, even if this new colorless self should set Sarah apart from other blacks, it does not mean that Sarah is *like* her white colleagues.

Sarah's white colleagues have failed to recognize that, in this society, their race accords them privilege. Peggy Mcintosh has written frankly of the "matrix of white privilege, [the] pattern of assumptions" passed on to her as a white person.[18] She describes white privilege as:

> an invisible package of unearned assets . . . an invisible weightless knapsack of special provisions, assurances, tools, maps, guides, codebooks, passports, visas, clothes, compass, emergency gear, and blank checks about which whites were meant to remain oblivious.[19]

Mcintosh is aware that while the notion of privilege mediates something desirable, critical interrogation of privilege systems reveal just how "misleading" this notion has become.[20] The "connotations [of the word privilege] are too positive to fit the [negative] conditions and behaviors which 'privilege systems' produce." [21] The system of white racial privilege "systematically overempower[s]" whites as a racial group at the expense of non-white racial groups, just as male privilege systematically overempowers males as a group at the expense of females.[22] This is raw privilege; it "simply *confers dominance*, gives permission to control, because of one's race or sex." [23] These kinds of privilege systems, Mcintosh asserts, accords people "license to be ignorant, oblivious, arrogant, and destructive." [24]

Nothing in our so-called meritocracy has prepared Sarah's white colleagues to understand that their race affords them an unearned, unfair advantage in society.[25] These men and women insist that they have attained their professorial appointments because *they* are educated, qualified, hardworking and, therefore, deserving individuals. This is so, Mcintosh writes, because "whites are taught to think of their lives as morally neutral, normative, and average, and also ideal."[26] Moreover, she contends, that when whites work to benefit others, this is seen as work that allows those *others* (that is, so-called minority or racial-ethnic groups) to be more like whites—to be more *normative, average,* and *ideal.* Nothing has prepared whites to acknowledge that unearned white privilege has not been good for white people's development as human beings or for the development of the society in which we live.[27]

If Sarah enjoys none of the privilege of whiteness, she pays a heavy price for being black. This price is what blacks routinely and exasperatedly call the *color tax.* The color tax is the price that white racism imposes on all blacks—simply for daring to desire to come on to the playing field. After centuries of coping with slavery, lynching, segregation, discrimination, and anti-black racism, blacks have internalized the unspoken expectation that they must pay for the attempt to succeed. Blacks know, from our mother's milk, that we must be better qualified than whites, males in particular; we must work twice as hard as whites, males in particular; we must take on tedious, drudge assignments without complaint. Blacks know that *only* after ruthless and repeated examination of *our* own behavior and performance can the charge of racism ever be laid.

Blacks pay for being black in white institutions in stress, anxiety, self-censorship, and over self-scrutinization. Blacks exercise constant vigilance—rarely, if ever, and never fully, letting down the racial guard. Blacks restrain themselves in personality and spontaneity. For insinuated in the color tax is our struggle to construct identity in a society that prefers to behave as if we do not exist. The long-term "price of this continual coping is not insignificant."[28] The color tax is one source of despair, self-defeat, hypertension, stroke, cerebral hemorrhage, chronic obesity, even suicide.

II

For more than a decade, theological education has been the topic of a growing number of studies. Few of these, however, address the notion of *collegiality* among faculty—particularly in relation to the presence of a small yet growing number of women and men of color who are joining the faculties of colleges, universities, and seminaries. Sarah's case brings into focus several unexamined assumptions that shape the reception of Native Americans, African Americans, Asian Americans, and Latino Americans as members of theological faculties. Chief among these is the way in which we faculty understand the meaning of being a colleague, the meaning of collegiality as a moral and ethical practice.

The word *collegiality* is derived from the word *colleague,* both are rooted in the noun *college.* Several images coalesce around this word: libraries, lecture halls, and laboratories; courses, examinations, and degrees. But the courses, the degrees, even the physical structures, are possible only because of the association of self-governing persons whose own education and training have equipped them with a very high level of expert knowledge and skill. In other words, a college is constituted by its faculty, that is to say, the men and women who, by virtue of their own education and learning, responsibilities and duties, comprise the college or that association of colleges, the university. These men and women identify and relate to one another as colleagues.

The exacting criteria by which post-graduate faculty, in particular, have been educated, the cultural power which that education accords us, and our intimate relation to human knowledge reaffirm our collegiality. Neither the responsibilities and duties nor the rights and privileges our positions grant are for ourselves alone; rather, they are for the preservation, transformation, and transmission of the cultural capital of civilization.

When we faculty refer to one another as colleagues, whether we intend to or not, we acknowledge and reaffirm a dense web of personal, cultural, and social relations. When we call one another colleague, we recognize that we share certain responsibilities and duties for the development of the fund of human knowledge, the educational institutions that our association creates, our students, and the way that we live our lives. We acknowledge our common accountability to history and culture, to probity and integrity in scholarship, to one another and, in the case of theological education, to the church. Because our educational preparation has the most direct bearing on the broad cultural and religious matrix of our civilization, we enjoy considerable social status, autonomy, and authority. Our responsibilities and duties, privileges and rights, form the nexus of our common enterprise and distinguish us as colleagues. Moreover, our colleagueship extends well beyond research projects or courses conducted within the walls of a seminary or college or even our disciplines. Our colleagueship influences our social and cultural tastes and choices, our friendships, even our life-partners and our religions.

Still, too many of us would admit that the "community of scholars" exists more as an ideal than a reality. As academicians, we have been trained to work alone in libraries and laboratories, to embrace solitariness, to guard our research and, sadly, to tear someone else's apart. These skills, while important, resist the very collegiality and community for which we yearn. Hence, most of us have no idea just how to practice collegiality and to create authentic community, whether or not women and men of color join our faculties. Yet, we honestly yearn for community, we want collegiality. Where we catch a glimpse of it, *there,* with those women and men, we want to be; *with them* we want to teach and to collaborate, to conduct our research, and to engage conversation. When this fails, we settle for the corner office, the two-course semester teaching load, and a graduate assistant. But when we settle, we lose and so does the common human good.

III

This case study incriminates the meaning of collegiality as an ethical and moral practice. To say that collegiality is a moral and ethical practice implies that it shares several of the features of virtue. Much like virtue, collegiality (1) must be learned by practice, (2) aims for excellence, (3) is expressed through concrete human acts, (4) concerns not only our doing but also our being, (5) involves human relationships and community, and (6) enables us "to attain the furthest potentialities of [our] nature."[29] To be virtuous, to be morally good, we must do more than refrain from harmful and evil acts or "only reluctantly follow out what we know we should do."[30] By fidelity to right reason, to prudential or practical judgment, the virtuous person knows, seeks, embraces, and carries out the good with alacrity, spontaneity, freedom, and joy. In the proper exercise of virtue, we realize our authenticity as human persons. This is equally true for our practice of collegiality; in the proper exercise of collegiality, we become good colleagues to one another.

To challenge the biased practice of collegiality may be exceedingly difficult, but it is worth the effort. As a practice, collegiality is carried forward in some basic human acts. I propose at least these: critical attentiveness, basic regard, and community.

Critical Attentiveness

Many seminary, college, and university faculty began their long graduate school apprenticeships at a time when both the scholarship and persons of blacks, other people of color, and women were absent from the academy. While it is important for white faculty to attend to the presence of blacks, other people of color, and women, it is perhaps more important for these men and women to attend to their whiteness. If blackness is a social fiction, so too is whiteness a social fiction. Because whiteness in our society is rarely marked in the same sense as blackness, white men and women enjoy the "majoritarian privilege of never noticing themselves."[31] Faculty will need to be critically attentive to themselves, their behavior, and the institutions they constitute. Critical attentiveness uncovers the subtle violence of the hegemony of what has come to be considered normal, average, ideal—namely, whiteness. Critical attention exposes and questions "behaviors of avoidance, aversion, expressions of nervousness, condescension, and stereotyping."[32] Rather than a call to interrogate blacks or people of color about their experiences in the academy, critical attentiveness turns the spotlight on the behavior of white men and women and the practice of collegiality.

Basic Regard

White racist supremacy breaks down the intersubjective spontaneity of human feeling for another human being. It intentionally estranges human beings one from another through divisive tactics of control and dislocation. Basic regard includes at least the recognition of difference without aversion or exclusion. This calls for authentic recognition of our common humanity.[33] Basic regard resists yielding human (race or gender or sexual orientation or age) difference to the lowest common denominator—

to indifference, to tolerance. Rather, in privileging face-to-face relations, we engage the concrete human other. Authentically engaging the difference of the concrete human other in all its uniqueness, variation, and fullness as *human* life debunks the myth that difference is the conceptual opposite to equality. Further, to authentically engage the concrete human other is to repudiate the tendency to universalize the particular, thereby eliminating difference—eliminating the concrete human other.

Community

Collegiality implies something very fundamental about community; critical attentiveness and basic regard generate minimum conditions for its realization. Sarah's situation confirms that community is never just an aggregate of individuals within a given boundary. Given the isolating character of our academic training, "creating community [will] involve [the] difficult work of negotiating real divisions, of considering boundaries before we go crashing through, and of pondering our differences before we can ever agree on the terms of our sameness."[34] Further, while collegiality assumes mutuality and reciprocity, black and other scholars ought not be called upon "to take primary responsibility for sharing experiences, ideas, and information. Such gestures place black people once again in a service position, meeting the needs of whites."[35]

For blacks and other people of color, the academy can be "a frustratingly segregated integrated professional world."[36] To change that world for blacks and other people of color changes it for all of us, and the commitment to change that world is a practice that changes us.

1. Because there are so few black Catholic theological scholars, this case, in particular, runs the risk of teasing the reader into trying to discover just who *is* Sarah. There is *no* Sarah. This case study is *not* about a particular person. Indeed, at this writing, I know of *no* African American Catholic— female or male—who has a doctoral degree in New Testament studies and teaches in a Catholic seminary. But, even if Sarah is fictional, the content

of the case is not. This case has been constructed from the *actual* experiences of several black faculty—women *and* men—teaching in private and public, Catholic and Protestant, colleges, universities, and seminaries. At the same time, it may be important to point out that Sarah's case is *not* peculiar or particular to Catholic institutions; Sarahs can and are found in public educational institutions and in Protestant seminaries. But African Americans, Catholics and Protestants, do teach in Catholic colleges, universities, and seminaries, and the behaviors described here can be and are found in those settings. *Finally, let me state, and most emphatically so, this case and my reflection on it in no way depicts my own university or my own colleagues.*

2. By naming the environment *over-male-identified*, I mean only to underscore the *gender* of those for whom the seminary has been established, the *gender* of those who benefit most from that establishment, and the *gender* of those who control it.

3. Peggy Mcintosh, "White Privilege and Male Privilege: A Personal Account of Coming to See Correspondence Through Work in Women's Studies," typescript, Working Paper No. 189 (Wellseley College: Center for Women Research, 1988), 3.

4. Bernard Lonergan, *Insight, A Study of Human Understanding* (London: Longmans, Green and Company, 1957), chapters 6 and 7. On Lonergan's account, bias is the more or less conscious and deliberate choice, in the face of what we perceive to be a potential threat to our well-being, to exclude further information or data from consideration in our understanding, judgment, reflection, and decision.

5. Hortense J. Spillers, "All the Things You Could Be by Now, If Sigmund Freud's Wife Was Your Mother," in *Female Subjects in Black and White,* eds., Elizabeth Abel, Barbara Christian, Helene Mogle (Berkeley: University of California Press, 1997), 145.

6. Ibid.

7. Michele Wallace, *Invisibility Blues: From Pop to Theory* (New York: Verso, 1990), 7.

8. Yolanda T. Moses identifies these as some of the typical problems encountered by African American women faculty and administrators in higher education in "Black Women in Academe: Issues and Strategies,"

Baltimore Project on the Status of Education of Women (Association of American Colleges, 1989). This research is cited by Ruth Farmer in "Place But Not Importance: The Race for Inclusion in Academe," in *Spirit, Space and Survival: African American Women in (White) Academe,* eds., Joy James and Ruth Farmer (New York: Routledge, 1993), 203–204.

9. bell hooks, *Talking Back: Thinking Feminist, Thinking Black* (Boston: South End Press, 1989), 67.

10. Ibid., 60–61.

11. Kellis Parker, "Ideas, Affirmative Action and the Ideal University," *Nova Law Journal* 10 (1986): 763, cited in Farmer, "Place But Not Importance: The Race for Inclusion in Academe," 201.

12. Farmer, "Place But Not Importance: The Race for Inclusion in Academe," 204.

13. Ibid., 202.

14. Seeing color is one of the most contested practices in a person's social formation in the United States. For some analyses see, Lewis R. Gordon, *Bad Faith and Antiblack Racism* (Atlantic Highlands, NJ: Humanities Press, 1995), idem., *Her Majesty's Other Children: Sketches of Racism from a Neocolonial Age* (Lanham, MD: Rowan & Littlefield, 1997); Charles W. Mills, *Blackness Visible: Essays on Race and Philosophy* (Ithaca: Cornell University Press, 1998).

15. Adrianne R. Andrews, in "Balancing the Personal and the Professional," (in *Spirit, Space and Survival: African American Women in (White) Academe*, eds., Joy James and Ruth Farmer [New York: Routledge, 1993], 179–95), reports the result of an ethnographic study of black female academics. On the issue of class, Andrews observes: "The vast majority of the tiny minority of Blacks (both female and male) in the academic profession come, primarily, from black middle-class backgrounds (distinct from the middle class of White America) and have internalized American middle-class values with some modifications based on cultural and socioeconomic factors. Therefore, class should be a less significant factor in shaping the experiences of Black women in academe than race and gender" (182).

16. Patricia Williams, *Seeing a Color-blind Future: The Paradox of Race* (New York: Farrar, Straus, Giroux, 1997), 4.

17. hooks, *Talking Back: Thinking Feminist, Thinking Black,* 67.

18. Mcintosh, "White Privilege and Male Privilege: A Personal Account of Coming to See Correspondence Through Work in Women's Studies," 11.

19. Ibid., 1–2.

20. Ibid., 12.

21. Ibid.

22. Ibid., 10.

23. Ibid.

24. Ibid., 12.

25. For a critical discussion of the meaning of merit and meritocracy, see Iris Marion Young, *Justice and the Politics of Difference* (Princeton: Princeton University Press, 1990), 192–225; K. Anthony Appiah and Amy Gutman, *Color Conscious, The Political Morality of Race* (Princeton: Princeton University Press, 1996), 119, 122–24.

26. Mcintosh, "White Privilege and Male Privilege: A Personal Account of Coming to See Correspondence Through Work in Women's Studies," 4.

27. Ibid., 2.

28. Ellis Cose, *Rage of a Privileged Class* (New York: HarperCollins, 1993), 56; see also 56–72.

29. Josef Pieper, *The Four Cardinal Virtues* (Notre Dame: University of Notre Dame Press, 1966); xii.

30. John A. Oesterle, "Introduction," in St. Thomas Aquinas, *Treatise on the Virtues* (Notre Dame: University of Notre Dame Press, 1966/1984), xiv.

31. Williams, *Seeing a Color-blind Future: The Paradox of Race,* 7.

32. Iris Marion Young, "Abjection and Oppression: Dynamics of Unconscious Racism, Sexism, and Homophobia," in *Crises in Continental Philosophy,*

eds., Arleen B. Dallery, et. al. (Albany: State University of New York Press, 1990), 205.

33. Young, *Justice and the Politics of Difference,* 238–39, 232.

34. Williams, *Seeing a Color-blind Future: The Paradox of Race,* 6.

35. hooks, *Talking Back: Thinking Feminist, Thinking Black,* 47.

36. Stephen L. Carter, "The Black Table, the Empty Seat, and the Tie," in *Lure and Loathing: Essays on Race, Identity, and the Ambivalence of Assimilation,* ed., Gerald Early (New York: Allen Lane, Penguin Press, 1993), 66.

Contributors

Richard Bondi is Pastoral Counselor at the Emanuel Center of Pastoral Counseling, Atlanta. He is the author of *Leading God's People* (Abingdon Press, 1989).

Diana Fritz Cates is Associate Professor of Ethics in the School of Religion at the University of Iowa and is the author of *Choosing to Feel: Virtue, Friendship, and Compassion for Friends* (Notre Dame University Press, 1997) and "Taking Women's Experience Seriously: Thomas Aquinas and Audre Lorde on Anger" in G. Simon Harak, ed. *Aquinas and Empowerment: Classical Ethics for Ordinary Lives* (Georgetown University Press, 1996).

M. Shawn Copeland is Associate Professor of Theology at Marquette University and has written "'Wading Through Many Sorrows': Towards a Theology of Suffering in Womanist Perspective" in Emilie Townes, ed. *A Troubling in My Soul: Womanist Reflections on Evil and Suffering* (Orbis, 1993) and "Violence and the Imagination: Preaching to the Wounds of My People," in John S. McClure and Nancy J. Ramsey, eds. *Telling the Truth: Preaching Against Sexual and Domestic Violence* (Pilgrim Press, 1998).

William Johnson Everett is the Herbert Gezork Professor of Christian Social Ethics at Andover Newton Theological School and has written "Ecclesial Freedom and Federal Order: Reflections on the Pacific Homes Case," *Journal of Law and Religion* (1996) and *Religion, Federalism, and the Struggle for Public Life: Cases from Germany, India and America* (Oxford University Press, 1997).

Margaret A. Farley is the Gilbert L. Stark Professor of Christian Ethics at Yale University Divinity School and has written *Personal Commitments: Beginning, Keeping and Changing* (Harper and Row Publishers, 1986) and "Divorce, Remarriage, and Pastoral Practice," in C. Curran, ed. *Moral Theology: Challenges for the Future* (Paulist Press, 1990).

Richard M. Gula, SS, is Professor of Moral Theology at Franciscan School of Theology of the Graduate Theological Union at Berkeley and has written *Ethics and Pastoral Ministry* (Paulist Press, 1996) and *The Good Life* (Paulist Press, 1999).

Vigen Guroian is Professor of Moral Theology at Loyola College, Baltimore, and has published *Life's Living toward Dying: A Theological and Medical-Ethical Study* (W. B. Eerdmans, 1996) and *Tending the Heart of Virtue: How Classic Stories Awaken a Child's Moral Imagination* (Oxford University Press, 1998).

Patricia Beattie Jung is Associate Professor of Theology at Loyola University, Chicago, and has recently written "Differences Among the Elderly: Who Is on the Road to Bremen?" in *The Christian Practice of Growing Old,* David Cloutier et al., eds. (W. B. Eerdmans, forthcoming) and "Dying Well Isn't Easy: Thoughts of a Roman Catholic Theologian on Assisted Suicide," in *Must We Suffer Our Way to Death?,* Edward DuBose and Ron Hamel, eds. (Southern Methodist University Press, 1996).

Shannon Jung is Director of the Center for Theology and Land, Wartburg, and the University of Dubuque Theological Seminaries. Among his publications are two recent books: *Moral Issues and Christian Response* with Patricia Jung, Paul Jersild, and Dale Johnson, 6th edition (Harcourt-Brace, 1998) and *Rural Ministry: The Shape of the Renewal to Come* with Sr. Pegge Boehm, B.V.M. (Abingdon Press, 1998).

Judith W. Kay is Dean of Students and Assistant Professor of Religion at the University of Puget Sound and has published "Politics without Human Nature?: Reconstructing a Common Humanity," *Hypatia* (1994) and "Getting Egypt out of the People: Aquinas's Contributions to Liberation," in G. Simon Harak, ed. *Aquinas and Empowerment: Classical Ethics for Ordinary Lives* (Georgetown University Press, 1996).

James Keenan, S.J., is Professor of Moral Theology at Weston Jesuit School of Theology and has written "Proposing Cardinal Virtues," *Theological Studies* (1995) and *Virtues for Ordinary Christians* (Sheed & Ward, 1996) and *Commandments of Compassion* (Sheed & Ward, 1999).

Joseph Kotva, Jr., is Pastor, First Mennonite Church, Allentown, Pennsylvania. His writings include *The Christian Case for Virtue Ethics* (Georgetown University Press, 1996) and "Hospital Chaplaincy as Agapeic Intervention," *Christian Bioethics* (1998).

Karen Lebacqz is the Robert Gordon Sproul Professor of Theological Ethics at the Pacific School of Religion and has written *Sex in the Parish* (Westminster Press, 1991) and *Word, Worship, World and Wonder* (Abingdon Press, 1997).

Shirley Macemon is a second career, graduate student at the Pacific School of Religion, after twenty years in data processing and computer services.

Gilbert Meilaender is Board of Directors Professor of Christian Ethics at Valparaiso University, in Indiana. He has written *The Theory and Practice of Virtue* (Notre Dame University Press, 1984) and "Grace, Justification Through Faith, and Sin," in *Ecumenical Ventures in Ethics,* Reinhard Huetter & Theodor Dieter, eds. (W. B. Eerdmans, 1998).

Anne E. Patrick, SNJM, is Professor of Religion at Carleton College, Northfield, Minnesota. She has written "Ethics for Church Professionals?" in *New Catholic World* (1983) and *Liberating Conscience: Feminist Explorations in Catholic Moral Theology* (Continuum, 1996).

Carlos Piar is Associate Professor of Religious Studies at the California State University at Long Beach and has written *Jesus and Liberation: A Critical Analysis of the Christology of Latin American Liberation Theology* (Peter Lang, 1994) and "Cesar Chavez and La Causa: Towards a Hispanic Christian Social Ethic" in *Annual of the Society of Christian Ethics,* 1996.

Charles Pinches is Professor of Theology at the University of Scranton and has published with Stanley Hauerwas *Christians Among the Virtues: Theological Conversations with Ancient and Modern Ethics* (Notre Dame University Press, 1997) and an essay, "Virtue" in the *Oxford Companion to Christian Thought* (Oxford University Press, forthcoming).

Samuel K. Roberts is Professor of Christian Ethics in the School of Theology at Virginia Union University and has authored *In the Path of Virtue: The African American Moral Tradition* (Pilgrim Press, 1999).

Paul J. Wadell is Associate Professor of Religious Studies at St. Norbert College, De Pere, Wisconsin, and the author of "Growing Together in the Divine Love: The Role of Charity in the Moral Theology of Thomas Aquinas" in *Aquinas and*

Empowerment: Classical Ethics for Ordinary Lives, G. Simon Harak, ed. (Georgetown University Press, 1996) and "Learning Lessons of Forgiveness: A Meditation on Oscar Hijuelos' *Mr. Ive's Christmas*," *New Theology Review* (1997).

Sondra Ely Wheeler is Associate Professor of Christian Ethics at the Wesley Theological Seminary in Washington, D.C. She is the author of *Stewards of Life: Bioethics and Pastoral Care* (Abingdon Press, 1996) and "Broadening the Concept of Justice in Health Care" in *The Changing Face of Health Care,* John Kilner et. al., eds. (W. B. Eerdmans, 1998).

William H. Willimon is Dean of the Chapel and Professor of Christian Ministry at Duke University. He has written *The Service of God: How Worship and Ethics Are Related* (Abingdon Press, 1983) and contributed three chapters to *Exilic Preaching: Testimony for Christian Exiles in an Increasingly Hostile Culture,* Erskine Clarke, ed. (Trinity Press, 1998).

p. 102 "who we are, not decisions
we make...."
p. 138
"The kind of person...."

_____

x woman being interviewed for a position
as head pastor (17-19)

x Conflict between call & marriage (56-57) <

Transformed in prayer (147-148)

Forgiveness (157-159) <

Bounday → Communion / Sacraments (186)

✓ Burn-out (225) <

Boundary → Homo sexual (239) <

✓ Compensation (280) <